# THE DOLLAR

The Americas in the World
Jürgen Buchenau and Steven
Hyland Jr., Series Editors

The Americas in the World
series publishes cutting-edge
scholarship about the Americas in
global and transnational history,
politics, society, and culture as
well as about the impact of global
and transnational actors and
processes on the hemisphere.
The series includes both works
on specialized topics as well as
broad syntheses. All titles aim at
a wide audience.

Also available in The Americas in
the World series:

*North American Regionalism:
Stagnation, Decline, or Renewal?*
edited by Eric Hershberg and
Tom Long

# THE DOLLAR

## HOW THE US DOLLAR BECAME A POPULAR CURRENCY IN ARGENTINA

Mariana Luzzi and Ariel Wilkis
Translated by Wendy Gosselin

University of New Mexico Press
Albuquerque

© 2023 by University of New Mexico Press
All rights reserved. Published 2023
Printed in the United States of America

ISBN 978-0-8263-6538-5 (cloth)
ISBN 978-0-8263-6539-2 (paper)
ISBN 978-0-8263-6540-8 (electronic)

Library of Congress Cataloging-in-Publication data is on file with the Library of Congress.

Founded in 1889, the University of New Mexico sits on the traditional homelands of the Pueblo of Sandia. The original peoples of New Mexico—Pueblo, Navajo, and Apache—since time immemorial have deep connections to the land and have made significant contributions to the broader community statewide. We honor the land itself and those who remain stewards of this land throughout the generations and also acknowledge our committed relationship to Indigenous peoples. We gratefully recognize our history.

This work has been published within the framework of the Sur Translation Support Programme of the Ministry of Foreign Affairs, International Trade and Worship of the Argentine Republic. (Obra editada en el marco del Programa Sur de Apoyo a las Traducciones del Ministerio de Relaciones Exteriores, Comercio Internacional y Culto de la República Argentina.)

Cover and interior design by Isaac Morris
Composed in Copperplate, Fairfield, and Madrone

Programa Sur

# CONTENTS

| | |
|---|---|
| VII | ACKNOWLEDGMENTS |
| 1 | INTRODUCTION |
| | A Social History of a Popular Currency |
| 22 | CHAPTER ONE |
| | Before the Dollar Became a Global Currency (1931–1955) |
| 43 | CHAPTER TWO |
| | Bretton Woods on the Streets of Buenos Aires (1959–1970) |
| 67 | CHAPTER THREE |
| | A Global Currency in Argentine Pockets and Pocketbooks (1971–1983) |
| 106 | CHAPTER FOUR |
| | Strong Dollar, Weak Democracy (1983–1989) |
| 135 | CHAPTER FIVE |
| | Legal Tender: A Neoliberal Experiment in Dollars (1991–2002) |
| 163 | CHAPTER SIX |
| | The Financial Crisis from the Southern Cone (2008–2015) |
| 189 | CONCLUSION |
| | The Dollar Beyond Its Borders |
| 199 | NOTES |
| 207 | BIBLIOGRAPHY |
| 222 | INDEX |

## ACKNOWLEDGMENTS

This book is a modified version of *El Dólar: Historia de una moneda argentina (1930–2019)*, published in Argentina in 2019. We are including here the original acknowledgments to recognize the colleagues, institutions, and family members who accompanied us during the five years of research and writing that culminated in this book.

The research for this book was done at two Argentine universities, Universidad Nacional de San Martín and Universidad Nacional General Sarmiento, and at Argentina's national research council CONICET. Funding was provided by Argentina's National Agency for Research, Technology Development, and Innovation. Juan Arrarás, María Clara Hernández, and Joaquín Molina provided their invaluable assistance for the press archive research.

Our immersion in the archives would not have been possible without the guidance of those who know better than anyone else the bibliographic and newspaper collections we consulted. We are grateful to the staff of the Biblioteca del Congreso de la Nación, Biblioteca Nacional, Centro de Documentación e Información—Ministerio de Economía de la Nación, Biblioteca Prebisch—Banco Central de la República Argentina, and Biblioteca Utopía—Centro Cultural de la Cooperación.

To understand the functioning of the illegal foreign exchange market in recent years, it was essential to consult the Archives of the Procuraduría de Criminalidad Económica y Lavado de Activos (Procelac). Our thanks to Carlos Gonella, Néstor García Paradiso, and Gustavo Latanzzio, who made this possible.

Agustín Díaz Fischer, in charge of the visual art archive of the Centro de Estudios Espigas (UNSAM), guided us to access the material from Mara Minujín's personal archive. Rodrigo Daskal generously opened the doors of the River Plate

## Acknowledgments

Club Museum, to explore their archives of player transfers and contracts. We were able to reconstruct the references to the US dollar in the history of Argentine theater thanks to the accurate information provided by Carlos Swarcer. To all three, our deepest gratitude.

This book would not have seen the light without the colleagues who shared tips on hunting down archive documents, recommended new readings, read early drafts, and helped give shape to our final ideas. We thus owe very much to Martín Abeles, Juan Cruz Andrada, Javier Auyero, Máximo Badaro, Viviana Barry, Claudio Benzecry, Maxim Bolt, Jimena Caravaca, Alan Cibils, Eduardo Corso, Claudia Daniel, Joe Deville, Matías Dewey, Alejandro Dujovne, Ximena Espeche, Alejandro Gaggero, Diego Galeano, Pablo Gerchunoff, Felipe González López, Jane Guyer, Mateusz Halawa, Kaveri Haritas, Mark Healey, Mariana Heredia, Orsi Husz, Deborah James, Gabriel Kessler, Alejandra Laera, Pablo Lapegna, Jeanne Lazarus, Valeria Manzano, Pablo Miguez, Marek Mikus, Eugenia Motta, Lucía Müller, Fabian Muniesa, Susana Narotzky, Federico Neiburg, Arturo O'Connell, Gustavo Onto, Horacio Ortiz, José Ossandon, Jorge Pantaleón, Fareen Parvez, Melina Piglia, Mariano Plotkin, Sarah Queen, Andrés Regalsky, Fernando Rabossi, Alexandre Roig, Hadrien Saiag, María Soledad Sánchez, Marcin Serafin, Magdalena Villarreal, Marcela Visconti, Jing Wang, Fred Wherry, and Caitlin Zaloom.

Viviana Zelizer backed this project right from the start and encouraged us to deepen our perspective on the sociology of money. We are especially grateful to her. Our dear friend and colleague Daniel Fridman offered generous feedback and sharp readings, besides proving an invaluable guide when it came to adapting our original work for a public unfamiliar with the history and culture of Argentina. We also had the privilege of working with Wendy Gosselin, who translated this new version of the book into English with the utmost care and professionalism. Special thanks also go to the editors of the "Latin America in the World" series at University of New Mexico Press, Jurgen Buchenau and Stephen Hyland, who were excited to include our work in the press's new books about the region.

Michel Millman, editor at University of New Mexico Press, provided unwavering support for the project right from the start. We are extremely grateful for his help: he allowed us to bring our book to a whole new audience.

Finally, our families accompanied us with love and patience despite all the time that the writing of this book stole from them. Our special thanks go then to Emilia, Sebastian (Mariana), Manuel, and Muriel (Ariel).

*Introduction*

# A SOCIAL HISTORY OF A POPULAR CURRENCY

"What was the official peso-dollar exchange rate on February 26, 2015?" The question twinkles in blue letters across the television screen. The game-show host of the Argentine version of Who Wants to Be a Millionaire? reads the answers to a contestant. The options on the screen are: A) 4.45, B) 14.55, C) 8.73, and D) 18.98. The contestant listens closely to the host and then responds. "Well, it's definitely not 18 or 14, because those have been the exchange rates under this administration. And 4.45 must have been in around 2010 or so. So I'm going with B, 8.73." "Is that your final answer?" asks the host. "Yes, it is," says the contestant with no hesitation. "The incredible thing about living in Argentina," the host quips, "is running into questions about dollars." Laughing, the contestant responds, "Not to mention the fact that there are four totally different numbers and any one of them could be right." Now comes a moment of suspense. Answer B, 8.73, turns yellow on the screen: the contestant has answered correctly.

A screenshot with the question about the dollar exchange rate immediately begins circulating on Twitter. An American Internet user tries to be ironic: "Can I phone a central banker?" Someone replies right away (also in English): "Only if you don't know a regular Argentinian."

On April 8, 2019, the day the game show aired, the dollar was worth AR$44.60 pesos on the local foreign exchange market. Four years had passed since the date referred to in the question, and all the answer options seem equally remote. However, the question itself was no surprise to local viewers. As expressed in that brief Twitter exchange, while only economic professionals or people with links to foreign trade keep up with exchange rates in other countries, ordinary people in Argentina closely follow fluctuations in the peso-dollar exchange rate, especially in times of monetary turbulence.

A topic of conversation and a preoccupation, the dollar is also a highly valued asset among Argentines. According to a report published by the Federal Reserve in 2006, Argentina topped the list of countries (other than the United States) with the most dollars per capita (Department of the Treasury et al., 2006). This comes as no surprise, given the economic dynamics of a country in which the national currency stands cheek by jowl with the US dollar, especially on certain markets. Since the end of the 1970s, the Argentine real estate market has operated in US dollars: not only are prices listed and published in this foreign currency, but also the transactions themselves are done in greenbacks.

During the second half of the twentieth century, the US dollar played a starring role in the international history of money. After the Second World War, victory on the battlefield and a booming industry made the US dollar almighty in international currency dealings, as seen in the intergovernmental agreements struck at the Bretton Woods Conference in 1944. The stability associated with the gold standard was to be short lived. Twenty-five years later, under Republican president Richard Nixon, the United States made a unilateral decision to sever the direct convertibility of its dollars into gold, thus ending the gold standard. Since then, the US dollar has invigorated the economic liberalization and financialization associated with neoliberalism.

Reflecting on this dynamic, anthropologist Jane Guyer (2016) has noted how in the 1970s, the US dollar reigned supreme as the global foreign trade currency, a common exchange medium, and, most of all, a store of value in different regional landscapes, giving shape to a new era of multiple currencies. Despite this general trend, this powerful global currency has penetrated national economies in different ways depending on the economic, political, and cultural history of each individual country.

How did the dollar come to play such a leading role in Argentina? What cultural, economic, and political processes made the US currency dominant on certain domestic markets? How did the dollar-peso exchange rate become an everyday part of life, something nearly everyone follows? In other words, how precisely did this global currency become a local currency on the other end of the Americas?

These are some of the questions that this book addresses. For some time, the global expansion of the US currency and its influence on the economic dynamics of different regions was understood as a natural offshoot of America's predominance in the world economy (Eichengreen, Mehl, and Chitu 2019). However, as the case of Argentina reveals, this process is more complex and, more importantly, exceeds geopolitics. While the dollar is, in fact, a global currency anchored in many countries, multiple articulations of local history, economy, and culture have allowed this grafting. By offering a new lens on the dollar, this book examines another dimension of the economic and political predominance of the United States, telling the story of the greenback as a popular currency outside its home country's borders.

## A Popular Currency

To respond to the questions posed above, we draw on the sociology of money to propose a sociology of the dollar's popularization in Argentine society. Two dynamics fall under the lens: the emergence of the dollar as an artifact of popular culture and its incorporation in the financial repertoires of a growing number of social groups. Each of these dynamics constitutes a specific dimension of the US dollar's social life in Argentina: its public existence—where the greenback is mostly a piece of information, a public number loaded with multiple social meanings—and its private, transactional life, where it is an asset as well as an object that can be seen, touched, hoarded, or burned.

Our approach draws on Viviana Zelizer's reflection on the social uses and meanings of money (Zelizer 1994). Showing how people constantly differentiate between money's connotations and uses according to the social relations in which it circulates, Zelizer has contributed to a deep understanding of the history of the US dollar as it grew into a national homogeneous currency in the late nineteenth century. Her work, which considers the rise of the American currency, provides a new perspective on the role money plays in social life.

However, a different approach is needed to capture how the US dollar later evolved into a global currency anchored in heterogeneous territories. In order to understand what occurs with the US currency outside America's borders, we need to go beyond Zelizer's classic work. Through the reconstruction of the social and cultural history of the US dollar in Argentina, we propose to home in on this phase of the dollar's history, showing how it became a particular "popular currency" even outside its country of origin.

The US dollar in Argentina was slowly but progressively popularized from the 1930s until the second decade of the twenty-first century. Over this period, information about the dollar, formerly of interest exclusively for financial agents or foreign trade experts, began holding political relevance for increasingly broader social groups. At the same time, the dollar was gradually incorporated to the financial repertoires of a growing number of Argentines. Yet without the highly decisive mediations that had preceded this phase, it would never have been possible for social actors with virtually no contact with the financial or exchange market to incorporate the greenback to their savings, investment, loan, and consumer practices. The building of the US dollar as a popular cultural artifact made it into a familiar currency, one capable of providing cognitive, emotional, and practical guidance for anyone venturing into an unfamiliar economic universe. Therefore, starting in the 1930s, but especially from the 1950s on, a new relationship between popular culture, financial practices, and the exchange market resulted in the dollar's increasingly central role in Argentine economy and politics.

In order to understand this process, a careful examination is needed of the cultural devices that helped establish the buck in the public's mind, integrate it to their financial repertoires, and allow it to persist over time. On the one hand, a sociology of this sort must reveal the cultural mediations that make money practices with a "strange" currency familiar, legitimate, understandable, and doable for a great many Argentines. On the other, it must acknowledge that as cultural devices, currencies add meanings and public uses to money that do not necessarily or automatically correspond to specific financial repertoires. The reconstruction of both the connection and the relative autonomy between the "two lives" of currencies (as cultural artifacts that operate in the public space and as stores of value and a medium for payment and exchange within financial repertoires) is at the core of this research into the process of a currency's popularization.

## Local Stories of a Global Currency

While the US currency did not achieve global hegemony until the Second World War, its rise dates back a few decades prior. As the United States rose to predominance in foreign trade, the dollar began competing with the sterling pound; at the same time, the American banking system expanded globally, flooding the financial market with bonds denominated in dollars (Eichengreen 2011). In the 1910s, the State Department launched a foreign policy known as "dollar diplomacy" that aimed to foster the interest of private American firms abroad, particularly in Latin America and Asia. Companies were thus encouraged to play a role in foreign trade and make investments outside the US (Rosenberg 2004). In these contexts,

> "dollar diplomacy" involved the promotion not just of trade and investment but of the dollar itself, a practice that we might call "dollarization diplomacy." With the exception of Puerto Rico, however, US policymakers did not . . . encourage the dollar to be adopted as the exclusive currency of foreign countries. Instead, they simply pressed for it to be used alongside the national currency abroad. (Helleiner 2003a, 409)

At the end of the First World War, the United States became the biggest lender to European countries struggling to recover from the war but also to Latin American countries affected by the collapse of trade with these countries. For that reason, over the course of the 1920s, reserves denominated in dollars at many banks worldwide began to overtake those of other traditionally strong currencies like the sterling pound. During the interwar period, New York rivaled London as a financial center, and the dollar contended with the pound as the foremost international currency (Eichengreen and Flandreau 2008). In Latin America, the rising leadership of the United States during the interwar period was also evident in the invitations extended to American economic experts to help the region's governments build local monetary, financial, and tax systems. These "money doctors" also helped the dollar make headway (Drake 1989).

The relative balance between the dollar and sterling pound during the 1920s would be suddenly interrupted by the Great Depression. The US economy during this decade was nearly autarkic, with protectionist policies that heavily reduced foreign trade. This period marked the transition toward a new world order that would come in the 1940s with the Bretton Woods agreement. Though rooted in the gold standard, the agreement made the US dollar the only convertible currency, effectively introducing what could be called the "dollar standard" (Aglietta and Coudert 2014). The equilibrium achieved at the war's end, however, would not last forever. In 1971, under the Nixon administration, the United States decided to end the gold standard. Far from undermining the buck's position as a global currency, this decision actually consolidated it.

The dollar has become a "savage money," to use the term coined by Australian anthropologist Chris Gregory (1997) when describing this new international phase of the global economy's strongest currency. Since then, the dollar helped accelerate the economic liberalism and financialization associated with neoliberalism. Free of any bounds in the search for profits, it operated in a "savage" way, seizing on volatile, unregulated exchange rates.

In many of the countries along the periphery, this process led to systems of monetary pluralism. If the process of African decolonization between the 1960s and 1980s provided particular insight into the complex exchanges, operations, and actors behind several coexisting currencies, the collapse of the Eastern Bloc provided yet another. Starting in the 1990s, the capitalist world had entered a new phase of multiple currencies, similar to what Africa had seen in the past (Guyer and Salami 2013, 13). But in this case, two overlapping phenomena appeared: on the one hand, the multiplication of the national currencies (twenty-two new currencies created in the postcolonial period and fifteen new currencies in the postsocialist period); on the other hand, there was a proliferation of the circuits in which the US dollar became the single, common currency (Guyer and Salami 2013, 4).

This second phenomenon spoke of a new economic and monetary configuration at the beginning of the 1970s: from the point of view of economic theory, the primordial monetary function was determined to be storing value (Guyer 2011; Orléan 2009). However, in terms of how monetary economies and economic practices were configured at the local level, the US dollar was consolidated as the currency used not only in foreign commerce globally, but also as a common account and exchange unit in different regions and nations.

This disaggregation of the monetary functions, no longer embodied in a single national currency but in different coexisting ones, is expressed in the common distinction between soft and hard currencies, where only those which serve as a store of value are considered "strong." The recent history of money in widely different nations can be understood as an expansion of monetary plurality that creates a lasting bond between a strong currency (the US dollar) and a weak local currency. Interesting cases in this regard include Israel (Dominguez 1990), Russia (Lemon 1998), Nigeria (Guyer 2004), Vietnam (Truitt 2013), and Latin American countries like Panama, Ecuador (Nelms 2015), Cuba (Marques-Pereira and Théret 2014), and El Salvador (Pedersen 2002).

This connection between the US dollar and "weaker" local currencies can, in some cases, lead to the former actually replacing the latter, as occurred in Panama (since 1904), Ecuador (since 2000), or El Salvador (since 2001). In other cases, the local currency is substituted only partially and for certain money purposes (as in Israel or Cuba, at certain points in time). At the same time, these are situations that can go on for decades—the case of Argentina, as will be seen in this book—or for only a certain period of time, like that of the former USSR at the beginning of the 1990s or Israel in the 1980s. Finally, the recurring use of the dollar can be de facto, as is most often the case, or enshrined in law, as it was in Panama, Ecuador, and El Salvador, or in Zimbabwe's and Argentina's currency board (1991–2001).

Countries that were former colonies or suffered a military invasion—or heavy foreign investment—by the United States (Panama, Haiti, Vietnam, and Cuba) are more likely to experiment with different types of dollarization; this is also the case for countries like El Salvador and Vietnam, which receive a good deal of remittances in US dollars sent by nationals living abroad. Other circumstances that can lead to a total or partial replacement of a local currency include extreme levels of inflation (as has occurred in many Latin American countries), foreign trade restrictions (Cuba and Nigeria), or disruptive political events like wars or the collapse of political regimes (as observed in the USSR or Vietnam).

As noted, the Argentine experience is different from that of most of the other countries. Argentina has never been occupied by the United States (the case of Vietnam or Cuba), nor does it fall within its geographical range of influence (as do Central American or Caribbean nations). Similarly, there is not a large community of Argentine migrants in America, so remittances in US dollars do not have a huge impact on its GDP (the case in El Salvador).

Generally, scholars and the press have focused on the country's economic history and macroeconomics when attempting to explain what makes Argentina unique. Two of these factors include inflation and foreign trade bottlenecks, which cyclically lead to a lack of foreign currency that could stimulate the economy. Effectively, since the 1940s, Argentina has experienced repetitive cycles of rising prices—some gradual, others sudden and extreme. At its worst, inflation reached an average of 340 percent between 1984 and 1988 in addition to two moments of hyperinflation in 1989 and 1990 (Bulmer-Thomas 2014), contributing to the dollar's consolidation as a reserve currency, used to protect Argentines against the depreciation of their local currency. At the same time, since the second half of the twentieth century, the Argentine economy has suffered chronic shortages of the foreign currency it needs to fund development, causing a nearly constant trade deficit. Finally, and especially since the 1980s, the weight of the foreign debt has exacerbated monetary pressures.

It should be noted, however, that the inflation Argentina has experienced is similar to that of other countries in the region like Brazil (Neiburg 2006; 2010), though the buck did not evolve into a "popular money" in these countries. Another factor emphasized in literature on the topic (Wainer 2021) is that foreign restrictions are also not exclusive to Argentina but plague the vast majority of semi-peripheral countries (Abeles, Lavarello, and Montagu 2013). Finally, although the greenback does have a certain presence in a range of other countries (like Israel), the greenback's persisting weight in society, politics, and the economy dates back decades and cannot be pinpointed to any single moment or period.

## A Sociological Reading

Any sociological interpretation of the dollar's prominence must consider the configuration of the economic structure, shifting public policies, the global economy, and the conditions these impose on the ways different social actors invest, save, and spend money. Yet it cannot be limited to these considerations alone.

The money practices of families and businesses are not automatic responses to any macroeconomic stimulus or restriction; they evolve in a historical process of economic socialization and education in financial repertoires that are socially produced and culturally meaningful. This is the point of departure for the perspective that will be constructed in this book. Its main contribution is to highlight the gradual processes that allow a financial repertoire to take root. In the case of Argentina, one of the main features of this repertoire is the articulation of different currencies—the US dollar and the Argentine peso—in everyday life, but also in the public and cultural sphere.

This way of understanding the overlapping processes of the US dollar's popularization, an economic socialization shaped by the dollar, and the construction over time of financial repertoires that make use of it rests on three pillars. First, it draws on the tradition of the sociology of money, a field that Viviana Zelizer helped to innovate in the 1990s. Second, it employs developments from contemporary economic anthropology and the anthropology of money, enriched by their unique approach to social universes characterized by multiple currencies and their different configurations over time and space (Hart 1986; Guyer 1995, 2016; Maurer 2006; Neiburg 2006, 2010, 2011; Wilkis 2017a). Third, it engages in dialogue with the institutionalist approach to money developed in France since the 1980s, an approach that takes precedence over more classical economic definitions, where money is treated as instrumental and fungible (Aglietta and Orléan 1998; Théret 2007; Orléan 2013; Blanc 2018; Alary et al. 2020).

"I finally understood the historical paradox that just as the U.S. state worked to achieve a single national currency, people were continually disrupting monetary uniformity by creating all sorts of monetary distinctions" (Zelizer 2016). Two decades after *The Social Meaning of Money* was first published, this is Zelizer's assessment of one of the most important discoveries of her book. Charles Tilly (1999) underlined this same finding when he noted that Zelizer's sociology of money had contributed to a "bottom up" theory of power that revealed the everyday practices of "those at the bottom" against the state. The paradox that Zelizer had noted rests in the discovery of people's enormous creativity when it comes time to use and give meaning to money. By placing the emphasis on the maneuvering room people have in the face of state power, Zelizer opened the door for a critical reevaluation of classical theories on how modern societies had taken shape.

In the past, classic sociology had contributed to an imaginary of homogeneous currencies associated with unified states. In the nineteenth and twentieth centuries, territorially homogeneous and exclusive currencies were issued across the Western world. This responded to the consolidation of nation-states and the goal of promoting the domestic markets while fostering certain technological advances (Helleiner 2003b). Under classic sociological theory like that of Karl Marx or Georg Simmel, currency homogenization was assumed to have negative effects on subjectivities and social relations. These critiques, however, served to reiterate the need for each nation-state to operate in a single currency. For these authors, the expansion of monetization was synonymous with currency homogenization and imposed moral uniformity across societies, forging the values and aspirations of the capitalist *homo economicus*. Within a certain branch of classic sociology, state unification, currency homogenization, and moral uniformity were mutually reinforcing processes (Wilkis 2018).

Zelizer's sociology of money questioned these theoretical imaginaries that associate homogeneous currencies with unified states and the moral uniformity of society. Based on the empirical context (the process of monetary unification within a society taking shape according to the modern capitalist society model) and the theoretical challenge she posed (questioning the ideas of classic sociology on the effects of modernity in interpersonal life), Zelizer approached "domestic currencies" as a privileged scenario for her theory of "special monies." The study of the uses and meanings of money in the intimate realm, outside the market, allowed Zelizer to test out her interpretation. This reading collided with the hypotheses of authors like Marx, Simmel, and Max Weber, who argued that market impersonality was a key part of monetizing modern societies.[1] Domestic monies were thus the privileged empirical locus for a sociological theory that went a step beyond the aporias of the classic theory of modernity. In her subsequent research, in fact, Zelizer continued to analyze money in intimacy or within the framework of intimate relationships (Zelizer 2005). In these investigations, she was able to show how interpersonal relations are not dissolved when money circulates; instead, people creatively redefine them. These monies provided the empirical evidence necessary to break down the seemingly impenetrable walls of classic theoretical narratives surrounding money.

The relevance of Zelizer's analysis on the social meanings of money, in fact, has also been evidenced in spheres outside the household, including banks and financial markets (Carruthers 2017; Polillo 2017). Although works by scholars such as these make a relevant contribution by testing Zelizer's sociology of money outside the intimate sphere, they make no attempt at rebuilding the connections between this sphere and the public, institutional realm. Others have proposed macrocultural approaches (Carruthers and Babb 1996) and macro-social analyses (Helleiner 2017) to study the meanings of money. Although these explorations have successfully drawn attention to public or institutional dynamics in the production of meanings about money, they make no attempt to link these "top-down" processes with daily practices at the "bottom." The disconnect between the macro- and micro-dynamics neglects questions fundamental to the circulation of the US currency in territories with heterogeneous currencies. How do people incorporate a currency? How does a "foreign" currency become familiar outside the borders of the state that issues it? This is a question that the sociology of money should be able to answer.

Zelizer's strategy to analyze the gradual establishment of the US dollar as the sole currency—and then critique the hypothesis on money in classic sociology—is limited to only one of the dollar's functions: its role as a medium of payment or exchange. A great part of the author's analysis focuses on the dollar's restricted circulation despite currency homogenization, and its variations in myriad relationships and social situations. Drawing on a conceptual and empirical proposal that makes use of earmarking, multiple currencies, etc., Zelizer questioned the universal fungibility that classic sociological theories attributed to modern currencies. Zelizer successfully showed how the dollar's circulation was confined despite the currency standardization and homogenization imposed by the US state, and argued that these restrictions were basically social (moral prohibitions, ritual practices, etc.). Therefore, her criticism of universal fungibility is well-founded, weakening the perception that money configures an impersonal society, or one indifferent to the attributes of interpersonal relations.

This important finding by Zelizer, however, leaves aside issues that become fundamental when attempting to analyze the transformation of the dollar into a global currency that circulates in territories with their own national currencies. Unlike the contexts where territorially unified currencies triumph, the phase of the dollar as a global currency implies multiple currencies that circulate simultaneously.

As many authors have noted, the generally accepted idea of a unified national currency is more of a political norm than a fact of modern societies (and its precedents, we could argue), which always tolerated multiple currencies to some degree (Servet, Théret, and Yildirim 2020). This multiplicity emerges from a range of payment methods (issued by different entities), in a continuous tension with a unified account measure. Jerôme Blanc has shown how central banks are the institutions that generally make this set of heterogeneous means of payment coherent by guaranteeing their convertibility into a single unit of account (Blanc 2009, 662). For these reasons, far from an anomaly, the multiple monies circulating within a single nation should be considered a normal feature of modern currency systems (Théret 2007; Servet, Théret, and Yildirim 2020; Théret 2008; Orléan 2009).

Following in the footsteps of renowned anthropologists studying the currencies of Atlantic Africa (Bohannan 1959; Dalton 1961), Jane Guyer has contributed to an empirically informed understanding of the multiplicity of money (Guyer 1995; 2004). Her research shows that the multiple currencies common to African economies are anything but exceptional, and her more recent works have taken these findings even further to show the diverse circles in which different monies circulate within a singular country. At the same time, Guyer highlights the conversion processes that prove key in this configuration of monetary pluralism (2016).

By incorporating contributions of this kind, the study of money can go beyond the model of a unitary, territorially homogeneous currency. At the same time, it can enrich the understanding of the functions of money, moving away from its image as exclusively a medium of payment or exchange. Money's role as a unit of account or store of value can thus be incorporated, creating a more suitable perspective for understanding how the dollar ends up circulating in multiple territories outside the United States.

Finally, in order to grasp how the greenback becomes a "special money," processes must be analyzed from the top down and the bottom up, in the public sphere and in ordinary financial practices. In order to forge connections between these two levels, it is important to bring in the contributions of a sociology of money that considers both its uses and social meanings. This perspective must also be informed by an anthropology that provides ethnographic insight into contemporary forms of monetary pluralism and the relationships that make it possible. Finally, monetary theory must also inform this approach, providing conceptual tools to think about the different forms money takes (Théret 2008), particularly with regard to different coexisting monies within a single territory. That is the challenge this book embraces.

## The Hegemony of the Dollar and Finance: A Bottom-Up Perspective

The sociology of money as laid out in this book relies on a long-term historical approach to examine the social, cultural, and political roots that allow a global currency to become a local money. This type of perspective is rare in literature focused on the hegemony of the greenback and its implications for both Latin America and the rest of the planet.

Much has already been said about the US currency's role in entrenching US hegemony since the mid-twentieth century. Books such as *Exorbitant Privilege: The Rise and Fall of the Dollar* (Eichengreen 2011), *The Future of the Dollar* (Helleiner 2009), and *Le dollar et le système monétaire international* (Aglietta and Coudert 2014) all reveal how the dollar acquired a central position in the world monetary system during the twentieth century. But its conversion into a "global currency" that circulates in multiple territories (not merely as a currency among elites) still needs to be explored. Other aspects of the dollar that remain to be examined include its integration as a unit of account or as a payment or exchange method among vast sectors of the global south in monetary repertoires that may or may not include other national currencies.

Far from considering the dollar as a unilateral imposition by the US government at the global level, this book helps reconstruct the transformations of capitalism and its institutions, the structural economic conditions of a semi-peripheral country, and the political-cultural dynamics of this process. Without them, the greenback would have remained the exclusive currency of the elites and never become a popular currency.

From this perspective, the argument presented here engages with two lines of thought on how Argentine society came to embrace the US dollar. First, the "popularization of dollar" could be considered part of the "informal imperialism" (Gindin and Panitch 2013) or the "dollar-Wall Street" regime (Gowan 1999) that characterizes the United States today. Yet both perspectives tend to overlook the social and economic conditions that helped American currency take root without the intervention of experts, elites, or international financial institutions. The classic by Ricardo Parbonni, *The Dollar and Its Rivals* (1981), also analyzes the outsized role of the dollar in the international economic system and elites' persistent involvement on the exchange market. However, this book goes a step further by observing the dollar not only within that restricted universe but also in people's ordinary, everyday lives.

By examining how culture, politics, and economy come into play in the popularization of the US dollar, this book innovates on the study of the hegemony of global currencies in both theoretical and empirical terms. It offers a detailed account of how the hegemony of America's currency takes root by gradually gaining the acceptance of ordinary people in peripheral countries.

Second, this book narrates a particular expansion of "financial capitalism" in the terms proposed by Costas Lapavitsas (2013). Social studies of finance have been one of the most prolific fields in economic sociology and anthropology in recent years. As institutions that globalized capitalism relies on, financial markets captured the attention of academic and nonacademic researchers alike (Zaloom 2006; Callon, Milo, and Muniesa 2008; Mackenzie 2008; Preda 2009; Ho 2012; Krippner 2012; Knorr Cetina and Preda 2012; Beunza 2019; Ortiz 2021). Yet this work analyzes a case—that of foreign exchange markets—that has received scarce attention in this literature, examining their role as a financial institution essential to peripheral economies and the economic and cultural life of citizens as well.

As elsewhere, individuals in Argentina, a peripheral country with scarce capital market development that has suffered from medium to high inflation for much of the last seven decades, are impacted by processes of financial expansion. In this case, however, the exchange market has played a fundamental and unique role in these processes. What is referred to herein as the popularization of the US dollar has been critical to allowing Argentines to adapt to the new phase of capitalism that began in the 1970s. In relation to the thesis on financial capitalism, this book shows the particular articulations between economic structure, the political system, and cultural mediations, making the popularization of the US dollar both a condition and an outcome of the financialization of individuals and households in Argentina.

## The Conditions of Democracy: A Latin American Concern

Over the course of the twentieth century, research on Latin America has honed in on the economic, social, and cultural conditions of political processes in order to understand the "atypical" path of countries in the region in comparison to those of other Western democracies. As part of this research agenda, studies on "classic" populism of the 1940s and 1950s (Juan Domingo Perón in Argentina, Getúlio Dorneles Vargas in Brazil, and Lázaro Cárdenas in Mexico) (Germani 1972; French 1989; Knight 1998) merged with literature on military dictatorships and the end to democracies (Petras and Zeitlin 1968; Rouquié 1981), and investigations on the "democratic transitions" of the 1980s (O'Donnell et al. 1986). Taking into account the importance of political processes in the study of the region's societies, this book examines the role that the meanings and uses of money played in said processes. In Max Weber's view, money occupies a very significant place in political sociology. For example, the payment corresponding to the administrative staff of each type of legitimate domination is one of its distinguishing factors. Weber explores both the type (regular, extraordinary, etc.) as well as the payment method (money, in kind) received by the administrative officials in charismatic, traditional, or legal-rational domination. The relationship between politics and money also appears in other works by the German sociologist, who understood democratization to be connected with the monetization of political life. All regular competition between political parties drives the monetization of its activities (Weber 1978). Money helps oil the political machinery (Wilkis 2017b).

Though it does not focus on the monetary dimension of professional politics, this book does examine the impact of the dollar's popularization on the game of politics. It also aims to explore how the uses and meanings that citizens attribute to money influence the interpretations and political decisions of career politicians. Despite how essential this approach proves to an understanding of the past forty years of democracy in Argentina, it has largely been overlooked in studies on the dynamics of participation in Latin American democracies. Money (in general) and monetary practices (in particular) have been emphasized in studies on political party financing (Leiras 2004) and research into the transactions that take place in client politics (Auyero 2001). Yet the question of how monetary cultures influence the political participation of citizens and thus condition the practices of professional politicians has yet to be explored.

Since Argentine democracy was restored in 1983, the economic, cultural, and political implications of the dollar's popularization have been patently clear. If the sociology of money sets out to underline the diverse connotations and uses of this object while exploring its roots, this book contributes by showing how the popularization of the US currency in Argentina resulted in practices and meanings that are also political. These can be seen in the way in which Argentines experience democratic processes and the state. People's close attention to the forex market is part of the financial decisions they will make, but it also figures into their political expectations and experiences. By following the fluctuations of this market, Argentines are able to participate in political life and assess the government's performance—or the opposition's chances in an upcoming election. On the other hand, the incorporation of the dollar in both household and corporate financial repertoires also denotes a singular and to some degree autonomous way of relating to the Argentine state. The knowledge and lessons that come with this autonomy afford protection against monetary regulations and the cyclical breakdowns of the state. In these uses and meanings of the dollar lies a political lesson on protecting oneself from—and resisting— the state.

Introduction

# The "Argentine Dollar" over the Years: Stages of Popularization

One of the tenets of the sociology of money is that money is never the same. The practices and connotations of the dollar in Argentina in the 1950s were not the same as those of the 1970s, 1980s, or 1990s. Each stage in the popularization of the dollar represents an innovation on the uses and meanings inherited from the past. As the dynamics changed, the dollar's reach varied: over time, more social groups dabbled in the exchange market (from the economic and state elites in the 1930s and 1940s to workers, retirees, women, and youth in the 1980s). The proliferation of the dollar also fluctuated: the use of this legal tender as a unit of reference or payment method increasingly spread to more markets and transactions, from the tourism market in the 1950s to the real estate market, art world, and automobile industry in the 1980s. In fact, during times of crisis like the hyperinflation of 1989, Argentines used the dollar as a payment method for everyday services like plumbing or psychology sessions, though these practices later faded. Finally, the intensification of its use varied as well. Originally the exclusive focus of foreign trade actors, the US dollar has become a central political indicator in all electoral campaigns since the return to democracy in 1983.

The process analyzed here extends over several decades through five periods of the dollar's popularization in Argentine society. In each of the periods identified, the public life of the dollar aligns with the transactional use of this same currency in a singular way. At the same time, the social expansion, economic proliferation, and political and cultural intensification of the dollar advanced at a different pace during each of these stages. Our central empirical aim was to understand the practices and implications that took hold and emerged in each stage of the dollar's popularization in Argentine society. By establishing the specific temporality of the dollar's double life—as both a public and household currency, connecting the public sphere to private financial repertoires—we are able to discover the diverse meanings and uses that have made the dollar a "popular" currency far from its home territory.

The 1930s and 1940s represent what we could call the prehistory of the buck's popularization in Argentina. Following the introduction of the country's first exchange market regulations—and a global economic crisis—the dollar became a prominent topic in the news. However, the elites alone were interested in the dollar, which did not yet stand out from other "strong" currencies (the sterling pound, the French franc) in those years.

The first stage of the dollar's popularization begins at the end of the 1950s and beginning of the 1960s. During those years of political and economic instability, the dollar made headline news, gradually evolving into a benchmark that allowed both market experts and novices to understand the economic state of affairs. This is the moment in which the dollar's public prominence is furthest from its actual use as a medium of exchange: although the exchange rate gradually becomes a number to watch among business executives as well as housewives, it rarely figures into household economies.

The situation changes radically in the following stage, in which the dollar becomes a pressing concern for the public and the authorities alike, as increasingly broader social groups begin buying and selling the foreign currency. The seventies bring successive changes at the regulatory level: a period of intense forex market regulations (1971–1973) followed by liberal financial reforms (1977–1980). During this decade, the dollar will be incorporated to the financial repertoires of families as a tool for savings and investments, a trend that will continue with renewed force in the following stage.

The eighties start and end in crisis (in 1981 and 1989). Though the latter proves much more extreme than the former, the dollar plays a prominent role in both. During this decade, high inflation will characterize the Argentine economy as well as that of other countries in the region (Frenkel 1990; Damill and Frenkel 1990), resulting in hyperinflation in 1989 and 1990. At its peak, the US currency will reign above all others in both public and private terms. The dollar's popularization comes to a head in this third stage, and it is widely used as a medium of exchange.

The fourth stage of the dollar's popularization begins in 1991 with the currency board, in which the US dollar becomes legal tender alongside the Argentine peso. In this period, the day-to-day financial repertoires of Argentine companies and families, even low-income households, incorporate the greenback. At the same time, the prominence of the dollar in the public's attention wanes as its use as a medium of exchange increases; the dollar ceases to be a topic of concern. This new balance, however, comes to an abrupt end with the end of the currency board and the 2001–2002 crisis. At the same time, besides returning as a constant in public debates, the uses of US currency shift during these tumultuous times: the dollar begins to be articulated as part of the language of rights and social protest.

Finally, the fifth stage of the dollar's popularization traces the years from the recovery of the 2001–2002 economic crisis until 2015. During this period, particularly between 2011 and 2015, the dollar's popularization intensifies in novel ways. While the use of this currency has now been instilled among large swaths of the population, the public and political discussion around the dollar escalates, with state actors taking on a new role. While in the 1990s, the dollar's use as a medium of exchange had risen as its salience in public debate waned, the two go hand in hand yet again in these years. The role of the dollar's popularization in democratic processes since 1983 becomes particularly evident in this final stage. In virtually all presidential elections of the period, the forex market proves a political flashpoint, and interpretations on the exchange rate influence citizen choices at the polls.

## Research Itinerary

In a country in which game-show contestants are expected to know the dollar-peso exchange rate, there is a surprising lack of research on the local penchant for the dollar. The investigation behind this book began in 2014, a year in which the news reported daily on forex regulation measures and the varying exchange rates of the US dollar. Beyond print and broadcast media, the official and unofficial (or "blue") exchange rates were key numbers on social media, cell phone message groups, and blogs.

At that point in time, the phenomenon we set out to explore was nothing new; we were aware that certain traits of the US currency had contributed to its local importance. It was more than a store of value: it was a powerful benchmark, a cultural artifact that encapsulated multiple meanings. Yet what aspects of this phenomenon were of particular interest? What social actors relied on the dollar as a financial tool? Who bought, sold, saved, invested, or took out loans in dollars? What were the settings where people knew these bills would be circulating? Other questions followed in relation to who was responsible for relaying the dollar's value. Where and when did this communication take place, and what was its purpose? What meanings and implications were associated with this currency?

As sociologists, we began by analyzing the sociodemographic aspects of this phenomenon, heading out into the field to discover how people from different social and economic universes related to the dollar. We wanted these individuals to show us how the dollar figured into their personal and professional lives at a time in which the greenback was a daily topic of conversations. The initial universe of contacts included builders, developers, and real estate agents; economists, accountants, and other financial professionals at banks; brokerage firms; forex exchange offices both legal and illegal; and financial companies. Farmers, agricultural technicians, grain co-op managers, and farm machinery vendors were also interviewed, as were tourism professionals and employees, and immigrants living in slums who regularly sent back remittances to their countries of origin. In total, 120 individuals gave us personal insights during these interviews while also reconstructing how the dollar circulated in their respective worlds.

At the same time, we set out to explore the social life of the dollar, its daily presence in economic news, expert debates, public discussion, humor, and other cultural productions such as literature, film, and television. The press, including both general media outlets as well as those specializing in the economy, was a prime source. Economic journalists also served as contacts, helping us to understand the logic behind the media's coverage of the dollar.

Our examination of the contemporary life of the dollar led us to points in the past when the US currency took center stage, like when new foreign exchange restrictions were introduced. Existing research pointed to the 1970s as a key moment in time: starting that decade, due to fierce and persisting inflation combined with financial liberalization, the dollar became a fixture of the national economy. The abrupt devaluation of the Argentine peso in 1975 by Economic Minister Celestino Rodrigo—known as the *rodrigazo*—became the first milestone we set out to reconstruct.

As happens in many investigations, the discoveries we made along the way sent us onto a different path. First, as we advanced with our interviews, we began to see that it proved difficult for informants to reconstruct their memory of the dollar, or this memory was limited to specific moments in time (like the rodrigazo or the hyperinflation of 1989). In all cases, the interviewees found it hard to pinpoint the role of the US currency, which they had entirely assimilated. On the other hand, discussions with those who had worked for years in the financial world or the media led us to rethink the period of time we would cover in the research. According to the personal memories and records of their professional activities, the dollar occupied a prominent place long before 1975. At the same time, media articles from the 1970s revealed that the affinity for the dollar was already a "chronic problem" in Argentina.

Just when did Argentines start fixating on the US dollar? It was necessary to go further back. What had started as a sociological investigation with a traditional qualitative methodology was reformulated as archival research. The general criterion remained the same: to identify moments in twentieth-century Argentina during which monetary policy in general, and forex regulation in particular, had been topics of public debate. The first foreign exchange controls, introduced in 1931 after the military seized power and appointed General José Féliz Uriburu president, became the new point of departure. Therefore, we decided to abandon our ethnographic approach to the topic, turning instead to the documentary sources we had gathered with the same questions we had initially formulated for the personal interviews. We thus undertook what could be referred to as an "archival ethnography" (Decker and McKinlay 2020) in our attempt to discover how the dollar became part of public life and personal habits in Argentina.

There was yet another reason to reorient our methodological strategy and expand on the body of documents employed for the research. Now that we realized we needed to go back further in time, the in-depth interviews were limited by the ages of our informants. In addition, personal interviews would give us only superficial answers to one of our main questions: How did the dollar become so popular among Argentines? How did Argentine men and women become familiar with the US currency, learn to maneuver an often-fluctuating exchange rate, find out where to buy and sell it, and contribute to building its multiple meanings? Our questions were as much about economics as they were about culture. Responding to these questions, then, required a detailed description of economic practices and calculations, and a careful analysis of the cultural devices that made the dollar into not only a public figure but also a core part of the financial repertoires of vast sectors of society.

Much of the corpus that informed this book provided monetary lessons, to borrow the term coined by Federico Neiburg (2006; 2010), teaching different sectors of the public how to participate in the exchange market. Though not all participated equally or got involved as quickly, these financial agents learned to move within the shifting borders of financial markets (Preda 2009) as a result of the tips, guides, and training these materials provided. By examining the national dailies, weekly news magazines (during the years they existed), and economic journals (targeting readers from the business world), we were able to reconstruct the dollar's gradual evolution into a newsworthy currency. Though the coverage of the buck varied in different news outlets, it clearly stood out from all other foreign currencies, progressively moving from the inside pages to headlines and then covers. Journalists reported on the economy, and the foreign exchange market was part and parcel; this reporting, which employed different techniques during the periods analyzed, made the forex universe understandable for the public at large. The positions of editorial boards of the major papers were another focus.

In terms of different cultural productions, print media was our foremost source, particularly the advertisements and comics. However, film and theater also proved insightful, as well as, more recently, social media posts and even memes circulating on WhatsApp. All were sources of information and fundamental channels for expanding the borders of legitimate access, participation, and interpretation on the forex market. Other valuable material was later added to our original corpus, like the archives of the government departments that battled the illegal foreign exchange market at different times, the records of art institutions or sports club, and documents from the first decades of Argentine television.

## A Blueprint of This Book

The history covered in this book begins in the early twentieth century and leads up to the present. While it touches on the foremost political and economic transformations Argentina experienced over these years (revolutions, changes in government, coups d'état), the timeline proposed herein corresponds to the pace and prominence of the US dollar. Each chapter covers one of the stages in which the greenback gradually developed into a popular currency of Argentina.

Chapter 1, "Before the Dollar Became a Global Currency (1931–1955)," describes how exchange market regulations in Argentina helped the country's economy emerge from the Great Depression. In those years, the dollar had not yet developed into a special money, to use the term coined by Viviana Zelizer. The public meanings attributed to the dollar—exclusively by the upper classes—were no different than those of other currencies. In fact, economic and political elites were still the only social groups with any dealings on the exchange market, which was then mostly limited to foreign trade and illegal activities.

The topic of chapter 2, "Bretton Woods on the Streets of Buenos Aires (1959–1971)," examines how the US currency, once the money of the elites, gradually became part of mass culture, though it was not yet completely incorporated into the everyday financial repertoires of diverse social groups. Using a range of sources, this chapter reconstructs the first stage of the dollar's popularization, uses, and meanings to reveal how the public and private life of the dollar were autonomous but interconnected, allowing it to evolve into a familiar currency for a great part of Argentine society.

Chapter 3, "A Global Currency in Argentine Pockets and Pocketbooks (1971–1983)," explores how political convulsions (coups d'état, a succession of military governments, weak democratic governments) and economic uncertainty (recurring devaluation, a rise in inflation, foreign trade restrictions) helped consolidate the process that had started in the previous decade. The US decision to suspend the convertibility of dollars into gold in 1971 ushered in a new model of capitalist accumulation and invigorated the financial sector. During this new stage, the dollar—now a global currency—would further penetrate the Argentine economy, politics, and culture. From the early 1970s to the early 1980s, even more social groups developed a relationship with US currency. In addition, the dollar itself became even more widespread, with more markets incorporating it as the benchmark currency for transactions, and more popular, with an increasing number of people fixated on its ups and downs. This led to a new watershed moment in the meanings and practices of the dollar to date and marked a new phase.

The popularization of the dollar across Argentine society during the first democratic administration that followed the country's last military dictatorship (1976–1983) is the topic of chapter 4, "Strong Dollar, Weak Democracy (1983–1989)." While the end of the 1980s saw the collapse of the Berlin Wall and a profound crisis of the Socialist Bloc, neoliberalism—especially the reforms introduced by the conservative governments of the United States and the United Kingdom—was taking root in the Western hemisphere. In Latin America, however, things had unfolded differently that decade. At the political level, a great number of countries governed by dictatorships had successfully returned to democratic rule. Economically, however, many had succumbed to instability, with unprecedented levels of inflation and even periods of hyperinflation that wreaked social havoc. Along with the political challenges associated with a return to democracy, the new Argentinean government faced economic difficulties that, though relatively recent, had compounded. While developed nations had kept inflation in check, often through strict neoliberal economics, Argentina would be plagued by a staggering level of inflation over the course of the 1980s, the worst in the country's history. The peak came in 1989 when inflation reached 3,080 percent annually, and, to the relief of all social sectors, the dollar became the currency of choice for everyday transactions and took center stage in public and political life. During 1989, the popularization of the dollar reigned supreme in Argentina.

In chapter 5, "Legal Tender: A Neoliberal Experiment in Dollars (1991–2002)," the focus is on the political, cultural, and economic experiences associated with the currency board (locally referred to as the *modelo de convertibilidad*) introduced in 1991. By acknowledging the US dollar as legal tender, the government ended the unofficial popularization of the dollar—and the headaches it entailed for previous administrations. The designers of the currency board saw this model as a way to institutionalize the different ways in which Argentines related to the US money, regulating both its meanings and daily uses. The ten years of the currency board covered in this chapter were characterized by relatively little fixation on the dollar in the public sphere, given that with a stable exchange rate, there was no need to be closely following its fluctuations. In the private sphere, however, people increasingly held bank accounts, certificates of deposit, loans, and mortgages in dollars; appraisals of properties and other durable goods were also done in this currency. In other words, this institutionalization of the dollar further consolidated its use in the financial repertoires of Argentine society. The currency board thus breathed new meaning into the dollar for Argentines, showing yet again how the uses and meanings of monies always fluctuate over time. As the dollar was now legal tender, Argentines came to consider this currency as a fundamental right.

This particular meaning will be key to understanding the aftereffects of the 2008 crisis that began in the United States and later spread worldwide, and the economic and political dynamics the crisis put into motion. Chapter 6, "The Financial Crisis from the Southern Cone (2008–2015)," describes the attempts to keep the local economy under control despite these tremors, revealing that the exchange market is not merely an economic instance but a core political institution of Argentine society. This chapter demonstrates how the lengthy, gradual process of the dollar's popularization, which this book follows from the 1930s to the present day, is both cause and effect of the workings of the exchange market precisely as a political institution in Argentina.

In the final decade analyzed in chapter 6, from 2008 to 2015, political actors from both the party in power and the opposition measured their chance of success or failure through the greenback's ebb and flow. The harder it became to control the US dollar–peso exchange rate, the slimmer the chances of reelection for any administration. It was simply impossible for Argentine citizens to not pay attention to the dollar, because all economic forecasts and likelihood of political alternatives depended on its fluctuations. Ignoring the exchange rate, which the national media reports on as regularly as it does the weather, would mean excluding oneself from public life. For that reason, it is no surprise that a contestant on the game show Who Wants to Be a Millionaire? was able to guess the peso-dollar exchange rate from a day four years past. If governing in Argentina means governing the dollar, for citizens, keeping up with the dollar is an imperative in political life.

The analysis of chapters 4, 5, and 6 reveals how since the end of the country's last dictatorship in 1983, the forex market became an informal institution (O'Donnell 1996) of Argentine democracy. It has operated as a regulator of citizen expectations and their electoral leanings, while serving as a gauge of whether either the ruling party or opposition will triumph at the polls. Therefore, the money culture shaped by the dollar's popularization—though absent in existing literature—has proven key to the evolution of Argentine democracy for almost forty years.

The conclusions parse sociology's conceptual contributions to the dollar's popularization in Argentina, noting its innovations with regard to the social studies of money. Specifically, this new approach contributes to an understanding of a less visible facet of this global currency: its cultural, political, and social embeddedness in heterogeneous territories. The conclusions also delve into the empirical understanding of multiple currency systems, emphasizing the myriad economic and noneconomic dimensions of this phenomenon as seen throughout the book. Finally, it lays out a new way of understanding the always problematic relationship between economic and politics in a region where perpetual crisis had thwarted economic development and jeopardized institutional stability in many countries. In short, this book proposes to move beyond economic considerations and international relations, providing a close-up of the cultural and political roots necessary for a global currency to become a local one.

*Chapter One*

# BEFORE THE DOLLAR BECAME A GLOBAL CURRENCY (1931–1955)

In March 1939, one of the big-name theaters in the city of Buenos Aires opened its season with a revue starring by Sofía Bozán and Marcos Kaplan, two of the most popular performers of the day. In reviews of the musical, *El dólar está cabrero* (The dollar is raging), critics noted how the song lyrics conveyed an obsession with "our diminished foreign trade with the United States." A decade later, the same theater launched its 1949 season with *La risa es la mejor divisa* (Laughter's the best currency), starring the same performers. The show poster featured a laughing heavyset man in a suit, probably a banker or a businessman, surrounded by bills and coins.

In the 1940s, a more urban revue known as the *revista porteña* had taken the place of the folksier song-and-dance acts of the past (*revista criolla*). The frivolous plays and musicals so popular before World War II had been gradually replaced by a drier humor, and comedy writers increasingly sought inspiration from politics and the economy. *El dólar está cabrero* and *La risa es la mejor divisa* were major productions with popular stars; the former is characteristic of the prewar style, while the latter shows how humor changed after the war. Although the US dollar did not stand out prominently from other currencies at the time, it was gradually becoming a motif in popular culture.

Globally, the 1930s would be the decade in which the dollar would become a global currency, overtaking the sterling pound. Once World War II had ended and the Bretton Woods agreement had been reached, this "exorbitant privilege" (Eichengreen 2011) would become evident. This chapter analyzes the proto-popularization of the US currency in Argentine society. In this analysis, it notes the connection with the dollar's rise as a global currency but also the unique conditions of the Argentine economy that fueled its spread.

In the 1930s and 1940s, Argentina saw the need to shift away from the export-led growth model that had enabled its incorporation to the world economy at the end of the nineteenth century. The country increasingly wagered on industrialization and government intervention as the path forward. The ideological conflicts that accompanied this process—as manifested in the political divide surrounding President Juan Domingo Perón (1946–1955)—also influenced this prehistory of the dollar's popularization in those years.

This period differs from the one that follows, in which the dollar definitively becomes popular Argentine currency, in two key ways. First, the dollar is not yet distinguishable from the sterling pound or the French franc, both of which were also relevant when Argentina originally introduced foreign market exchange restrictions, creating a "shortage" of foreign currency. On the other hand, these affairs were relevant to foreign trade and the country's monetary policy, topics for debate among political, economic, and financial elites, but not yet for the public at large.

This chapter describes how the topic of foreign exchange becomes prominent in the 1930s and then turns to the end of the 1940s, when the US currency began standing out from other international currencies. On the other hand, it addresses how the dollar in public debate becomes explicitly connected to the living conditions of different sectors of society. These sectors are not yet participating on the foreign exchange market as they will in the coming decades, nor have they developed a particular interest in staying abreast on the dollar's worth. In other words, though the visibility of the greenback was far from what it would be in later years, it did acquire a certain public and social role during this period.

## The First Foreign Exchange Controls (1931 and 1933)

In September 1931, as part of a series of measures designed to offset the Great Depression's impact on the domestic economy, the Argentine government decided to introduce forex controls (Salera 1941; Arrarte, 1944; Gerchunoff 2010), following suit with many countries worldwide (Eichengreen 2015). Until that time, meat and grain exports had kept the national economy awash in foreign currency. England's withdrawal from the gold standard and the subsequent devaluation of the sterling pound meant urgent measures were necessary for countries like Argentina where Great Britain had a major influence (Aglietta and Coudert 2015). Administrations set out to contain the crisis that had shaken the agriculture export model to its core; it was a model that had given Argentina a prominent role globally, stimulating its growth and development (Rapoport 2008; Cortes Conde 2005). Foreign exchange controls ushered in a new stage, one in which the tenets of economic liberalism were increasingly drawn into question (O'Connell 1984).

## Chapter One

On October 3, 1931, *La Nación*, one of the country's oldest and most read papers, ran a cover story entitled "Seeking a Realistic Exchange Rate for the Dollar." José Félix Uriburu had been ruling Argentina since the coup d'état that put him into power in 1930.[1] Besides limiting people's access to foreign currencies, Uriburu eluded the devaluation of the sterling pound by limiting currency trading of the Argentine peso to the US dollar and the French franc, both of which were still backed by gold. One official source cited in the newspaper suggested that the government's new forex controls aimed to combat the "psychologically disorienting" effects of "capital evasion" and the "alarm and confusion" this fostered (*La Nación*, October 10, 1931). *La Prensa*, the other major paper, quoted the president of Banco Nación; in his view, the controls sought "to neutralize perturbing factors without perturbing exports or legitimate transactions." Given that "supply and demand are [currently] suffering pathological symptoms," he continued, "limits are needed to encourage prudence and keep the psychological factor from overcoming the economic factor" (*La Prensa*, September 11, 1931).

The decree on foreign exchange control cited the "expectations" surrounding Great Britain's withdrawal from the gold standard. A devalued British pound paralyzed exports, creating "an opportunity for speculators." Therefore, it was "necessary to end this calamitous market anarchy by introducing a centralized method overseen by our most capable men." The foreign exchange market was the perfect setting for a government with authoritarian, nationalistic tendencies to introduce an anti-liberal approach to the economy.

The measures adopted by the administration ended floating exchange rates, fixing them to avoid fluctuations. An Exchange Control Commission was also created to oversee foreign currency transactions at specially authorized banks. Exporters were obliged to hand over all foreign currencies obtained from sales abroad. Importers could apply for exchange permits, which the commission granted according to a list of priorities. Foreign currency the government (national, provincial, or municipal) needed to pay its debts was highest on the priority list, followed by the purchase of raw materials, fuel, and indispensable consumer goods; remittances sent abroad by migrants residing in Argentina; travel expenses; the purchase of nonessential goods; and the repayment or amortization of non-overdue trade obligations (Salera 1941; Arrarte 1944; Gerchunoff 2010).

The aftereffects of the Great Depression had led to increased monetary intervention at the state level, and this would have repercussions of its own. As part of the New Deal, President Franklin D. Roosevelt issued an executive order suspending the gold standard in April 1933 (Eichengreen 2015). The devaluation of the US dollar was felt the world over. A comic strip in *Caras y Caretas*, an emblematic Argentine weekly that had covered politics and culture since 1898, poked fun at the situation. Two men in suits and hats, both looking very high class, have this conversation.

"What are those numbers you're doing?"
"Every day, I note how the dollar is falling. Because I'm hopeful."
"Hopeful that what?"
"That one day, I'll be able to buy them for free." (May 6, 1933)

That same year, the government set out to amend the problems that had arisen since the forex controls had been introduced in 1931. Given the drop in the dollar's value worldwide, those against the controls considered them exceedingly strict. "Our currency's value is artificial," complained members of the Rosario Stock Exchange, an important hub for agricultural trade. According to meeting minutes from November 1933, members considered the controls detrimental for farmers "because they are forced to sell their products at ten times less than they would get on a free market." Just two years earlier, the officials in favor of forex controls had suggested that the "real" exchange rate would emerge once the "economic factor" had curbed the "psychological factor"; now the system of forex controls was being blamed for the currency's "artificial" value.

Importers unable to obtain foreign currency for their purchases were hardest hit by the system introduced in 1931 as they constantly accrued debt. According to Federico Pinedo, economic minister between August 1933 and December 1935,[2] the amendments to the system were aimed at "importing what we can afford." In other words, the demand for imports would simply have to adapt to the availability of foreign currency. In keeping with the new amendments to forex controls, importers would request permits far enough in advance to assure access to the foreign currency they needed and thus avoid accruing debt with foreign banks (mainly in the United States), a problem they had faced since 1931. According to those responsible for its design, the amended system was the stepping stone to an unrestricted forex market like that of the past. The amendment also contemplated negotiations for the debts of importers, allowing them to purchase treasury bonds in dollars that could be converted to sterling pounds provided they received approval from British banks.

Those who supported the amendment also sought to link the Argentine peso to the British pound. In their view, "the policies of Great Britain are healthier and [it represents] Argentina's largest trade partner." In addition, Argentina's foreign debt in sterling pounds had risen, informed *La Prensa* on November 9, 1933. The amendments to the forex control system began taking effect on November 10. The decree on the amendments stipulated,

> The public evidently benefits when the exchange rate of foreign currencies reflects the real market value of national currency. . . . The real value of the peso is not that of the rigid exchange rate that has been in place since November 26, 1931, until the dollar was withdrawn

from the gold standard and has since been set at a constant number of French francs . . . The moment has come for a natural exchange rate for the Argentine peso.

Besides devaluating the peso 20 percent with regard to the French franc, the new system created two foreign exchange markets. The "official" market was reserved for those exports considered "traditional" and imports from countries with which Argentina had payment agreements, while nontraditional exports, foreign investments, and exports to neighboring countries would take place on the "free" market. Foreign currency could only be obtained on the free market for a percentage of imports (from countries with which Argentina had no trade agreement) and remittances sent to those countries; to determine who qualified, a bidding system was designed. A fund was created with the difference between the exchange rate the government paid exporters and the selling rate: the funds accrued from this "exchange rate margin" were used, in part, to finance the Regulation Boards for Meats and Grains, an entity also created during this period that purchased agricultural products at subsidized prices (Rapoport 2008; Cortes Conde 2005). In the official announcements of the exchange rate reform, the economic minister described it as follows:

> The plan we are introducing reflects the reality of our currency today. It is essential to free Argentina's currency from obstacles limiting its movements, allowing it to reach its real value and enabling agricultural products to also be priced in the corresponding currency.

The press covered the implementation of the new system closely. In an article entitled "Reasons for the Relative Exchange Rate Reforms" and published on November 29, 1933, *La Nación* shared "opinions and impressions" of officials and financiers who supported the reform. According to one of the arguments cited, "Everything within our power has been done to move toward a free exchange market while ensuring audit measures to avoid capital evasion and the speculative withholding of foreign currency on the part of exporters." An editorial published that day in the same paper insisted that the government was introducing "transcendental reforms," celebrating the initiative as the first step in a broader plan to rekindle the economy: "The executive branch has taken the necessary measures to proceed with a controlled opening of the international currency market so that foreign exchange rates represent the real economic value abroad of our national currency." Yet according to the editorial, the bidding system "brings new uncertainty and problems due to the bidding wars that will follow: an investor will always prefer to settle, even at a loss, than to chance uncertain loss/gains."

A few months after the introduction of the new regime, some began to accuse the government of "arbitrariness" and "manipulation." In a series of editorials, the newspaper *La Prensa* emphasized the shift in the state's interventions on the foreign exchange market. On January 24, 1934, an editorial entitled "The Dark Room of (Ex) changes" questioned why Congress had not been consulted on the new exchange regime, noting that

> the government has assured arbitrary exchange rate margins . . . It auctions off currencies, but keeps the country in the dark . . . Transactions take place in a dark room. . . . No one knows how much currency is available . . . and no one knows whether these are done at a gain or a loss, only price averages. . . . The government always wins and the merchant always loses . . . This auctioning system [is] not public but secret and random for those bidding because only the government has a window into the dark room of currency exchange for exports.

Three days later, a new editorial reported that the government was keeping the difference between the bid-ask spread. It also challenged the decision to tie the Argentine peso to the pound. In February, *La Prensa* again posed the question, "Why is the exchange rate going up? What is the government's objective: to increase its illegal earnings? To devalue our currency as a political move? The discovery of these malicious acts contributes to the malaise. The very prestige of the executive branch is at stake. And it is important to remember that there is no legal basis for these actions and that the lack of clarifications further complicates the situation." Around this time, businessmen voiced similar issues with the law. The Association of Fabric Importers informed the government of the detrimental effects the forex system had on its members. According to the association, the system was arbitrary and uncertain, favoring those who could bid the highest on foreign currency and thus fostering speculation and driving up prices. As an alternative, they proposed a fixed exchange rate system.

Argentina, like the rest of the Western world, spent the first half of the 1930s trying to recover from the international crisis while the government gradually began to play a new and more proactive role in the economy. This coincided with tumultuous political times, including the coup led by Uriburu in 1930. This was the backdrop for the introductory exchange controls, making the forex market a topic of public debate and political disputes. The difference between the peso's "real" and "artificial" value served both the critics and the supporters of forex market regulation. In the debates at the beginning of the 1930s, the world of foreign currency depended almost exclusively on the relationship between economic elites and the state. The incidence of other social sectors with some involvement in the foreign exchange market—like immigrants, who sent remittances to their countries of origin—was absent from the public debate.

## Perón: "Any of you ever seen a dollar?"

As World War II unfolded, the role that the United States was to play in the global political system in the coming decades became increasingly clear. In 1944, the Bretton Woods Conference laid the groundwork for this new role through a series of agreements on the international monetary and financial system. In the push to position the United States at the center of this configuration, a payment system was established based on the dollar, now the sole world currency convertible into gold and the benchmark for all other currencies. Besides starting the International Monetary Fund and the World Bank, the United Nations thus made the US dollar the global currency of reference (Eichengreen 2010; Aglietta and Coudert 2014).

The development of Argentine industry that had begun in the 1930s accelerated over the next decade. As a new economic model was consolidated, so was a new social structure comprised of the proletariat and an urban subproletariat (Germani 1954). This was the result of internal migration to cities, where job and consumption opportunities abounded. At the political level, industrialization and social integration would be both cause and effect of Juan Domingo Perón's rise to the presidency in 1946.

Perón was the political leader of the movement that has been historically associated with the Argentine working class since its founding in the 1940s. He served as president three times (1946–1951, 1951–1955, and 1973–1974). As a political movement, Peronism defended worker rights, promoted government intervention in the economy, and defended national industry. Peronism depended on strong, charismatic leadership and the support of industrial and farm workers, small and medium-sized business owners, and certain other sectors of the urban middle classes (Germani 1972; Torre 1990; Sidicaro 2002; Murmis and Portantiero 2011).

During the postwar period, the countries that had fought the war cut back on imports and focused on recovering and then increasing prewar production levels. As a result, after enjoying a healthy trade balance throughout World War II, Argentina developed a trade deficit that rose in 1947. In order to continue industrialization, the Peronist government attempted a triangular trade scheme that had worked in the past (Fodor, O'Connell, and Santos 1973). The country received foreign currency from its exports to Great Britain and Europe that it then used to purchase goods and equipment from the United States. Since exports could not keep pace with imports, the Argentine trade deficit with the United States increased drastically in 1947 and

1948. The drain on the Central Bank was evidence of this process, dropping from US$1.7 billion in 1946 to US$1.1 billion in 1947 and nearly half that in 1948.

In June 1947, *La Prensa* ran an editorial entitled "Shipping Gold to the United States." This newspaper, clearly biased against the Peronist administration, contextualizes the postwar changes and the new role that the United States had assumed in foreign trade:

> In fact, our country buys extensively from the United States. Yet in order to close those sales, dollars are needed, be they in form of foreign currencies or deposits credited to banks in that country. Like the deposits, the foreign currency is obtained through sales to U.S. merchants. Let us be clear: the dollars for U.S. purchases can only be obtained by selling to that nation because the translation of the sterling pound to the U.S. dollar is still a problem for which there appears to be no immediate solution.

At the same time, legislators from the non-Peronist parties in Congress asked the government for a report on gold remittances sent abroad and on the movements of the foreign currency account. In June 1947, the government announced it was suspending permits to import automobiles as well as champagne, whiskey, and rayon. At the same time, a new preferential exchange rate was set for the importation of buses and trains. In the face of rumors that began circulating about the peso's devaluation following these changes, the Central Bank announced that "these measures were adopted, in one case, because the existing supply of vehicles could meet the country's needs for a reasonable period and, in the other cases, because the merchandise was considered a luxury" (*Clarín*, June 21, 1947).

Not everyone shared this opinion. An editorial that ran on June 18 in *La Nación*, another newspaper critical of the Peronist government, noted: "It's important to note that automobiles are no luxury: they are an indispensable item for doctors, merchants, and a long list of other workers who require a speedy method of transportation." The topic prompted a comment from General Juan Domingo Perón himself at a talk on June 23 at the headquarters of the Employees of Commerce Union to celebrate a new collective agreement. Standing before the workers, the president insisted on the need for economic independence, because "until we have achieved that, there's no reason to work any longer, no reason for us to make the country richer, when all those riches are taken abroad." He then added,

> They say we've got no foreign currency and that's why we forbade imports of perfume, whiskey, silk and luxury automobiles. We already experienced one postwar period. Looking back to 1918, that was child's

play compared with what is happening in the world today . . . For two straight years, all we talked about was how the fruits of our labor went abroad and now they want us to use those same measures to get back to the same situation we were in in 1920, when instead of buying machinery, steam engines and trains, we pilfered the money on perfumes, whiskey, wine, etcetera . . .

We won't sell bonds to get foreign currency. And logically, those who do business with foreign currency are protesting. Today, our currency has support it didn't have in the past. Our peso is backed by gold 151% and this is unprecedented in Argentina. To get to a point where that backing is just 33%, the way it was back then, we have to hand out a lot of gold. Some say we shouldn't get rid of the gold and I wonder, if famine strikes, can we eat gold? . . . What is the state going to do with the piles of gold in the Central Bank? If we left them right where they are, five years from now, they will not have yielded any profit. Isn't it better to exchange a few of those piles for steam engines that will pay us back in freight costs four years from now? (Argentine President's Office, Information Department, National Press Bureau, June 23, 1947)

In the days following the president's speech, the ban on certain imports was extended to more goods. The Central Bank also announced another dip in its reserves of gold and foreign currency that backed the Argentine currency. In seven months, reserves had fallen from six billion pesos to AR$4.9 billion. On June 16, *La Nación* emphasized that a guarantee on national currency "should have no negative repercussions" if "gold and foreign currencies are employed to better production facilities" and "facilitate the various articles inhabitants need."

A month later, *La Nación* expressed concern given that reserves continued their downward spiral: "It is evident that our monetary regime is in dire straits. More currency is circulating, with less gold and foreign currency to back it." The author of that editorial, dated July 15, blames the shortage on an "erred economic policy that starts with the foreign exchange control regime." *La Prensa* also took up the issue, though from another angle. According to an editorial entitled "The Dollar, a Currency There's Not Enough Of," the scarcity of greenbacks was an issue for the international economy: if it hit Argentina hard, it hit the European economies in the process of postwar reconstruction even harder. Despite acknowledging the global nature of the problem, the newspaper again lambasted governmental policy, as outlined in the first paragraph of the editorial:

The difficulties our Central Bank faces in terms of foreign currencies—difficulties that should and could have been easily prevented—are, in fact, a chapter of an international monetary problem that the scarcity of funds usable in the United States has made patent everywhere.

The debates continued throughout 1947. During the first half of that year, Perón seized on nearly every public appearance to address the "shortage of foreign currency" and respond to critics. Those who circulated these "rumors" were "saboteurs" and "agitators," leaders of a "campaign" against the country's "economic independence," as the president himself solemnly declared on the country's Independence Day, July 9, 1947, in San Miguel de Tucumán. There was one particular realm, a battlefield where these "rumors" spread and multiplied: the foreign exchange market.

One year after launching the First Five-Year Plan, which laid out the Peronist administration's economic plan for 1947–1952,[3] Perón explained that the lack of dollars could be attributed to a broader government strategy to promote industrialization and improve the living conditions of workers. "That's why we don't have dollars, but we do have the vehicles and the machinery," said the president on June 16, 1948, in a speech to a gathering of trade union delegates.

> They talk about the lack of purchasing power, about how the peso is down. What's lacking, they say, is foreign currency. What does that matter: we don't need foreign currency to buy bread or milk or wine! The lack of foreign currency is thus a concern of some very specific groups: "There's no dollars on the market." "On the black market, the dollar's six pesos." But the people buying those dollars are the ones traveling abroad. So let them pay. . . . In short, this is a campaign waged by people looking out for their own interests.

According to Perón, those responsible for this anti-government campaign "make their living off foreign currency," "men who get up at ten in the morning and leave their homes to make their rounds, [saying] 'No dollars to be found! Isn't that appalling? No wonder we're in the state we're in'" (closing remarks at the Assembly of Civilian Government Workers, June 28, 1948). Yet, as Perón asked a group of military men, "what can a handful of profiteering businessmen on the foreign currency *bolsa negra*[4] do to our credit?" (speech at the annual Armed Forces camaraderie dinner, July 5, 1948). On August 21, in a speech to bricklayers, General Perón took up a similar line of argumentation in what would become one of his most remembered remarks: "Some of the traffickers operating within the country are saying we have no dollars. So let me ask this: any of you ever seen a dollar? The history of dollars is simply foreign pressure exerted to assure we never achieve economic independence"(speech at the Bricklayers Union Rally, August 21, 1948).

## Anti-Peronist Currencies

"Before the Currency Problem Existed" was the title of an editorial *La Prensa* published on January 14, 1949. The first few paragraphs sought to illustrate the reader on the day-to-day problems generated by "the lack of many goods and the high price of others. The public deserves an explanation for the lack of foreign currency or exchange." Yet the article took its argument further, noting the preoccupation at local shops: "Younger folks are surprised to hear middle-age people saying that there didn't used to be any foreign currency issues in Argentine. These are lessons for new generations within a broader context that, at least economically speaking, erases even the recollection of individual rights."

According to *La Prensa*, which would soon suffer a government expropriation, 1931 had been a pivotal year, one in which individual liberties had been lost in Argentina. That year, the authors explained, the country had suffered a "gradual drop in the standard of living of Argentines": the "shortage of foreign currencies" was then directly tied to the loss of individual rights. Since "Argentina has been subjected to a regime of exchange rate controls," concluded the editorial, "the lack of currencies has thwarted national development and the shortage of foreign currency can be attributed to national administrations that have acted for the past eighteen years as though they were the natural owners of all foreign currency."

As illustrated in the previous section, this dispute during the years of Peronism brought the public's attention to the foreign exchange market. The question at stake in the many pieces *La Prensa* published has to do with which currencies had a real impact on the population's well-being and the country's development. Despite a growing spotlight on the dollar, however, the "shortage of foreign currencies" is what was generally cited as the problem. This economic and political tension played out at the Maipo Theater in the show *La risa es la mejor divisa*.

During the first years of Peronism, worker purchasing power increased significantly, unions grew stronger, and companies profited from a prosperous domestic market and low-interest loans (Milanesio 2013). However, starting in 1949, the economy slowed to a halt until 1952. During those years, annual inflation averaged 33 percent, several percentage points higher than other countries in the region. The country was entering its first "stop-go" cycle. The drop in exports reduced the foreign currency available, leading to a reduction in imports and a cycle of economic stagnation. It had become evident that the "shortage" of foreign currency threatened the Peronist plans (Gerchunoff and Antúnez 2002).

At the beginning of September 1949, the executive sent a bill to Congress aimed at reforming the Central Bank's charter. One of the most controversial points of the bill was a proposed change to the country's money supply in relation to its reserves. At the time the bill was introduced, foreign currency holdings were limited to 20 percent of the Central Bank's reserves. This idea, as summarized by economic historian Marcelo Rougier (2018), was to eliminate this limit and do away with the requirement for 25 percent of all money in circulation to be backed by gold and foreign currency reserves in order to maintain the peso's value. Financial Minister Gómez Morales explained the objectives of the bill to the press:

> A bilateral offset agreement yields not foreign currency but purchase power.... Under such conditions, we create not foreign currency but raw materials and machinery ... yet there are obstacles that prevent us from building up monetary or foreign currency reserves.... In this context, the state needs a flexible monetary regimen. It must develop monetary policy that ensures its workforce is employed ... Purchase power depends not on gold reserves but on a state that maintains domestic order through a balanced budget and labor prosperity ... Eliminating this guarantee means eliminating a requirement that will have no effect on the monetary issue ... This is a precautionary measure, one subject to the ups and downs of the global conditions for buying and selling. (*Clarín*, September 9, 1949)

Then, gingerly, the Peronist official added, "Everyone knows the measure could have psychological repercussions."

Arturo Frondizi, a legislator for the Radical party, who would go on to become president a decade later, asked Congress to postpone debate on the bill in order to have time to pore over it. In his words,

> There is an article in the bill that would end our gold and foreign currency backing. There are little over fifty articles that come down to eliminating the backing of the peso.... This bill has two fundamental aims. First, it gives the Executive free rein to spend what little gold and foreign currency the Central Bank still has. Second, it gives it free rein to continue issuing currency without limitations of any sort. (*Clarín*, September 9, 1949)

According to an editorial in *La Prensa* that ran on September 10, the bill coincided with paltry gold reserves at the Central Bank. The public "has the right to know why their pesos have lost so much of their value and what to expect in the future." The daily *La Nación* concurred with Frondizi: the amendments outlined in the bill had but a single aim: "to facilitate the government's use of foreign currencies currently set aside to back the peso."

The bill reached the lower chamber of Congress, and the press closely followed the lengthy debate. During the discussion of the Central Bank reforms, Peronist legislator Eduardo Rumbo argued that "the government's idea is currency as political will, not a commodity: currency should be at the public's service." For his part, Frondizi confirmed that neither he nor his fellow Radicals would vote in favor of the bill. When Financial Minister Gómez Morales took the floor, he reiterated the arguments (and rhetoric) of the president: "They say we're pilfering our foreign currency reserves . . . The country now owns its public debt, had nationalized public utilities, built a powerful merchant navy, and equipped the transportation industry. What better path is there for the country?" Finally, after more than twenty-nine hours, the reforms were approved.

The local economy would be further shaken by international turbulence. In September, the announcement of a 30 percent devaluation of the sterling pound led to a temporary freeze on foreign exchange rates. After the president met with his ministers, a communique was released stating that the peso would not be devaluated and Argentines thus "[should] not be startled by the moves speculators make" (*Clarín*, September 20, 1949). Despite the affirmations to the contrary, some in banking circles and on the stock exchange worried that the exchange rates would be modified. And the more time passed that no foreign currency transactions were allowed, the more the preoccupation grew.

Finally, on October 1, the rumors were confirmed: a new communique informed the public that exchange rates would be modified and new "exchange rate categories" for exports and imports would be established, four for buyers and two for sellers/importers. The goals of these controls remained the same: to defend consumers and protect jobs by upping the price of luxury goods. Later that same month, *La Prensa* returned to the fray with new criticism of exchange rate controls: "a regime that was established to prevent the country from running out of foreign currency and dollars has led to a shortage of everything." (*La Prensa*, October 10, 1949).

Toward the end of that year, Perón responded to these accusations in several speeches. The importance of monies continued to be a topic of controversy and dispute:

> Used for political ends, the issue of foreign currency is entirely made up. They say the peso isn't worth much, but what do I care how the peso compares to the dollar or the British pound: I don't use pesos to buy or sell any international goods—I use dollars and pounds. . . . The peso is for the domestic market. In order to buy on the international market, we don't rely on pounds or dollars: we rely on wheat and meat, neither of which will ever suffer from devaluation. . . .
>
> People will talk and they talk about foreign currencies. Agriculture relies on foreign currency. I agree. But what I want to

> know is, when did foreign currencies go to agriculture? Because if they had been giving foreign currency to agriculture, the countryside would have had the equipment it needed fifty years ago instead of doing things the same as they did four centuries ago. Foreign currencies used to go to men traveling to Europe. Some of them sailed on a transatlantic, even taking their cow along so they could have milk in their coffee. They are the ones spending the foreign currencies that never went to agriculture. They spent them in French cabarets while our poor farmers and field workers wasted away from hunger. (speech at the opening of the VI Argentine Farming Conference, November 8, 1949)

These arguments were particularly relevant to a debate on the currencies used for international trade—a debate that had grown particularly intense since the end of the war.

> Some are saying—with a straight face!—that a dollar costs fifteen pesos. And to them I say, who has to pay fifteen pesos for a dollar? Anyone who goes to the United States! Well, then they shouldn't go to the United States. The dollar doesn't cost me anything because I don't buy dollars.
> Now, when the country has to buy or sell abroad, we don't use currencies that lose their value. We pay with wheat, leather, meat—all of which hold their value. We're not going to use currencies backed by the gold standard because currencies lose their value. We know the game: it's about the value of gold rising. We pay with the fruits of our land and our labors, which have never lost their value anywhere in the world. (speech by President Perón to the Railway Workers Union, December 19, 1949)

In the following years, this type of argument persisted. *Mundo Peronista* was a biweekly magazine published between 1951 and 1955 that promoted Peronism nationwide. Along with regular sections like the "Peronist Calendar" and "The Peronist Children's Page," the magazine ran comic strips, including one entitled *Mister Whisky and Soda*. The main character of the comic strip was a journalist from a foreign news agency sent to cover Argentina under Perón. Depicted as an alcoholic who provided wayward accounts of events, *Mister Whisky and Soda* was a character who got paid in foreign currency. This was no minor detail for the Peronist imaginary. By associating this character with foreign currency, the comic strip established him as staunchly anti-Peronist.

Since 1931, the foreign exchange market in Argentina had been more than just a market. During those years, government intervention in forex rules and regulations made it a flashpoint for political disputes, imaginaries of progress and decline, and ideas about how Argentina should relate to the world. Due to political polarization under Peronism, these disputes intensified in a society whose social structure was experiencing transformation. Though most of society remained unaware of it, a new market that would play a central role in the dollar's popularization was taking shape: the black market for currency exchange.

## The *"Bolsa Negra"* Boom under Peronism: Illegal Currency Exchange

> A few moments later, he reached the Plaza. He found his friend at a table in a lively conversation with the others. Paglioretti introduced them. Milani greeted everyone cordially. He not only knew the man from some time ago: he had relied on him at the time as a middleman or something of the sort. It wasn't that the mutual society was in any trouble; it was business as usual but there was increasing uncertainty in the insurance sector. Some expected a crisis; others, that the government would nationalize the companies and take charge of all insurance policies across the country, as it had announced it would do on several occasions. The plan Milani had in mind was to move toward capitalization or financing collective enterprises; but for that to happen, new capital was needed, and that is where Paglioretti came in. . . .
>
> This Paglioretti fellow had stumped the police for a time. To start, he was unable to give any satisfactory explanation for the recent fortune he had amassed. Finally, Paglioretti admitted that he owed his fortune to illegal business transactions, speculation, and trading on the *bolsa negra*. His shady and misguided relations with Milani seemed, for a time, a clue in the investigation, but Paglioretti was able to prove that he had left the Plaza after the crime and had nothing to do with it.

This excerpt from the Leopoldo Hurtado story "Pygmalion" was published in a 1953 collection of detective stories edited by Rodolfo Walsh, who would be assassinated under the dictatorship for his work as a journalist and activist in 1977. The pioneering compilation also included a story by Jorge Luis Borges and Adolfo Bioy Casares. At the beginning of the 1950s, readers and moviegoers alike were increasingly drawn to detective stories. Besides their unique narratives style, this genre also provided insight into people's daily lives and opened a window onto shady, illegal practices not usually found in other types of fiction. "Pygmalion" is one of the first works of

Argentine literature that mentions the *bolsa negra* for trading currencies and other cash transactions.

Economist Raúl Prebisch, a key member of the United Nations Economic Commission for Latin America and the Caribbean (ECLAC) created in 1948, served as vice secretary of economy from 1930 until 1935. In 1935, he was appointed chair of the newly founded Central Bank, a post he would retain until the military coup of 1943. Both of these roles provided him with insight into the foreign exchange market. At a press conference given at Banco de México in 1944, the economist analyzed the consequences of the restrictions introduced in 1931:

> All those unable to obtain the foreign currency they needed to pay for their imports in full or send remittances abroad, either for services or to friends or family, quickly discovered that exporters and other merchants were willing to sell them currencies on the *bolsa negra*. The same applies to people looking to send remittances or make a capital investment in Argentina: they also bought and sold currencies at high prices on the black market. (Prebisch 1993)

Many observers or analysts of the period concurred with Prebisch, associating the existence of the bolsa negra with the exchange controls Pinedo had introduced in 1933. Prebisch himself went so far as to liken the exchange market reforms as using free trade to effectively "legalizing the *bolsa negra*." However, even when exchange market restrictions eased, the illegal transactions had continued.

As early as 1934, *La Prensa* had begun to emphasize the public's "preoccupation" in response to reports of "malicious acts" associated with exchange control regulations. An editorial in the paper gathered recent news about a trading ring comprised of exchange control officials from the Argentine Exchange Controls Commission, seven forex traders, the vice manager of the Bank of London, and a wire transfer officer at the same bank. The ring would purchase import permits and resell them to "private parties" with a markup of between 25 percent and 30 percent. According to the Ministry of Economy, the first step in the illegal transactions consisted of drawing up a list of importers (with their respective registration numbers) who only exchanged foreign currency from time to time. The commission officials then obtained copies of the signatures of these importers to forge currency requests; these were drafted at the homes of the accused. Sixty forged permits were mixed in with other urgent requests as part of daily remittances to the Bank of London. The bank employees involved had to bribe two other employees because the currency requests needed seals under Argentine law. Once the foreign currency had been purchased, "underground negotiations began, without any involvement of the authorized banks, at a much higher [exchange] rate."

The importance attributed to this crime is reflected in the economic minister's decision to make a public announcement; additionally, the press covered the story extensively, probing the connections between state officials, bankers, and financial agents. This public/private connivance laid the foundation for the bolsa negra. According to newspapers, the ring had made between AR$200,000 and AR$250,000. One of the men accused confessed that his boss was a forex broker with "a desk at 121 San Martin Street," in the heart of the Buenos Aires financial district. Upon his arrest, said individual declared that he had carried out the transaction at the request of a financial intermediary. The Chamber of Financial Intermediaries responded with an announcement that none of its members had been involved in the affair (*La Nación*, January 27, 1934).

In the early years of Perón's first term, the press covered a few telling cases that help understand how these "con games" or "speculation" with foreign currencies contributed to a booming illegal market. This coverage and state documents reveal the networks, rationale, and actors who—like the character in the Hurtado story—did business on the bolsa negra. In January 1949, for example, the largest Buenos Aires papers reported on a swindle involving the sale of checks in US dollars for amounts totaling AR$400,000. *La Prensa* attributed the crime to the "scarcity of foreign currencies," making the connection between national monetary policy and illegal transactions.

According to the chronicle, a man by the name of Félix Varela had contacted a Mr. Pucci, who supposedly had contacts "high up" at the Department of Health, to help "two friends of his" who needed dollars. Mr. Pucci handed over three checks (for US$3,000, US$15,000, and US$29,000) drawn on New York banks. However, "the men were astounded to discover that the checks were fakes and Pucci did not have a dollar to his name." A few months later, another crime caught the public's attention due to both the people involved and the calls to deport some of those responsible. The police reports describe the profile of the delinquents, the rationale behind their transactions, and the connections between the legal and illegal markets. Information on this case allows for a clearer picture of how this type of crime developed over time as international networks dating back to the 1930s involved perpetrators from Uruguay, Chile, the United States, and Switzerland.

In their respective editions of November 15, 1949, *La Nación* and *La Prensa* reported that the defendants would suffer the "penalties for currency speculation," including deportation in the case of four of the miscreants. The National Bureau of Price and Supply Controls had already received reports of speculation outside the remits of Law 12,830, passed in 1946, which made it a crime to sell at prices above those set by the government. The following year, Law 12,893 was enacted, allowing the executive branch to impose fines, prison time, and deportation against those found guilty of speculation, criminal gains, and illegal pricing practices. The

National Bureau of Price and Supply Controls had been created in 1948 to fight against "speculation and illegal gains," with the aim of defending the purchase power and consumption level of the country's workers (Elena 2011).

Once the crimes had been investigated, the head of the bureau called the journalists in for a meeting at police headquarters. He gave them a copy of Executive Decree 28,337/49 describing illegal transactions, the people involved, and the sanctions established. The document provided precise details on the workings of the illegal currency trade network. This "vast international organization" was overseen by a Frenchman, Renato Carlos Lefay, a "skilled and established financier . . . with no official authorization who worked exclusively trading currency on the market known as *bolsa negra* or black market." According to the decree, "the transactions, some on his own behalf and others for third parties, consisted of the purchase and sale of foreign currencies in the capital [Buenos Aires] and the interior, without the involvement of the official institutions that 'control' exchange rates." The decree noted that Lefay boasted a "profound knowledge of monetary affairs, the result of years of work, [since] he was also involved in 'financial futures' or 'chalkboard transactions,' as they are also known, speculating on a rise or drop, especially of the dollar." One of Lefay's transactions involved the purchase of checks or other securities, almost always in dollars, that credited to accounts abroad; in other cases, he used colleagues also operating on the black market for new purchases. The decree added that "Lefay began his dealings on the black market in 1932 and since 1942, he had worked in association with Andrés Carlos Lestoille, another French native who is a financial advisor on stocks and currency exchange. The two shared the earnings from these dealings, which totaled astronomical sums each month."

The "organization" that Lefay and Lestroille had formed operated with "collaborators from different agencies." The identified individuals included an Egyptian, Jacobo Salomón Koldobsky; a Paraguayan, Félix José Luis Evaly; and two Argentines, German Díaz and José María Eduardo Ruiz. Koldobsky owned a currency exchange office operating at 312 San Martín Street; Evaly worked for the well-known currency exchange agency Casa Piano; Díaz, for Société Générale; and Ruiz was a currency exchange manager for Banco Holandés Unido. All "also dealt on the black market" and obtained "hefty earnings from the illegal trafficking of national and foreign currencies, generally dollars."

The decree also reflected on the difficulty of determining the exact amount of the "mobilized funds," since the transactions were only "recorded in their books erratically so as to cover up [the crime]." However, the analysis of the documentation revealed that "the amounts these transactions involved were, quite literally, astronomical." According to the recitals of the decree, the executive branch "must take decisive action against the underhanded maneuvering described in the documents . . . maneuvers typical of [currency] speculation." As a result, the punishment for the crimes included prison sentences, fines of up to AR$100,000, and the deportation of those born abroad (Lefay, Lestoille, Koldobsky, and Evaly). On December 27, 1949, Ministry of Technical Affairs Decree 32,214 was published in the Official Gazette, confirming "fines for perpetrators of illegal foreign exchange." The Central Bank's report on the "currency trafficking" network run by Renato Carlos Lefay formed the basis for the new decree. According to the police report, between March and September 1949, Lefay purchased a total of US$6,523,058 and sold US$4,902,142 on behalf of several individuals and entities in both Buenos Aires and Montevideo. The difference in price for these transactions in comparison to the official exchange rates was 50 percent.

Lefay helped one of the defendants, José María Eduardo Ruiz, purchase US$287,000 and sell US$2,243,152. In comparison to the average price on the official exchange market, the earnings on the dollar totaled AR$1,333,640. The defendant had also bought and sold shares on behalf of himself and others for a total of thirteen million pesos in 1948 and 1949.

Another defendant, Jacobo Salomón Koldobsky, relied on Lefay to buy US$398,050 and sell US$208,000. Eduardo Fernando Battillana had worked continuously and almost exclusively on the "parallel market [sic]," though his modus operandi varied. From August 1948 to February 1949, he partnered with Lefay, with whom he shared checking accounts at the Bank of New York. At the same time, he served as a middleman for the Chilean company Victorio Ugarte, handling numerous transactions on the black market. In other cases, he did transactions on his own. It was not possible to determine precisely how much Battillana had made, but again, the earnings were sizable.

José Martínez Fandiño, the owner of the foreign exchange office located at 418 Corrientes Street, was involved in many of Lefay's black market transactions for amounts totaling one million pesos, and admitted to involvement in similar transactions with companies in Montevideo. David Faradjic was an employee at a foreign exchange office acquainted with Lefay. At his job, he took Lefay's calls and who offered him US$25,000 at AR$9.15, suggesting by Lefay reach out to a Montevideo company offering the same amount for AR$0.15 higher than what he had offered first. He was hoping for a "tip" from Lefay if the transaction went through, though it did not, due to a delay.

No additional charges were filed against Jorge Horacio Harispe. An employee at the Provincia Cambio agency, he was an acquaintance of Lefay. Based on a hunch that the dollar would be going up, he went to see Lefay and purchased US$20,000 at AR$9.32, with a maturity date in November. By that time, the dollar had reached twelve pesos; Harispe would have made AR$75,000, but Lefay did not pay him the difference. A letter from Andrés Carlos Lestoille dated November 18, 1949, is included in case file of the National Bureau of Price and Supply Monitoring. In the letter, Lestoille asks the bureau to reconsider the fine for his crime and pardon him for not paying it, given that "the rise in the dollar has been my ruin."

> May the record note that I was not Mr. Lefay's partner in the dollar transactions. In one year, I have made but a single purchase and two transactions in dollars in Buenos Aires. That is because I have openly defended the peso and advised all my clients not to buy dollars or gold . . . How is it possible that a man who had gone to extremes to defend the peso be punished with a fine and taken to trial for economic reasons? As a patriot and an Argentine, after nineteen years living here, I believed this was precisely the way to build ties with the homeland.

In March 1950, another decree describes more shady transactions. Armando Luis Julio Berardi stood accused of putting together a de facto corporation with six individuals. Together, they set out to conduct foreign currency purchase and sale transactions on the "parallel market." The decree emphasized the "serious and verified acts of speculation" and their "noxious effects on the national economy, which is plagued by systematic capital and foreign currency evasion . . . Indirectly, the resulting financial imbalance has a negative impact on the country's legal industry and trade . . . artificially enhancing the quality of life [of some] to the detriment of the poorest population."

## The Peronist Dollar: Just Another Currency

Starting at the beginning of the 1930s and for a good part of the following decade, control policies made the foreign exchange market an arena of dispute where the economic, political, and ideological tensions of a society in transformation played out. Globally, the world economy was suffering from the crisis set off by the stock market crash of 1929 and later, the Second World War. This is the setting of what we refer to as a proto-popularization of the dollar in Argentine society; the dollar does not begin to stand out from other currencies until the end of this period and even then is not yet a part of the financial repertoires of vast social sectors.

During the first two terms of Perón (1946–1951, 1951–1955), the public debate was divided between the president's supporters and opponents. Those against Peronism insisted that a scarcity of foreign currency and its "artificial" value had severe repercussions for the country's economy and the population's living standards. The government, its allies, and supporters focused on the disconnect between the volume of foreign currency reserves (and their value) and Argentines' economic situation. Media outlets and political sectors dead set against the Peronist government fanned these public controversies, as did the statements by Peronist officials, legislators, and the leader himself. This was the seed of the dollar's popularization.

In those years, however, the dollar had not yet developed into a special money, to use the term coined by Viviana Zelizer (1994). Its public meaning was limited to the more general topic of the "lack of dollars." Finally, the only social groups with any dealings on the exchange market—dealings mostly limited to foreign trade and obscure illegal activities—were the economic and political elites. This would change in the coming decade.

*Chapter Two*

# BRETTON WOODS ON THE STREETS OF BUENOS AIRES (1959–1970)

I believe that all of us have become financiers for a very specific reason. Think about it like this: when a guy used to have some money put away, he would open up a little factory or shop, he'd buy some land and raise chickens or plant tomatoes—those things people do in poor countries. Here, though, everything is different. You've seen San Martín Street, where the exchange offices are located: everyone is outside staring at the board. Workmen, masons, field hands, tailors, musicians, artists. Guys who used to work hard have now become economists and they're all standing there with a bundle of money. As soon as the exchange rate changes up on the board, they push their way into the office. One calls out, "Give me three dollars." Another says, "Give me four dollars." . . . They run out and go into another exchange office and before they go home that day, they've sold their dollars. They spend the whole day doing that, buying and selling, and when they get home, exhausted, they collapse onto the couch, pull out the money and count it, and say, "Honey, honey, come here! I made fourteen bucks today without doing a thing!"

Tato Bores (Mauricio Borensztein, 1925–1996) was an Argentine comedian and the host of a Sunday late night show. Aired on different Argentine television channels from the beginning of the 1960s into the 1990s, the Bores show suffered only a few interruptions, most due to issues with the censors. In 1962, with his wig, tuxedo, thick glasses, and cigar, Bores had already developed the TV character that would make him a celebrity. His signature weekly act was a series of fast-talking monologues on current affairs. Bores had a knack for making people laugh even when he touched on issues that seemed anything but funny—like the devaluation of the Argentine currency or the exchange market.

Like many comedians, Bores held up a mirror to viewers. In torturous times, comedy was a way of interpreting national life but also of taking a step back from it. Only a few of Tato Bores's programs from those years—like the one quoted above, which aired on August 30, 1962—are found in archives. This particular one continues to be shared on social media even today. In the brief monologue, the comedian notes a shift that was only just beginning but that would continue in the years to come. In fact, Bores's forecast was prescient: the dollar would soon be integrated to the repertoire of Argentine financial practices, an easy-to-understand reference both economic and political for increasingly larger swaths of the population.

The comedian's monologue is indicative of a profound change at the end of the 1950s and beginning of the 1960s in the relationship between mass culture, financial practices, and the exchange market. Starting in these years, the dollar was gradually incorporated to the financial repertoires of sectors that previously had only limited contact with the financial world and exchange market. At the same time, it became a beacon of popular culture, a familiar and easy-to-decipher reference providing cognitive, emotional, and practical guidance for people with scant experience in the financial universe. During this slow cultural development, the media—particularly the print press—played a fundamental role. Through the news—and also advertising—the dollar gradually became a relevant topic and, later, a character all its own, one that inhabited clearly established terrains and had economic, political, and symbolic repercussions.

Different authors have shown that after the Second World War, the US dollar consolidated its hegemony as an international currency (Eichengreen 2011). This chapter homes in on a dimension of that process that remains unexplored, focusing on how, during the 1950s and 1960s in Argentina, the US dollar also became a popular local currency as well. In the first decades of the twentieth century, US policymakers had promoted a "dollar diplomacy" toward Latin American countries (Helleiner 2003a; Rosenberg 2004). After Bretton Woods, however, this regional policy dwindled. The exploration of the dollar's popularization in Argentina shows how the expansion of America's legal tender went far beyond politics and diplomacy (Helleiner and Kirshner 2009). At the same time, it is important to underscore that the history of international currencies depends not only on diplomatic and international agreements but also on the cultural mediations and social mechanisms embedded in the economic and political histories of each country. These are the topics explored in this chapter, which focuses on the first stage of the slow yet progressive transformations of the US dollar into a "special money" (Zelizer 1994) for Argentines.

## Arturo Frondizi and the First Major Devaluation

In 1955, General Pedro Eugenio Aramburu[1] overthrew President Juan Domingo Perón in a carefully staged coup d'état (O'Donnell 1997). Three years later, in February 1958, the de facto regime called for elections; the economic challenges Argentina faced would be a priority on the campaign agenda of all candidates. Some of the most pressing concerns included policies that would finally set Argentina on the path to development, the need to choose between a more laissez-faire approach or the state regulation of certain key markets, and strategies to help keep the cost of living under control. When consulted by the press about the policies they would introduce if elected, the candidates of the different parties—except for Peronism, which had been subject to a ban that would remain in place until 1973—all discussed these topics, though without any direct references to exchange policy or the dollar's value.

Things changed drastically toward the end of 1958 when the volatility of the dollar-peso exchange rate made newspaper headlines (Díaz Alejandro 1966). In February, one US dollar had been worth AR$37.70; on December 3, it had reached the unheard-of rate of AR$70. It was relevant enough to top the ranking of "Major National Events" on the cover of *Clarín*, a national daily that would become the top-selling paper in Argentina.

At the same time, inflation was a looming concern for the public and a headache for politicians. In June 1958, shortly after being sworn in as president, Arturo Frondizi[2] ordered an "emergency" salary hike and launched a "battle to reduce the cost of living," setting price ceilings for basic goods and halting imports. Meanwhile, the news began treating the dollar-peso exchange rate as the benchmark for the national currency's devaluation. Business chambers were quick to criticize the government's announcements: in their opinion, this marked a return to state intervention in the economy, a measure vociferously opposed since Perón had been overthrown in September 1955. For many business leaders, including those of the Chamber of Commerce, public sector largesse and state meddling in the economy were the root of out-of-control inflation. In order to reflect on how far Argentina had fallen, some harked back to what the country had been like in 1943, that is, shortly before Perón had come to power. Back then, "a dollar cost approximately three Argentine pesos, the country had copious gold and foreign currency reserves, and price fluctuations were minimal" (*Clarín*, June 4, 1958).

In times of political tension (Portantiero 1977; Cavarozzi 2006), worker protests against the drop in real salaries, and the repression of union reps, Congress passed a law at the beginning of December to authorize foreign capital investment in Argentina. At the same time, under another newly passed law, oil deposits became the "exclusive, inherent and inalienable property of the national state" (Act 14773,

October 10, 1958), and a call for bids was issued to private companies for the drilling of some 4,000 wells. In December, the country was finalizing the details on its first agreement with the International Monetary Fund, negotiating financial assistance with both the United States and the Paris Club simultaneously.

As part of the economic measures introduced by President Frondizi's developmentalist government (Altamirano 1998b), the Stabilization Plan was announced. Its goal was to drastically reduce fiscal deficit and keep the national currency stable through a set of new economic rules and regulations. The liberalization of the forex market—a measure several actors had clamored for since the coup overthrowing Perón—was one of the most important.

At 9:00 p.m. on December 29, Frondizi spoke to the Argentine people about the features and scope of the economic reforms, which would be covered in the papers in the following days. Before the forex market could begin operating in this new context, the government imposed a twelve-day "holiday" on currency exchange in order to give the economic team time to draft the new regulations. The planned measures included import taxes on all nonessential goods and duties on the country's top exports, meat and grain, both of which were also household staples in Argentina. The aim was to prevent price hikes on the domestic market.

During the first days of 1959, Fidel Castro's rebel forces seized the city of Havana, overthrowing the Fulgencio Batista administration and capturing the attention of the world press. In Buenos Aires, newspaper covers alternated between the latest happenings in the Caribbean and the introduction of the new economic measures, including speculation as to what the dollar-peso exchange rate would be once the forex market reopened.

The liberalization of the foreign currency market was no small matter. It was the first free-floating exchange rate for all economic activities since the 1930s, and Argentines were eager to see what the liberalization would bring at the end of the two-week hiatus. As a result, when forex trading finally resumed on January 12, people on San Martín Street—the heart of "la City," as the Buenos Aires financial district is known—elbowed one another to get a peek at the boards and windows of the exchange offices. That day, the dollar closed at AR$68.70, an exchange rate quite similar to that of the black market before the state-ordered holiday at the end of December.

All the major newspapers covered this unusual occurrence in "la City." The cover of the second section of *Clarín* offered a spectacular chronicle of the first day of free-floating currency. In a departure from the usual reporting in the economic section, which rarely included pictures, the spread included six photographs of the crowds. There were pictures from San Martín Street near the well-known trading office Casa Piano and outside the Central Bank, and also shots from inside the offices, including cashier counters, jittery clients, and the boards with the exchange rate. *La Nación* also used close-up photographs in its account of the day's events, though its coverage was less flashy. An overhead shot of the windows of Casa Piano on San Martín Street is included bottom-center; the caption notes that these are the exchange offices "where passers-by gaze into the office windows, carefully tracking the fluctuating prices of different currencies."

At the end of the 1950s, photographs remained rare in the print press and were generally reserved for certain sections or the coverage of major events (Gamarnik 2016). In the big national papers like *La Nación* or *Clarín*, stories on weekend soccer matches and international news stories sometimes included a photograph or two. War, natural disasters, or technological milestones—including the Space Race between two Cold War rivals, the United States and the USSR—merited a picture, as did political events like ministers taking office, the start of legislative sessions, and visits by foreign leaders. However, economic news almost never included images. With the exception of big announcements or international economic news important enough to make the front or back cover, most financial information in papers was provided in charts and graphs: the going rates on local and international markets for the country's principal commodity exports like meats and grains, stock market trading, forex rates, etc. The major papers ran articles on the state of the economy on weekends, usually Sundays, barring exceptional circumstances during the workweek. Given the technical vocabulary these articles employed, they seemed to target relatively expert readers looking for a summary of the week's economic activity.

Thus, the illustrated coverage by the two largest Buenos Aires–based newspapers on the reopening of the foreign currency market in January 1959 is particularly striking. The incorporation of images to foreign trading news ushered in a new way of reporting on the economy.

## The Passionate Crowds of San Martín Street

Three years before President Frondizi announced the Stabilization Plan, amendments to forex market regulation had already made the news. At the end of October 1955, the so-called Liberators' Revolution had seized power, defeating Perón and driving the former president into exile. The de facto regime was determined to gradually liberalize the foreign exchange market by introducing a model with two different exchange rates. The government-controlled rate would apply to commodity exports and the import of essential goods, while all other transactions would rely on a free-floating exchange rate. The transition to the new model also included a major devaluation that would quickly have an impact on prices: the dollar went from AR$5 for the basic official rate and AR$7.50 for the preferential official rate (depending on the economic activity of the exporter/importer) to AR$18 for both, while the free-floating rate skyrocketed to around AR$32. The reasoning given for this system would become commonplace when defending similar decisions in the years to come. According to the minister of finance at the time, it was necessary to do away with "fictitious" exchange rates "sundered from economic reality," and thus restore the peso's "true exchange value."

In 1955, the announcement of economic measures had been followed by a government-imposed freeze on foreign exchange until the details of the new regulation were finalized. On this occasion, the expectations surrounding the market's reopening did not result in such extensive media coverage. In the first days of November, the foreign currency exchange rate chart briefly made covers but later returned to its regular section with little fanfare. However, the novel news coverage the forex market received as the Stabilization Plan was launched in January 1959 would reappear at other critical junctures over the course of the 1960s in the face of cabinet shake-ups, new directions in economic policy, and successive devaluations by different ministers as they attempted to restore balance to an economy in crisis.

In addition to the use of photographs as a reporting resource, another novel aspect of the coverage was the chronicle, a novel style of writing for economic news. In a sharp contrast with the graphs and charts of the past, images and feelings began to be interwoven with the exchange market in January 1959. In the photographs, crowds are pushed up against the glass windows of exchange offices in downtown Buenos Aires, some anxious to see the dollar-peso rate and others eager to complete a transaction. The expectation overshadowed not only the visuals but also the tone of the chronicles:

> When exchange market transactions resume this morning, after nearly a two-week freeze imposed in order to give the system a chance to adapt to the distressing reality of Argentina's economy, the country will feel its heart beating to the rhythm of the numbers noted down on the receipts. The clatter of the switchboards at the nerve center of the money business and the rumbling wave of foreign currency symbols building up in the exchange offices will offer a glimpse into the initial reaction to the myriad and complex elements involved in attempting to reconstruct the Argentine peso after nearly three decades in which it languished beneath the guise of government controls and contrived exchange rates. (*La Nación*, January 11, 1959)

Two days later, the black-and-white photographs published by the main Buenos Aires–based newspapers drew attention to three aspects of the story: the crowds on San Martín Street, the efforts of passersby to get a glimpse inside the offices, and customers elbowing their way up to the cashier counters. Except for the panoramic shots of the office marquees and the hordes out front, most of the photographs are close-ups of the people vying for a spot in front of the glass windows and counters. Most are adult men wearing suits and often hats, presumably office workers. Their avid interest in the changing numbers up on the boards comes across in the photographs, as does the emotion on the faces of those asking the cashiers questions. The lively conversation between strangers outside the offices is another feature of the pictures.

In the days that followed the scheduled reopening of the forex market, the news stories explained how exchange rates fluctuated, reporting not only the opening and closing rates but also the ups and downs over the course of the business day. This narrative model, in which a series of usual actors can be identified, would gradually become hegemonic over the course of the next decade. Detailed descriptions of Central Bank measures during periods of regular market interventions and the identification of the actors responsible for the supply and demand of each business day—or for a sudden spike or drop in the peso's value—are an essential part of the narrative. Though their prominence in the chronicles varies over time, certain recurring actors appear in these stories, including the large public banks that buy or sell a great quantity of currency; Banco Industrial, which guarantees imports; and meat and/or grain exporters, which liquidate or withhold the amounts corresponding to their sales abroad.

These big market players, most of which have some relationship to the state, operated with what was referred to at the time as the *dólar giro* or *dólar transferencia* (the dollar at a special exchange rate negotiated with the banks). Another minor character is also a common sight at the exchange offices operating with the *dólar billete* (the actual dollar bill, exchanged at the official rate): the "pocket economist," a man content with small margins who dabbles in what is known as *especulación hormiga* or *pequeña especulación* (two-bit speculation). The pocket economist seizes on the opportunity to do business at times of currency turbulence when exchange market regulations are amended or the peso suffers a sudden devaluation. Political upheaval, when members of the economic team and/or high-ranking officials are replaced, also represents an opportunity for the pocket economist. He—for during these years, the people exchanging on San Martín Street were almost exclusively men—is the true protagonist of these chronicles of small-time Argentine investors always set in "la City."

In January 1959, *La Nación* referred to San Martín as the street "where piddling speculators work up a sweat." *Clarín* reported that the demands of "small investors (or should we say *especulación hormiga*?)" far exceeded the capacity of the exchange office personnel. Over the next few years, these descriptors became common when referring to customers at currency exchange offices. Although most of their transactions were small, they made the foreign exchange business more visible to the public at large, putting a face to an activity that had previously been associated only with major imports and exports or the veiled world of banking. In 1962, these same characters would inspire the Tato Bores monologue cited at the beginning of this chapter in which the comedian claims that all Argentines "have become financiers." Over the course of that decade, the prominence of the dollar-peso exchange rate would rise in the national media and even make newspaper covers at times of peak instability. Yet the numbers and the transactions would not be the only focus of journalists. At moments of economic stability, coverage of the forex market continued to be conspicuously technical. However, whenever that same market experienced tremors, the meticulous descriptions of local movements and the social climate returned to the papers, building a prototype for this kind of story and the images associated with it.

In April 1962, for example, when former vice president José María Guido[3] temporarily headed the country in the wake of President Frondizi's forced resignation, the currency was devalued anew. The papers covered the new devaluation closely, with a new series of photographs on San Martín Street. As with the images published three years earlier, groups of men in suits are again crowded in front of the exchange rate boards. In some close-ups, the anxiety on the faces is apparent. The same scenes, shot from almost identical angles, would reappear in April 1964 when the forex regime was again modified under new president Arturo Illia[4] and when bank accounts in foreign currency—previously available to any Argentine who had wanted one—were suddenly prohibited. In its chronicle, *Clarín* refers to "an intense day on the Buenos Aires Wall Street" and "*hot money* [sic] that chars the fingers as it passes across the counter" of exchange offices. March 1967 marked the one-year anniversary of the coup d'état against President Arturo Illia. Now, under the de facto regime of General Juan Carlos Onganía,[5] Economic Minister Adalbert Krieger Vasena[6] announced what he hoped would be the "last major devaluation" of the national currency, taking the worth of one dollar from AR$290 to AR$350. Once again, the papers treated the story to special coverage, with photographs of what was happening and play-by-plays of "la City," which had now become a synecdoche for the exchange market.

At these critical junctures of major changes to market regulations, the recurring image of the office windows and exchange rate boards underscores the reigning sense of anxiety and expectation surrounding the reopening of the forex market. The photographs also draw attention to another increasingly common urban figure: that of the curious onlooker. All those crowded outside the office windows in these photographs could not possibly be looking to buy or sell foreign currency, though there were undoubtedly some regular customers among them. Passersby and office workers interested in seeing the exchange rate for themselves, and in bearing witness to the market's fluctuations, were also part of the throngs. The exchange market had thus become more than an arena where specific transactions take place: it was a spectacle starring the US dollar exchange rate. In these years, the forex market experienced two important simultaneous changes. First, it ceased to be an impenetrable universe reserved for knowledgeable players and opened its doors up to the newly arrived "pocket economists." Second, the dollar-peso exchange rate was rendered comprehensible to an ever-increasing public, a number meaningful not only to those who dealt in currencies but also for the simply curious.

A new exchange market perspective and narrative are cemented during this period, one in which currency exceeds the numbers and unfolds in a series of texts and images. The average newspaper reader thus receives familiar references for something that was once expressed solely as a figure on a chart. The stories and photographs that now accompany the numbers trace a landscape where exchange market transactions take place. Although not all these transactions are done at the same location, the exchange offices on San Martín Street gradually become the setting par excellence for foreign exchange. At the same time, these representations help put a face—or at least a body—to the main players on this market, allowing corporate actors (i.e., exporters, industrialists) to be distinguished from those who perform only bit roles. Finally, these narratives provide insight into the specific mechanisms that enable these transactions, drawing on abundant resources—especially written descriptions of sound—to describe technical devices and procedures. Thus, for example, the "clatter of the switchboards" conveys that the dynamics of supply and demand exceed the boards and are expressed—and above all—via telephone, connecting actors across different locations.

This chronicle, with its folksy description of the dynamics of "la City," and printed at its most critical moments, would play a key role in teaching readers about certain economic practices, the places where they unfold, and the figures they involved. In this regard, starting in the 1960s, the mass media becomes a source of what Federico Neiburg has referred to as "economic pedagogy" whose lessons will take different forms.

## Economics, Exchange Market, and a "New Journalism"

The 1955 coup ousting President Juan Domingo Perón ushered in political instability that would stretch out nearly three decades, preventing a single constitutionally elected president from finishing a term. The recurring interventions of the armed forces in politics (in 1955–1958, 1962–1963, 1966–1973, and 1976–1983) and a strict ban on the Peronist party were two features of this period, as elected administrations were inevitably overthrown by military regimes. Even when democratic elections were held, however, the country's strongest political force—Peronism—was not allowed to run (Cavarozzi 2006; Potash 1996; O'Donnell 1988).

The country's economy was not immune to this unrest. Foreign investment in Argentina brought industrial expansion and modernized production in the 1960s, yet the decade was also characterized by profound economic instability, fundamentally owed to a poorly balanced production apparatus. In a widely read essay on Argentina's exchange rate, engineer and economist Marcelo Diamand (1972) characterized the Argentina economy as "comprised of two sectors" with opposing needs: the agricultural-export sector, which produced and sold at international prices, and the industrial sector, which imported exclusively and whose production costs and prices were higher than those abroad. In Diamand's view, the disequilibrium between a quickly growing industrial sector dependent on foreign currency (to import machinery, fuel, and other materials) and an exporting agricultural sector that grew at a snail's pace (but represented the only source of foreign currency for the Argentine economy) resulted in recurring crises in the country's trade balance.

The response to the foreign currency constraints was the devaluation of the peso, a measure aimed at stimulating exports and slowing industrial growth. However, a devaluation had other offshoots: it drove inflation—or *carestía de la vida* (dearness), the term used in the 1960s to refer to the phenomenon—which gradually evolved into one of the country's most troubling concerns (Heredia and Daniel 2019). The devaluation of 1959, the principal measure in Frondizi's Stabilization Plan, would be the first of three major reductions in the value of the peso over the next decade (1962, 1967) as well as a series of scheduled mini-devaluations (Rapoport 2008; Gerchunoff and Llach 2018). The first of these came at a critical moment in which the public broadly debated the topic of foreign currencies: the lack thereof, their value, and the rules and regulations for accessing them.

In this context, the print media began expanding its coverage of the economy while seeking new ways to keep readers abreast of this type of news, part of a broader set of changes to the media during this period. A new media outlet, the weekly news magazine, appeared in these years, along with special interest magazines dedicated to areas like the economy and the business world. This meant a more expanded offer of information but also new journalism styles and techniques for Argentine media. Beyond the differences in their approaches to the news, illustrated magazines like *Análisis* (1961), *Primera Plana* (1962), *Panorama* (1963), and *Pulso* (1967) prioritized photographs over sketches or engravings but also took on new topics and revamped narrative reporting styles (Gamarnik 2020; Taroncher Padilla 1998). While these publications continued to cite intellectuals and experts, they also used a plainer language more appealing to the new generations of readers who represented the majority of their readership.

At the same time, the appearance of these new media outlets led to changes in the editorial style of the country's major newspapers (Ford and Rivera 1985; Ulanovsky 2005). One was the addition of regular columns by experts; in the past, newspapers had only invited specialists to contribute pieces on occasion. Articles before that decade often included word-for-word speeches by well-known figures on key topics, but in the 1960s, the dailies began incorporating the experts to the editorial team. The result was well-informed columns that aimed to give readers technical insight into specific areas. While coverage of the economy had been quite limited in the past, it proved especially fertile ground for journalistic innovations of this sort, and keeping up with the dollar soon became a mainstay in news reporting.

*Clarín* was the first national paper to publish columns signed by experts, a trend previously limited to special interest magazines (Sivak 2013). During the first half of the 1960s, the Economy section of its Sunday edition incorporated two regular columns entitled "Dólar" and "Circulante" ("Dollar" and "Circulation"). Facing one another on opposite pages, both had a similar structure, were drafted by a well-known expert (as opposed to an anonymous staff writer), and began with statistics that formed a series as the weeks passed. In the case of "Dólar," the column began with a chart showing the exchange rate of the US dollar over the past week, which was always the reference period of the article. The "Circulante" column consisted of a small graph entitled "Where does our money go?" that reported on how much money circulated in the areas of government, the private sector, currency reserves, and others. The two columns provided summaries of indicators viewed as essential to the fluctuations of the national economy, attempting to enlighten a relatively broad readership but still making regular reference to statistics and using strikingly complex vocabulary. Many of these columns reveal the tension between the deft technical critiques of economic measures introduced by the Ministry of Economy—an area of government where cabinet shake-ups were frequent—and the push to make the workings of specific markets comprehensible to average readers. Thus, in addition to its technical-political descriptions, the "Dólar" column often included practical explanations of the mechanisms most frequently mentioned—but not explained—in the cursory daily coverage of the exchange market.

> It's important to stay on top of the exchange market, especially because speculation is a key part of this market's workings. During the trading hours on Monday, a technique known as *dólar calesita* (the merry-go-round dollar), in which a purchase is made at one price to then sell at a higher price, was on full display. This transaction can be repeated as many times as the exchange rate changes, yielding incalculable profit margins. (*Clarín*, July 1, 1962)

> Despite limits on the amount of dollars travelers can buy, the demand appears inelastic. In fact, there is already a parallel market "for tourists and travelers" where the exchange rate for the U.S. dollar varies according to demand. The [government-imposed exchange] limit, then, should be reconsidered, because if speculation is difficult to control on the exchange market, it is entirely impossible off that market. (*Clarín*, April 19, 1964)

The "Dólar" column—along with "Circulante"—was a clear example of how important economic topics had become in the local press during the 1960s. It was also indicative of how media outlets took on the challenge of informing an increasingly broader readership of an area involving such technical language and concepts.

Over time, the major papers would find and train journalists with market savvy, thus ending the information monopoly professional economists had held on the state of the economy. Yet in the early years, few reporters were up to the task. One noteworthy exception is economist Enrique Silberstein, who was known for conveying expert knowledge in layman's terms and combining humor with in-depth knowledge during the 1960s and until his untimely death in 1973. Silberstein published a series of brief weekly texts entitled "Charlas económicas" ("Chats on the economy") in several media outlets (including the paper *El Mundo*). The title of each piece was always structured as a "What is . . . ?" question. Using a chatty tone and drawing examples from everyday life, Silberstein set out to present the fundamental theories of the world's foremost economists, explaining technical terms with ironic commentaries on habits and customs from an economic viewpoint. Although these texts usually did not refer to the current state of affairs, they did bring up the exchange market and, more specifically, the US currency. In his "chats" published in the print press, Silberstein made mention of foreign exchange limits, the dollar, the parallel market, healthy currency, the gold standard, monetary policy, and black money.

The new addition to publishing, weekly magazines, also made important contributions in this regard. In *Primera Plana*, for example, the extensive Economy section included both up-to-date information on the economy as well as opinion pieces by specialists in the field. In these pieces, expert commentary on the current state of affairs was combined with meticulous descriptions for novices. The forex market was particularly important here:

> Apart from normal transactions like exports, imports, and financial payments, the foreign exchange market is a particularly propitious site for speculation. The small-time speculator on San Martín Street is not the one who truly benefits from the economic lurches caused by the

big-time speculators. The man on San Martín Street is a psychosocial phenomenon who reveals demoralization, a lack of faith, and a step back from collective responsibilities, but he has little sway over the day's exchange rates. You need to move millions to influence the exchange rate or have the power to postpone the conversion of export payments into local currency. (*Primera Plana*, February 4, 1964)

Thus, both the chronicles of the exchange market as well as columns written by experts gradually expanded the coverage of economic affairs in the country's foremost print media outlets. This expansion was about more than the number of pages of the Economy section, the quantity of information provided, or the priority given to this news in the publication's layout—the economic instability that characterized the period made it a priority—and involved a progressive transformation of the reporting style. While once reserved for the "business world," forex market news was expanded to appeal to other potential readers, not only market players big and small. Instead, the aim was to inform the "curious onlookers" (e.g., the readers who had just started leafing through the Economy section to see what it conveyed about not only the financial state of affairs—but about national political life as well).

## From the *Bolsa Negra* to the Parallel Market

During the 1960s, the transformation of economic journalism could be seen not only in narrative styles but also in the type of financial topics the print press covered. Thus, just as the forex market becomes part of daily chronicles during times of crisis, ways of depicting the business of foreign exchange—particularly, transactions on the illegal currency trading market—would also gradually be modified.

At the beginning of the 1930s, the illegal currency market that rapidly sprung up in response to the country's first foreign exchange controls rarely made the news. Known as the bolsa negra, this black market surfaced in the Crime section from time to time until the end of the 1940s, though only when the authorities successfully managed to intercept and/or temporarily disband the networks that kept it running. Starting in the 1950s, the tone of these narratives on the illegal market shifted. The illegal market was no longer an obscure universe operating in the shadows that was described in pejorative terms. Instead, it was connected to the exchange market and relevant, particularly with regard to the benchmarks it provided. Even before the liberalization of the exchange market in October 1955, the rates of the US currency on what was now referred to as the "parallel market" or "collateral sector" would prove essential to guessing the value of the dollar once the official market reopened. This would become a trend whenever the government shut down the forex market in preparation for a new set of regulations. In the days after Frondizi's Stabilization Plan was announced, the press reported on the happenings as follows:

> Though official transactions have been suspended, there are clear signs that the parallel market is alive and well, especially in the positions liquidated at month end, generally at between AR$66 and $67 on the dollar on Tuesday and Wednesday. Yesterday, *this vigorous sector within the currency business* continued operating, though to a limited degree, and most of the transactions were carried out at a selling price of between AR$68.50 and $69 pesos. (*La Nación*, January 4, 1955; emphasis added)

Something similar could be seen in 1962 during Guido's presidency:

> Given the confirmation that no transactions would be permitted over the holiday, an attempt was made to develop a collateral market. The dry runs were limited to the exchange of limited quantities of currency and in general, the price agreed to for the exchange did not exceed AR$124 per U.S. dollar. (*Clarín*, July 3, 1962)

This shift in the depiction of the bolsa negra accompanied its increasing consolidation as a predictable and legitimate illegal market, generating a need to explain its workings to the average reader. In a stark contrast to the reporting of previous decades, the tone of this chronicle reveals the assimilation of illegal trading as a run-of-the-mill business, though many journalists continued to be critical of it. Silberstein, for example, was more focused on understanding the workings of the economy than lamenting the current state of affairs. In mid-1964, in one of his "chats" for *El Mundo*, he noted that "what is a parallel market for one country is legal in a neighboring country"—that is, Uruguay, where tax law had historically been laxer than in Argentina. In his piece, he described all the market maneuvers possible on a speculative market:

> One dollar on Argentina's official exchange market is worth 170 pesos but on the parallel market, 280 pesos. As a result, it behooves producers to export Argentine products but invoice them at a lower price and ask the buyer to deposit the difference in a bank in Montevideo, Zurich, or New York. That way, the producer sells some of the dollars on the Argentine market at 170 and the difference in Montevideo for 280. With the 110 pesos left over on every dollar, he pays the upkeep on his houses in Punta del Este.[7] Another option is to import products at

a higher price and pay for them on the official market, that is, paying what one owes at 170 pesos on the dollar before selling the remaining dollars at 280. In other words, the carousing never ends on the parallel market. (Silberstein 1967, 166–67)

Months earlier, a similar narrative can be found in a column entitled "A black market with 200 counters" in the Economy section of magazine *Primera Plana*. Before criticizing an economic policy "that has pushed the vast majority of foreign exchange transactions onto the parallel market, thus making it the true free market," the journalist offers a matter-of-fact description of the workings of this particular underworld:

> San Martín Street during business hours. A self-assured looking man enters a foreign exchange office and approaches the counter. When the cashier comes over, the man says,
> "I need to sell 300 dollars but I don't want a receipt . . ."
> "No problem. That will be . . ." (typing some numbers into the calculator) "42,000 pesos. We pay 140 pesos on the dollar."
> The money is exchanged without further ado. Transactions on the parallel or "black" forex market are brisk. There may be just a momentary pause while the office employee "sizes up" the client, if this is the first time he's seen him. Otherwise, the transaction proceeds with no hesitation. (*Primera Plana*, May 12, 1964)

Progressively, then, over the course of the decade, the press ceased to question the legitimacy of the parallel market and, in fact, offered normalized depiction of it, often as a vigorously active part of the exchange market. At times when regulations limited certain transactions on the official market, the papers homed in on the illegal market, and went so far as to publish the exchange rates from both markets daily. As journalists noted, the under-the-table exchange market had become so important that it continued operating even when there was no real reason for it, like in March 1967 when a measure by Krieger Vasena made the official dollar exchange rate even higher than it was on the parallel market.

## The Dollar Becomes a Household Staple in Argentina

In April 1964, not yet a year into Radical party president Arturo Illia's presidency, economic instabilities led to a new currency crisis. On the first day of the month, the cover of newspaper *Clarín* drew readers' attention with the following headline:

"Dollar: The exchange rate rises as exports continue to be withheld." In order to address the lack of foreign currency, the Ministry of Economy and the Central Bank introduced a series of modifications to the foreign exchange regimen. First, it banned bank accounts in foreign currency—such accounts had been available since 1957, when the Central Bank had lost control over deposits—and ordered that all existing deposits in foreign currencies be translated into Argentine pesos.

At the time, only a handful of experts reacted to the measure. The lack of a broader public response is likely owed to the relatively low number of foreign currency accounts in the financial system at the time. Experts, however, were up in arms over the measure. The legal expert and economist Alberto Schoo, for example, gave a speech on the decision upon his incorporation as a standing member of the National Academy of Economic Sciences. Facing the academy's experts, he affirmed,

> The confiscation of deposits in foreign currency—and I say confiscation because there is no other way to refer to this impulsive ban—is surely no way to inspire trust either domestically or abroad. . . . As we shall seem, this ban is motivated by a simplistic, grandiloquent aim: to increase the foreign reserves of the Central Bank by removing them from private hands. And by private hands, I mean companies holding foreign reserves in anticipation of upcoming maturities and earning interest in the meantime, or even simple investors who saw the law as a shield that would protect their money against the catastrophic depreciation of our national currency. And our state is the one to blame for this catastrophic depreciation, stoking its flames in every way imaginable. (*Anales de la Academia Nacional de Ciencias Económicas*, vol. IX, pp. 61–62)

As Schoo's keen argument reveals, inflation was the topic that had truly captured the attention of both experts and laymen alike. In his speech, in fact, he referred to the inflation first as *galopante* (runaway) and then as *delirante* (unhinged). Additionally, the dollar's ups and downs became increasingly associated with inflation. The same month that the government ordered the conversion of all foreign deposits into pesos, *Clarín* ran a comic strip by the Argentine writer and graphic artist Felipe Miguel Ángel Dobal that offered a humorous take on people's concerns. In the doorway of a shop, a merchant explains to a worried-looking passerby: "Well . . . Since I couldn't sell foreign currency, I had to find something else valuable to sell." Next to him, the sign on his shop has suffered an alteration: "FOREIGN EXCHANGE shop" has been crossed out so it now reads "MEAT shop."

This was not the first time that the press made a connection between meat—a household staple for Argentine families—and the US dollar. Between the end of

1958 and the beginning of 1959, in a period marked by a major devaluation, liberalization, and the introduction of a single foreign currency market, the daily *Clarín* had come up with a novel way to highlight the spiraling prices of certain mass consumer goods. On the cover of December 17, 1958, one of the top new stories was summarized as follows: "Tenderloin: US$ . . . In Buenos Aires, the price of a kilo of tenderloin is pitted against the dollar exchange rate. Yesterday, on the butcher's price board, tenderloin cost AR$60. On the exchange rate boards, the dollar closed yesterday at AR$67.30. Tenderloin thus went up thirty pesos, while the dollar has risen AR$4.60 in the past forty-eight hours." The price of tenderloin merited a place on the list of "Major National Events," the following day. "Tenderloin: US$ . . . The price of tenderloin continues its dizzying ascent toward the U.S. dollar rate, as first reported yesterday . . . Will the tenderloin exchange rate reach that of the dollar?" A day later, the "competition" between the tenderloin and the dollar made the cover yet again, as did a slight uptick of the US currency. Yet there was another "trend" included in this day's "important events": the "democratic hake will replace the now opulent tenderloin at meat markets on Mondays and Fridays."

At the beginning of 1959, when the lengthy foreign exchange holiday ordered as part of the Stabilization Plan was nearing its end, the tenderloin was compared with the dollar yet again. The impact of the peso's devaluation on prices was an enormous concern as underscored in a range of stories in the press. One was titled "Buenos Aires residents say goodbye to fifty cent coins"; another covered three soccer teams that could not afford the train fare needed to get from Rosario to a match in Buenos Aires after a rate hike. The connection between the rising cost of beef and that of the dollar was also noted in this text: "The most recent dollar exchange rate—before the economic changes—was sixty-nine pesos. This is just a reminder because it's likely that today, beef will break the dollar-peso barrier and enter a new orbit: the beef-dollar" (*Clarín*, January 5, 1959). The following day, in another cover story, the paper informed readers: "As anticipated by this paper, tenderloin has surpassed the dollar" (*Clarín*, January 6, 1959). Toward the end of January, the dollar-tenderloin exchange rate continued to make headlines: "The price boards at meat markets trembled yet again yesterday when tenderloin hit sixty-five dollars per kilogram. Continuing with what has become a frequent comparison, the dollar closed at AR$66.20" (*Clarín*, January 23, 1959).

By comparing the value of the US currency with the price of a beef cut in order to draw attention to rising prices between the end of 1958 and beginning of 1959, the daily *Clarín* reveals yet another dimension of the dollar's initial popularization in Argentine society. While news coverage of the forex market helped make the dollar familiar for increasingly broader segments of the population, the "tenderloin-dollar" comparison reveals how the US currency became a reference not only for foreign exchange experts and *especuladores hormigas*, but for consumers as well. While the chronicles of the forex market gradually turned San Martín Street into a familiar setting—no longer the distant realm of certain financial sectors—this comparison removed the dollar from its usual habitat of the foreign exchange office and brought it into the sphere of the household and homemaker decisions. By using the dollar to gauge the value of beef, the US dollar entered the realm of daily life and became part of the household economy. In response to the rise in the cost of a kilo of tenderloin, which had become as expensive as the dollar, consumers could choose more reasonably priced fare such as hake, which the papers also promoted. At the same time, by constantly comparing it to beef, a household staple whose price is common knowledge, the dollar and its fluctuations are placed with the public's grasp; ultimately, understanding the foreign currency was merely a question of studying a different price board.

The tenderloin-dollar comparison, along with comic strips like Dobal's foreign exchange meat shop from 1964, also lent themselves to a gradual popularization of the dollar. Soon after, a broad public would be well versed in exchange rates. At the end of the 1950s, this way of depicting the rise in the price of household goods such as beef conveys a lesson: by noting that the price of tenderloin can climb as high as the dollar, it helps make readers understand what constitutes an "exorbitant" rise in prices.

## A New Advertising Icon

"YOU and the DOLLAR . . . are closely connected by the worth of the Argentine peso. This is why you were able to buy a piece of land for just sixty pesos per month when a dollar was worth thirty pesos. But now that same dollar goes for over seventy-five pesos . . ." The text is from an advertisement by the company Geofinca S.A. promoting the purchase in installments of lots in Mar del Plata, the seaside city known as "the pearl of the Atlantic" and also "the Argentine Biarritz." The ad consists of three panels in which different images—a dollar bill, a peso bill, and a bird's-eye view of a piece of land—appear inside a black-and-white silhouette of a man with a hat and cane. The second panel, the one with the peso bill, reads:

> YOU and the PESO have seen your purchasing power diminish and that same lot is now worth AR$170 per month. However, at the rate inflation is rising, AR$170 will be VERY CHEAP VERY SOON. So what should you do? Follow the anti-inflationary rule that saved the United States from crisis: BUY BETTER. That is . . . BUY LAND, the only way to effectively PROTECT YOUR MONEY against devaluation and INSTANTLY assure that your current and future savings QUA-DRU-PLE.

In the third panel, in which a piece of land is overlaid on the masculine silhouette, the ad concludes: "That's why the solution is between . . . YOU and MAR DEL PLATA . . . Where for just 138 monthly installments of AR$170, you can buy one of the STUPENDOUS LOTS AT PARQUE GEOFINCA MAR DEL PLATA."

At the end of the 1950s, the purchase of lots or apartments in seaside cities of Argentina became an investment alternative in a financial system in which inflation and strict state regulation of interest rates meant scanty yields on bank savings (Corso 2014). As the trend expanded over the two following decades, some economists attributed the coastal real estate boom to this search for a solid return on investment by Argentina's urban middle and upper-middle classes (Pastoriza and Torre 2019).

The eye-catching advertising by Geofinca S.A., a company with branches in Buenos Aires and other cities, demonstrates just how prominent such practices had become during this period. At the same time, it evidences how companies worked to capture not only seasoned investors but also potential ones who needed to be trained on where to put their money before they could be convinced. Although the dollar was still nowhere close to becoming the dominant currency on the local real estate market—as it would be in the 1980s—another key takeaway from these investment lessons was the greenback's growing relevance.

In the advertisement for lots in Mar del Plata, Geofinca S.A. proposed that potential customers use the dollar as a benchmark. The company thus promoted not only a product but also the calculations a buyer would need to conclude that land was the best investment, the sure way to "protect your money from devaluation." This message is reiterated in the advertisement's claim for a prospective buyer: "you and the dollar . . . are closely connected."

Like the journalistic pieces that associated the dollar with the rising prices of key consumer goods like meat, this type of advertisement contributed to making the US currency a benchmark beyond the foreign exchange market. As a way to protect against the peso's devaluation, the dollar as benchmark would become a key consideration among actors with little a priori knowledge in investing or the forex market.

At the same time, the dollar would also figure into the calculations of those accustomed to dealing with other currencies, though this does not necessarily suggest involvement in foreign trade or regular dabbling on the foreign exchange market. Instead, these were Argentines who traveled abroad: members of the local aristocracy who had doted on Europe since the nineteenth century (Losada 2008), but also a growing urban middle class that set out to explore the world in the 1960s as part of modern-day global influences in culture and consumer practices. A special travel report published in the magazine *Primera Plana* and entitled "1964 Traveler's Guide" in January of that year caters to this crowd. The five-page spread lists not-to-be missed sites at several key destinations along with practical tips for travelers on packages, transport, and the most convenient way of taking money abroad: traveler's checks.

In letters sent almost daily to his wife Silvina Ocampo and their daughter while away in Europe from August to December 1967, Argentine writer Adolfo Bioy Casares describes visits, restaurant menus, and purchases. In a letter postmarked in Geneva on October 29, he encourages them both to join him when the school year ends: "You can come simply so that we can make the trip home together or even to spend some time here together in Europe—provided winter doesn't scare you. To pay for the trip, you have the dollars I mentioned. If you come, come by ship. Get a comfortable cabin with a bathroom. I want you have a pleasant journey."

For Bioy Casares, and for many other Argentines who had the money to travel abroad in the 1960s, the dollar was simply the currency for tourism, independently of the legal tender in their chosen destination. In those years—and for some time—travel agencies always listed their airfare and vacation packages in the US currency. Thus, in 1958 a ticket from Buenos Aires to New York went for US$420 on the Chilean airline Cinta, while airfare to Miami cost US$345. Aerolíneas Peruanas offered "the most economical rate" on flights to Mexico: US$432. As for travel agencies, one promoted its 128-day grand European excursion for US$1,695 in 1962, where passengers would travel abroad a "majestic Arlanza motor vessel." Another option by the same agency was a "dreamy excursion to the Orient in fall," a 64-day journey flying on a Pan American jet for US$3,250.

In a decade characterized by regular currency devaluations and growing concern about inflation, the dollar became a rudder for maneuvering different transaction universes. Banks also took note of the dollar's growing importance in their ads, trying to keep customers abreast of changing regulations on foreign currency deposits and to capture all the dollars that Argentine citizens were saving. In April 1962, when new changes were introduced to the forex market, Banco Popular Argentino ran the following ad: "If you have foreign currency in Argentina or abroad, get a GOOD INTEREST rate." Month later, a new Ministry of Economy urged *Clarín* readers: "DON'T TAKE YOUR FOREIGN CURRENCY ABROAD. Collaborate with national recovery and get profitable interest rates on your deposits."

Advertisements on savings and investment options in dollars become relatively common starting in March 1967, when the de facto regime under General Onganía announced what it promised would be the "last devaluation," along with a series of measures geared toward "stabilizing" and "modernizing" the national economy. These measures, combined with other initiatives, liberalized the foreign currency market anew after three years of state intervention. In addition, the Central Bank announced that banks could again offer saving accounts and certificates of deposit in foreign currency, thus nullifying the 1964 ban on such instruments by the Illia administration. Less than a year after the 1966 coup, the stories on the crowds at foreign exchange offices reveal just how many "savers" had money tucked away. During the first few days after the reopening of the forex market, media outlets describe dollars abounding as a result of the "individuals with currency to sell," as seen in this story in *Primera Plana* magazine:

> [Minister] Krieger Vasena's initial 40 percent devaluation combined with the liberalization of the exchange market was quite the paradox. The announcement was met with elation on San Martín Street. A tide of people with dollars to sell flooded the four foreign exchange offices (Baires, Exprinter, Piano, and Mercurio) that opened that same Monday. Over the course of the day, all had to close their doors for two or three hours because they simply did not have enough pesos to exchange for the dollars, which came in an assortment of makeshift wrappings. (*Primera Plana*, March 21, 1967)

According to the magazine, exchange offices had purchased US$7 million that week. This is the backdrop to a wave of advertisements by banks and financial entities seeking to attract US dollar investments. As seen here, besides fostering the integration of the dollar into the financial repertoires of existing bank customers, these ads are indicative of a broader trend. In an ad by Banco Ganadero Argentino, for example, a man is seen from behind, his hands clasped in a pensive gesture. Question marks accompany a text bubble that reads:

> And now? How do you know what the best savings option is? A certificate of deposit? Dollars? A mortgage? There are many types of savings and investments available. You can't keep up with them all but we can, because we're bankers. Come see us. Talk to us. At our new Investment Information Center, we'll tell you the savings options that allow you to make the most of your money. This unique service is free for you, whether you're a saver or an investor.

From the moment in which the Central Bank authorized banks to accept dollar deposits, considering that some individuals and companies had foreign currency tucked away—as demonstrated by the arrival of dollars to exchange offices "in an assortment of makeshift wrappings"—several entities began promoting investments in foreign currency. Banco Comercial de Buenos Aires, for example, offered "dollar deposits with compensatory interest. Savings accounts in dollars, foreign transactions in dollars, purchase and sale of dollars. Transactions in dollars: an 'extra' service by the bank that always offers something 'extra.'" Another entity, the First National City Bank, attracted potential clients with the following text: "We are looking for people who deal in foreign currency. We offer the world's most comprehensive and efficient service for all type of transactions in foreign currency: deposits, certificates of deposit, purchases, sales, bank drafts, wire transfers, remittances, underwriting, traveler's checks." IVERCO S.A.F. ran an ad illustrated with a hundred-dollar bill targeting a similar customer at the end of March that year: "If you have dollars, interesting transactions are now available to you. IVERCO can conveniently advise you based on the latest changes to foreign currency exchange. Working for investors since 1954."

Finally, Economic Minister Adalbert Krieger Vasena's 1967 plan laid the groundwork for yet another role of the dollar in the financial repertoires of social groups that clearly went beyond the borders of "la City." In a context in which the value of foreign currency rose in lockstep with domestic price hikes, advertisements from the period reveal that US legal tender was a way to keep abreast of the changing values of certain goods and services. On March 12, 1967, Bellizzi Turismo released an ad reading, "You keep the difference: one U.S. dollar for AR$251." The travel agency offered to calculate the cost of airfare and boat trips to Europe and the United States in pesos at the dollar's pre-devaluation rate. The strategy of promoting goods and services at the "old" dollar rate reveals how the greenback was becoming a rather broad price benchmark. The dollar did not necessarily have to be used for a transaction in order to play this role as a unit of account, that is, a touchstone for prices. Nor was it restricted to transactions involving other countries. "Pay for new dollars at old prices" promised an ad for Cosentino, a shop offering photography equipment. The price in pesos of each item was based on a dollar worth AR$250 when the foreign currency rate had reached AR$350 on San Martín Street.

Bellizzi and Cosentino charged their customers in pesos, not dollars, and vowed to continue pricing their products and services based on the pre-devaluation dollar. Thus, both companies assured customers that their prices would not rise to the tune of the peso's devaluation. A similar ad by a home appliance store captured the public's attention in the following ad: "IS THE DOLLAR UP? No matter! At Kuligowsky, the home king, your pesos are worth more. We're still selling TVs." Zenith and Philco televisions, among other brands, were both available at the home appliance store for a "small down payment" plus installments.

All three ads reveal, first and foremost, the direct impact that each devaluation had on domestic price development—especially imported goods—and, therefore, on all commerce. Yet above all they demonstrate that the dollar already encompassed a set of meanings easy to decipher for the readers of major national newspapers and news magazines. Kuligowsky's ad relied on the dollar as a familiar gauge of the economy that consumers closely followed. At the same time, it utilized this knowledge to underscore the opportunity for customers to be able to purchase home appliances despite spiraling prices.

As this type of advertising grew, the experts took notice. The *Primera Plana* edition of March 21, 1967, included a lengthy article on the liberalization of the foreign exchange market and the peso's devaluation. It provides insight into how advertising had adapted to the context: "Traveler's checks returned to the spotlight again on Tuesday when the First National City Bank ran its first advertisement since the introduction of the government's new monetary controls." The advertisement promised that "this money is good worldwide" and that, in Argentina, "you can now buy everything you want." The article continued, "This is not the only case in which advertising has seized on an opportunity: two days later, the Cosentino shop began offering still and film cameras and slide projectors in pesos but based on a dollar at AR$250." In an interview with the weekly magazine, shop owner Ubaldo Cosentino remarked that his store's sales had doubled in just two days. According to the article, "the modest but effective ad campaign—costing him just 40,000 pesos [around 100 US dollars]—not only yielded an immediate rise in sales but also contributed to the future expansion of the business." This was because, in the merchant's own words, "If we hadn't said anything and just kept selling at the same price, only our usual customers would have reaped the benefits, but these ads helped us extend the opportunity to the public at large. Commerce, not speculation, is what we're about."

By invoking the dollar to promote the prices of his products, Ubaldo Cosentino was able to considerably boost sales, no small achievement at a time of monetary uncertainty. Interestingly, it was not necessary to require payment in US dollars in order for the strategy to work. The fact that the public had adopted the buck as a unit of account sufficed. In 1967, a Cosentino customer looking to buy a still or film camera did not need US dollars. Yet he or she did have to rely on the dollar as a framework for interpreting the object's economic value. This "effective campaign" rested on the dollar's role as a benchmark for transactions not associated with the forex market. The dollar thus reached increasingly broader sectors, expanding beyond those able to invest in foreign currency or travel abroad, or the customers of banks that allowed dollar deposits.

Like the "tenderloin-dollar" comparison at the end of the 1950s, advertising in the 1960s reveals how the dollar became a reference for interpretations and calculations off the foreign exchange market. Advertising discourse not only puts a series of practices on display—the incorporation of certain household goods and services, the promotion of cultural products, the dissemination of lifestyles—but also provides a window into the existence of other practices, with the codes and meanings it relies on to convey its message. In this regard, advertising matters in terms of not only what it directly promotes but also that which it takes as a given: economic practices, values, customs. Thus, advertising allows us to appreciate the two parallel ways in which the dollar was popularized. As the foreign exchange market became more familiar, the uses of US legal tender increasingly exceeded this sphere, taking root on different markets and integrating the calculations of an increasingly broader universe of actors. Over the following decade, this trend would intensify.

The changes noted in the way the media covered economic topics between the end of the 1950s and during the following decade had an impact on the language, themes, and figures that helped to redefine the borders of the foreign exchange market in Argentina. The print press and advertisements during the period, as shown here, contributed to making the dollar a benchmark for heterogeneous markets and diverse publics. The media became the setting for a campaign of a veritable economic pedagogy (Neiburg 2006) that provided frameworks for interpreting and evaluating the dollar as a key to maneuvering new incidences of economic turbulence. During the years examined here, a novel relationship began to unfold between popular culture, financial practices, and the exchange market. The making of the dollar into a bellwether by the press, advertising, and television thus fosters a consideration of popular culture's role in establishing the US currency as a resource in the financial practices of diverse social groups. This is done through a historical process of economic socialization and the establishment of financial repertoires that are socially produced and culturally significant.

The understanding of this initial phase of the dollar's popularization in Argentina required us to go beyond the observation of money uses and differentiation as analyzed by Viviana Zelizer (1994). In the case studied by the author, a single currency (the dollar) issued exclusively by the US federal state had legitimately achieved dominion over US territory. Zelizer's analysis of the use of this currency by individuals and households thus begins by accepting the currency itself as a given, without delving into the cultural and institutional mediations that enabled its acceptance. The understanding of the popularization of the dollar in Argentina, in contrast, brings the need for another approach. The interpretation we proposed here involved analyzing the way in which the US currency was established—in public culture and in ordinary financial repertoires—as a competent currency that served as a supplement to the national currency (the peso). The chapters to come will delve into how the dollar's popularity grew in the following decades and how its reach expanded to broader swatches of the population.

*Chapter Three*

# A GLOBAL CURRENCY IN ARGENTINE POCKETS AND POCKETBOOKS (1971–1983)

Javier Portales: "What about you? What do you expect from the new administration?"

Alberto García Grau: "For the dollar to go down . . . Right down the drain! And for us Argentines to finally believe that the Argentine peso is worth the same as the dollar!"

[laughter]

"Wait a minute. I thought—because you've bragged about it yourself for some time now—that you had all your savings invested in dollars. You used to buy dollars . . . So what happened, did you sell all the dollars?"

"Nope, I fixed all that."

"Is that right? You sold them?"

"Nope. I exchanged them for German marks, Spanish pesetas, sterling pounds . . . And a French franc or two. Up with the European common market! Down with Yankee imperialism! Out with the dollar area! In with the marks! In with the pounds! I'll buy, I'll buy, I'll buy, I'll buy."

In 1973, Argentine viewers rarely missed the television program *Polémica en el bar*. In a simple but effective formula combining gravitas with humor, *Polémica* featured several men sitting around a café table and discussing a range of topics. Sports (mainly soccer) was one theme, along with national politics, the economy and finance (the country's, but also their own), and women. The characters, played by famous comic actors, each represented a familiar urban stereotype: the intellectual, the *chanta* (con man), the student, the middle-class employee, etc.

## Chapter Three

This particular program aired shortly before Peronist Héctor Campora was sworn in as president on May 25, 1973; he had won under the party ticket when the ban on Peronism was lifted after eighteen years and nine military regimes.[1] Humor seemed like an effective way to convey what people expected the future would bring. Actor Javier Portales played the role of moderator on the program and the voice of reason. After wishing the new administration good luck, he asked the other comics what they thought about the situation. The first to answer was the one who played a character defined by the series writers as a "middle-class" man. This character was not concerned about the return to democracy, the lifting of the ban on Peronism, or an end to the political violence that had been increasingly plaguing the nation. Instead, he hoped that under President Cámpora, the dollar might go down. The parody, emphasized by the laugh track, lay in the fact that this character, as Portales noted, had "bragged for some time" about investing all his savings in dollars. Yet there was nothing contradictory about this. Given that the new administration had strong support among left-leaning Peronist youth groups, this character had simply adapted: he now preached anti-imperialism, selling his US currency and buying other foreign currency instead.

While in 1962, comedian Tato Bores had gotten a laugh when he noted that "everyone is outside staring at the board" of the exchange offices on San Martín Street, television humor had shifted a decade later. It still relied on the dollar, drawing attention to certain practices and meanings associated with the US currency, but had adapted to the times. In other words, a man declaring that he will stop buying dollars to adapt to the new status quo becomes a source of laughter in a context in which buying dollars seems like the safest investment option. The viewers of this popular program felt this character was familiar: he represented a segment of Argentine society that already knew the ins and outs of the greenback by 1973.

The dollar had become a pop culture icon. It was on television and radio, and soon it would be found in rock music. The final years of the so-called Argentine Revolution, the military regime that had seized power from democratically elected President Arturo Illia in 1966, had made an important contribution to this process. In this context, the sketch on *Polémica en el bar* conveyed the public meanings attributed to the dollar by the beginning of the seventies and its increased presence in the financial repertoires of at least a portion of Argentine society.

In its edition of March 2, 1973, the weekly *El Economista* ran a story entitled "1972: Inflation overpowered savers." The story, published in the run-up to the first presidential elections since 1963, noted that not a single investment option had outperformed inflation in 1972. Between 1970 and 1973, Argentina's inflation had tripled, making it one of the highest worldwide. Besides considering stock options, *El Economista* also addressed the "parallel dollar." The "investor" who had purchased dollars on the "parallel" market in 1972 had seen returns of 23.6 percent; though this was much lower than annual inflation, an estimated 58.5 percent, it still yielded more than savings accounts (18.4 percent) or certificates of deposit (22.8 percent). The returns on more sophisticated investment instruments, like securities, shares, and government bonds, were higher, but none even kept pace with inflation. The article concluded, with no small degree of irony, that Argentina's "national spirit" should be elated by the scare success of "black dollar" investments. Yet there was another unintended irony in the piece: it treated the "parallel" dollar like any other legitimate form of investment.

This chapter covers the evolution of the dollar from the beginning of the 1970s to the beginning of the 1980s. It is a period quite unlike any other in Argentine history, due to persistent military intervention in politics (O'Donnell 1997; Cavarozzi 2006; Novaro and Palermo 2003): the only elected presidents to serve in those years did so from 1973 to 1976. At the same time, as part of enormous political convulsion, youth organizations were growing increasingly radical (Landi 1978; de Riz 1981; Gillespie 1982) and the economy, increasingly unstable (Rougier and Fiszbein 2006; Basualdo 2013; Gerchunoff and Llach 2018). During these years, the US currency would enter a whole new stage in its progressive expansion in public life. This process was influenced by global monetary and economic transformations—the US decision to abandon the gold standard in 1971 and the commencement of financial globalization (Eichengreen 2010; Amato and Fantacci 2012; Aglietta and Coudert 2015)—as well as the local economic and political cycle. Over the course of this decade, the dollar would cease to be merely a benchmark of the domestic economy or a topic in the news: instead, it became part of the financial repertoire of the "average" Argentine. The greenback would no longer be just a headline story; it would be tucked into local wallets. This jump in the dollar's popularization was also fostered by the financial liberalization instilled as part of the economic policy of Argentina's last dictatorship during the second half of the 1970s. This winding path is the subject of this chapter.

## The Early Seventies: Capital Flight, a Booming Parallel Market, and the Repression of the Dollar

Juan José Redruello was forty-five years old and had worked as a "professional" for the past twenty. His line of work involved transporting large sums of foreign currency to and from Argentina. On August 5, 1971, he arrived to Ezeiza airport, about fifty kilometers outside Buenos Aires, on a flight from the United States. His friend Roberto García, a married man of forty-six, was waiting outside in a red Peugeot to drive García to the Piano exchange office in the heart of "la City." They left the airport and got on the highway. About halfway to their destination, their car was forced off the road by a green Ford Falcon with three passengers, a Fiat 600 driven by a young blond, and a white Peugeot 404 with another three passengers. Two men leaped out of the Falcon and approached the Peugeot. One forced García and Redruello into the back seat and climbed in next to them; the other took the wheel. (*Clarín*, August 6, 1971)

This dollar heist in the early seventies took place at five o'clock in the afternoon, amid intense traffic just a half mile from the city limits. As detailed in the chronicle, the robbers drove García and Redruello to the middle of nowhere and forced them out of the car. They even took Redruello's jacket, where they assumed he might be hiding part of the stash. After warning the two men to stay put for the next fifteen minutes, the seven robbers made off with the briefcase full of cash in the four cars. When they reached the police station, Redruello asked Casa Piano to send an employee to ascertain the exact amount of dollars in the stolen briefcase as he claimed not to know. At ten o'clock that night, the Casa Piano employee still had not shown up at the station.

Whether legal or illegal, the dollars in Redruello's briefcase would be unloaded onto an insatiable forex market. At the end of 1971, the government had ordered the sixth "micro-devaulation" of the year. The 1970s had started with a series of important monetary measures designed to keep inflation in check. On the one hand, a new currency had begun circulating on the first day of 1970: the *peso ley 18,188* (one was worth one hundred of the old pesos). On the other hand, in June of that year, the exchange rate was "reset" to AR$400 ("old pesos") per dollar. According to market observers at the time, this decision meant "the end of the stability" ushered in by the "great devaluation" of 1967. The introduction of the *peso ley* came on the same day the next president of the de facto regime, General Roberto Marcelo Levingston, was sworn in, replacing General Juan Carlos Onganía, who had been in power since 1966. The new president had been appointed by a military junta that had withdrawn its support for Onganía. Levingston remained in power until March 1971, when he was replaced by General Alejandro Agustín Lanusse.[2] The devaluation came as a surprise to the banking and business sector. It had a "negative psychological impact" with "unpredictable economic aftereffects" (*Clarín*, June 19, 1970), as emphasized by the Chamber of Commerce, the stock market, and Argentina's Industrial Union (UIA). The Rural Society and the Association of Argentine Economists issued similar statements. However, Washington and the International Monetary Fund considered the measure "wise."

In this context, Minister of Economy Carlos Moyano Llerena explained that the devaluation was not strictly necessary from an economic point of view but that the government wished to avoid "capital flight" (*Clarín*, June 19, 1970). According to his calculations, some US$400 million had left the country during the second half of 1969. In response to critiques, the minister stated that "one very important factor" of the measure was being overlooked. "If a number of individuals or companies that together represent considerable economic power have a sense of uncertainty regarding the future value of the peso, their psychological attitude could cause the nation serious damage. Although it may be unsubstantiated," Moyano Llerena continued, "mistrust" could be as detrimental as "adverse economic events." At the same time, he claimed that the measures were not about "small-time speculators who buy bills at exchange offices"; instead, there were "important members of the business community," who, seeking to avoid "major losses," were swapping their pesos for dollars. Therefore, the minister concluded, in order to keep "this unfounded psychological attitude of mistrust" from repeating itself, the government had opted for a 14 percent devaluation.

However, this did little to stop the "currency exodus," forcing the administration to announce further "micro-devaluations" in the following months. On July 30, 1971, the cover story of the *El Economista* was entitled "The dollars gone." The Ministry of Economy had presented a plan for a Repatriation for Development bond. The article emphasized that "the departure of that money can be attributed to our fear of political mishaps and schizophrenic taxes." Therefore, those dollars "won't return until Argentine politics inspires real, long-term trust" (*El Economista*, July 30, 1971).

In August that year, ads by the real estate company Geofinca in the daily *La Opinión* encouraged the public to "earn by comparing." Unlike the ad campaign the company had run at the end of the 1950s, where a rise in the dollar was associated with a loss in the peso's value, the buck was now presented as an investment option comparable to real estate investment. According to the ad, "buying dollars, you earn up to 20% per month; buying land, 150% annually." However, economic journalist Roberto Roth—who wrote for the same paper—did not agree. Roth analyzed the consequences of the "mini-devaluation" policy on the forex market, noting how the US dollar continued to rise, representing an attractive investment option: "With each new devaluation, the peso's worth on the black market grows by leaps and bounds. Each devaluation obliges yet another since a difference of over 20% between the cost of pesos over or under the table becomes intolerable" (*La Opinión*, August 3, 1971).

Given this state of affairs, it came as no surprise that the dollar would become the most profitable investment option: "The interest rate on bank deposits is 18%, mortgage rates are at 24%, and personal loans, 36%. Yet the purchase of dollars dances to the beat of the economic authority at 42%." Roth saw dollar bonds, a financial instrument that was being floated as a way to avoid "leaks" in the system, as a "coherent" option on the part of a state that fostered divestment. "By buying [the bonds], citizens are protected against the 42% devaluation and even make 9% profits. With all this, why work, why invest?" Comedian Tato Bores helped Roth understand what was happening with this dollar bonds: "The question of these bonds reminds me of a theory that Tato Bores presented years ago when he asked why the state prints pesos when they could be printing dollars." By issuing dollar bonds, the state was effectively crossing that line. "If the state begins conducting transactions in dollars today, citizens will follow suit tomorrow, thus doing away with the peso's standing and, as a result, with its remaining worth" (*La Opinión*, August 3, 1971).

In mid-August 1971, in the context of a set of anti-inflationary economic measures, US president Richard Nixon announced the end of dollar's convertibility into gold. It was a unilateral decision to terminate the Bretton Woods system, which had regulated international monetary relations for nearly three decades. The announcement shook the world economy to its core. As occurred in other countries, Argentina shut down currency trading for several days. The government attempted to translate the US decision to the national context, and the Ministry of Economy released a statement noting that the decision to suspend the gold-dollar parity

> serves as a lesson for those who believe that foreign currency is the only safe investment. Being realistic, what should be defended is the Argentine peso. Not only to protect Argentine savers and ensure a healthy, robust economic structure, but to maintain the image of a nation-wide commitment to what is ours. (*La Nación*, July 19, 1971)

When forex trading was reinstated a few days later, one dollar was worth five hundred of the "old" pesos. According to the government communique, the decision corresponded to a "realistic attitude" and aimed to adequately "adapt" the Argentine peso's official exchange rate and thus ensure "authentic" parity following the international measures. This 6 percent devaluation was the seventh in a five-month period.

The latest minister of finance, Juan Quilici, had only been in his post for two months after his appointment by General Alejandro Lanusse, who had succeeded General Levingston as head of the de facto regime in 1971. According to the new minister, the financial system should "increase global savings channeled through the banking system"; to achieve this, it was necessary to "discourage speculative purchases of currency in order to prevent the bloodsucking that undermines fruitful, creative investment" (*Clarín*, August 26, 1971). Among the possible measures to contain the speculation, one rumor was that the government would forbid news outlets from reporting on the black market exchange rate.

At the same time, the Central Bank carried out several bank inspections, uncovering "illegitimate" transactions between banks, stockbrokers, and exchange offices. At each step of the transaction, the exchange rate rose. Banks were taking full advantage of the market freedoms, turning a blind eye to the fact that certain transactions had been banned. There was little hope that the latest devaluation would do much to keep the dollar from rising. On the black market, the hub for all unofficial transactions—including the importation of nonessentials—the new exchange rate of AR$500 did not carry much weight: the dollar soon reached AR$590. According to an editorial in *Clarín*, "Like the 'mini' and 'midi' devaluations, this one [implemented last Tuesday] appears isolated from any economic context that would suggest reactivation." The critiques of the new economic measures continued: "once again, the 1967 stabilization plan is failing. Since the beginning of the so-called Argentine Revolution, one dollar costs double its price in pesos." In addition, "the way things are going, the peso's real exchange rate will trend upward."

According to Julio Nudler, an economic columnist at *La Opinión*, the speculative modus operandi of certain local business sectors was changing.

> In some cases, [these sectors] have applied their cash balances to businesses like construction or used them to acquire land or apartments. Based on the currency configuration of investment opportunities, speculators are opting for other channels. One of the fundamental ones is exchanging pesos for dollars or other currencies. The disintegration of the political regime has motivated this capital flight. (*La Opinión*, August 31, 1971)

These trends were clearly visible on the parallel market. On September 2, a *Clarín* headline read "Dollar hits record on parallel market: AR$601." Five days later, the dollar had climbed to AR$631 and was making headlines across the country. *La Opinión* went a step further in its assessment, concluding, "The dollar is today's most profitable investment." The example offered in the article was the following: anyone who had purchased dollars on the parallel market at the beginning of the year had paid AR$400. Now, they could sell those dollars at AR$630, reaping a profit of over 50 percent that far exceeded the 20 percent rise in the cost of living. According to the article, the "wave of speculation" was inextricably tied to the sense of political instability.

In the days that followed, the dollar continued its ascent. In a comic strip in *Clarín*, a man gazes up at the sky with a monocle while another asks, "What are you searching the sky for? The Concorde 001?" The man answers, "No, the Dollar 670!" (*Clarín*, September 18, 1971). Comic strips regularly made use of the dollar's rise. In *Clarín*, one shows the peso lying on the divan while telling the psychologist about the "anguish" his devaluation has caused him. In another, a dollar is waiting to take a special elevator up while a butler attends to him. Next to him, an angry-looking peso is waiting for an out-of-order service elevator (*Clarín*, September 18, 1971).

An editorial on capital flight published the same day as the "Dollar 670" comic deemed the "foreign exchange arena" critical to "our economic and financial reality" (*Clarín*, September 18, 1971). According to the editorial, the "dizzying" demand for dollars, which had averaged US$6 million per day for the past three weeks, was about much more than inflation. What happened on the parallel market, the article continued, could be attributed to investor mistrust of "controls and directives on the part of the state." Exonerating capital investors from any blame, the editorial noted that they had been "induced" to speculate, hoard, or take their money abroad. The consequences of this trend were alarming: capital flight had reached US$120 million. Given this state of affairs, the Central Bank decided to suspend imports. In government circles, the belief was that within two months, this measure would stop the unremitting flow of imports. Following the announcement, on September 13, dollars ran out on the parallel market when the unofficial exchange rate hit AR$685.

The demand for the Repatriation for Development bonds put more pressure on the market: companies bought dollars on the black market and then laundered them by purchasing bonds. *La Opinión* referred to the state of affairs as "the worst economic crisis" since 1962. The aggravating factors included "mass capital flight" and "speculation." As the dollar rose quickly, analysis continued to argue that forex speculation had become "the best business for anyone looking to save." In eight and a half months, the exchange rate had risen 60 percent while people's purchasing power had fallen by 30 percent.

As another strategy to slow the rising exchange rate, the government opted to divide the forex market. It would continue to control the "trade" market, maintaining one dollar at AR$500 for all foreign trade, while taking a laissez-faire approach to the "financial" market. At the same time, the limits on foreign currency purchases for tourism were eliminated, though anyone wishing to purchase foreign bills for a trip abroad was still required to present their passport and ticket. When the market opened the next day, this effectively produced another 50 percent devaluation in the peso's worth: one dollar was now worth AR$745. Now the parallel market was trading below the "financial" market, at AR$710.

National papers provided extensive coverage of this split exchange market. On its cover, *La Nación* observed how "the opening day generated great expectations among importers, exporters, and bankers, but also among the general public, which crowded out front of exchange offices to see how the exchange rate for the financial dollar would evolve" (*La Nación*, September 21, 1971). A photograph included in the article showed a group of men in suits standing before the boards at Casa Piano; the caption noted the "public's exceptional interest" and the forming of "small crowds" in front of the exchange offices, "complicating traffic on the streets of the financial district." For its part, *La Opinión* described the situation as follows: "Confusion reigned on the first day of the split foreign exchange market. The dollar is more expensive on the official market than on the parallel." The article in this paper quoted the manager of "a major bank," who confessed, "After a quarter century in the banking industry, I'm entirely confounded by this turn of events" (*La Opinión*, September 21, 1971). The public, unclear on the new regulations, had rushed to banks and exchange offices believing there were no restrictions on buying dollars on the financial market, but this was not the case.

One day later, *La Nación* noted that the divided exchange market had reversed the trend: it was no longer possible to "spend a week in Mexico or Miami at no cost" by acquiring foreign currency on the official market and reselling it on the parallel market. Under the new measures, it had become "great business to stock up on the parallel market," with an advantage of fifty or sixty cents per dollar (*La Nación*, September 22, 1971). Beyond all estimates, it was evident that the "parallel" dollar continued to rise.

Table 1. Evolution of US Dollar Rates. September–November 1971

| Markets | Sep. 22 | Oct. 28 | Oct. 29 | Nov. 2 | Nov. 3 |
|---|---|---|---|---|---|
| Trade dollar | 500 | 500 | 500 | 500 | 500 |
| Financial dollar | 605 | 770 | 770 | 775 | 775 |
| Parallel dollar | 672 | 933 | 900 | 920 | 920 |

Source: El Economista, November 5, 1971.

Despite the fact that the government considered the "black market" to be "small"—and thus capable of reaching "a boiling point" whenever the demand for dollars spiked—the parallel dollar was considered the most solid investment option in 1971. An editorial in the historic economic weekly *The Review of River Plate* summed this up in an example: a homeowner who had sold for AR$10 million in April of that year could have purchased US$28,000 on the parallel market. If, eight months later, he had exchanged those dollars for pesos, he could now buy a property worth AR$22 million. The editorial then concluded: "This example is not about hoarding currency: it is but a simple purchase and sale transaction in an eight-month period" (*The Review of River Plate*, September 23, 1971). The annual balance sheet, explained the weekly publication, flew in the face of all forecasts the government had made with regard to what would happen with the dollar.

A report by an influential Argentine think tank (Fundación de Investigaciones Económicas Latinoamericanas [FIEL]) reached a similar conclusion: the spike in interest rates during October had been small in relation to the "strong revenues offered by speculative investments on the parallel market." At the same time, the report emphasized that "any investor who wagered on the peso has suffered doubly."

The argument was that Argentine "investors make decisions based on what they anticipate will happen with the price of the dollar" (*La Nación*, August 24, 1971).

Finally, on November 25, the black market dollar exceeded AR$1,000, an amount with enormous symbolic value. It was a number that, in the words of *La Opinión*, signified "the country's economic breakdown and the end of an era." The government reacted quickly to tamper down on the forex market. The following day, in fact, Central Bank officials and police visited banks and agencies to conduct inspections. These new measures revealed the administration's growing preoccupation with the parallel market dollar. In fact, authorities had begun discussing a limit on foreign exchange transactions at banks. According to *La Opinión*, a rumor was circulating on the market that the government inspections were motivated by a suspicion of fraudulent transactions at banks. The "speculative maneuvering" consisted in transactions "changing hands," that is, making a single transaction appear to be many different ones, thus increasing the price of the foreign currency each step of the way (*La Opinión*, November 25, 1971).

While the inspectors worked to crack down on black market transactions, "history has shown that these inspections do not yield the expected results, as it is easy to elude the requisition." The greater the restrictions, according to *La Opinión*, the more the "parallel market" boomed. Therefore, "the parallel market, which normally operates in well-equipped offices, can just as easily function at a café table. In this case, it would be even less transparent, allowing for better business deals" (*La Opinión*, November 27, 1971). In the opinion of forex market sources consulted by *La Nación*, the rising cost of the dollar on the parallel market could be attributed to the expectations associated with the 1972 economic plan.

The pressure on the parallel market continued in the days that followed. In early December, *El Economista* reported that "the black dollar will apparently be struck from the public chalkboards" and reflected on how the black market had evolved. Before the 1955 coup, it explained, Peronism had "learned to live" with the black market. However, there was one substantial difference between that time and 1971. Prior to 1955, that market was "clandestine" and involved a risk of "true criminal prosecution"; "foreign currency is bought and sold, but in the shadows." In those early years, the press did not report on the black market exchange rate. By 1971, the "black dollar" had acquired a "regular status," "like a third legal market." The lack of concern on the part of both the Central Bank and the government was "part of the anomalies of the national system." It was "legal" and "necessary" to strip this market of "spotlights and coverage," thus restoring its "traditional place underground." This journalist had no idea why "the state and citizens not involved [on this market] tolerated these speculative deals," though he ventured that "this [could be] the last time we are allowed to mention the [black market] exchange rate" (*El Economista*, December 3, 1971).

Just a few days later, the press reported that although "the foreign exchange psychosis" continued, there was "no longer supply on the parallel market." *La Opinión* described an air of "fear and precaution" on the market, underscoring that the official news agency was no longer publishing the black market exchange rate. However, according to the forex market sources cited in the article, despite the fact that "the counters had been empty the previous day," operators had been making phone calls to schedule meetings with their clients. The sources did admit that by stemming the flow of under-the-table dollars, the controls prevented any large transactions on the "parallel market" (*La Opinión*, December 6, 1971).

Finally, the government also enacted the Criminal Exchange Act (Law 19,359), noting the need for "enhanced prevention of exchange regulation breaches and continual, efficient deterrence." In order to put the law into effect, different state bodies assembled a series of rules and made certain infractions crimes. According to the drafters, "the [new] law will put an end to the boom in crimes that go practically unpunished." The repercussions of the "new criminal foreign exchange regime" evidenced extreme mistrust of criminal prosecution as a strategy to quash the illegal market. In an editorial published on December 11, 1971, *Clarín* noted:

> The sole effect of a system like the one [Argentina has] introduced will be to render organizations more effective at evading the law, as always occurs in circumstances such as these. If the state is unable to stop drug trafficking, it will be unsuccessful at putting an end to currency trafficking, provided there is a demand for foreign bills. There is not a single country in the world—starting with the socialist countries—that shows otherwise. The parallel market will become a black market and there in the shadows, transactions will become even more lucrative; fewer people may be involved, but they will be more powerful and more organized.

In the column entitled "Changes," *La Nación* noted that the new law had been "implemented in 'la City' with little fanfare," despite the fact that the legislation aimed "to combat a small, highly speculative, and scarcely representative market." The columnist affirmed that the legislation had created "a typical kind of policing that fails to address the core issue." At the same time, it noted the "emotional or political motivations, not technical ones" behind the measure. According to the article, despite being "very small," the parallel market did not cease to be a "real market born from our economy's faulty structure": "As inflation and mistrust grow, capital flight increases; when transformed into black dollars, this fosters investment and economic development in other regions outside our territory." Additionally, this was not a new problem. "As shown in Argentina's experience over the past twenty-five years, police operatives are ineffective at detecting under-the-table transactions in dollars."

Chapter Three

# The Third Peronist Presidency (1973–1976): Fighting Speculation and Crisis

The de facto regime known as the Argentine Revolution (1966–1973) had little success at controlling inflation, fostering economic growth, or overcoming the foreign trade bottleneck (O'Donnell 1982; Pucciarelli 1999). All of these issues figured strongly in the campaign for the 1973 presidential election, the first in which Peronism was allowed to present a candidate after an eighteen-year ban on the party (Landi 1978; de Riz 1981). Presidential candidates from across the political spectrum cited the "lack of foreign currencies," "foreign exchange controls," and "Argentina as a currency-sending country" in their assessments of the national economy and the solutions they proposed. The Justicialist Liberation Front (Frente Justicialista de Liberación), which represented Peronism in the elections, proposed "strict controls aimed at minimizing foreign currencies, as these are a primary focus of the economic authorities." Candidates from the other political parties, which were strongly at odds with Peronism on other topics, agreed on this assessment of this national economic conundrum. This was the case of the New Force (Nueva Fuerza) party founded by Álvaro Alsogaray, who had served as minister of economy after Frondizi was overthrown. "Only New Force can stop inflation" was the campaign slogan of the party, which promised to make "Argentina a currency-hosting country" yet again. The campaign of the traditional Unión Cívica Radical (Radical party) promised "strict control on all foreign currency that enters or leaves the country."

During the election campaign, the forex market was presented as a place geared exclusively toward "speculation." This would be the term the new administration would use to build public awareness of foreign currency transaction and make it a political talking point. Peronist candidate Héctor J. Cámpora swept the election and took office in May 1973; when the party's original leader, Juan Domingo Perón, returned from exile, Cámpora resigned and Perón took office in October of that year. Introduced under Cámpora, the administration's first economic policy was based on a "social pact" between unions and businesses with the aim of limiting both price increases and worker demands for higher salaries (Torre 1983). This pact kept inflation in check until mid-1974. At that point, workers were clamoring for raises, challenging union reps who toed the party line; at the same time, businesses were no longer willing to keep prices down. Both led to a breakdown in the social pact. The death of Juan Domingo Perón on July 1, 1974,[3] only added to the uncertainty, limiting the administration's ability to handle the pressures on the economy. Country reserves began to fall, inflation began to grow, and the trade balance moved into the red yet again (Rougier and Fiszbein 2006).

In this context of political instability and economic malaise, the black exchange market again became a focus of attention. Analysts of the period who tracked the movements of the "parallel" market agreed on the sway it had over the population. At the beginning of August 1974, Peronist officials and legislators took a series of measures that denoted its preoccupation with the revival of the "black market." Central Bank officials summoned the forex market's largest operators to inform them of the type of collaboration it expected. According to the daily *La Opinión*, operators were informed at the meeting that the banking authority could order exchange offices to close if "gambling of the sort suspected does in fact exist."

Additionally, the Central Bank increased the amount of foreign currency travelers could acquire to keep them from resorting to the black market. A piece in *La Nación* in August entitled "More dollars" makes use of an argument typical of economic liberals on the "persistence" of "parallel markets" due to "inadequate regulations." From this perspective, the Central Bank's decision would in fact "reduce unauthorized transactions." At the same time, the article warned, it was important "not to choose the path of illogical tax hikes on currencies sold to travelers." Were that path taken, the "black market exchange rate would rise, meaning more illegal and overvalued transactions, not to mention the negative psychological effect on the country's economic and financial outlook" (*La Nación*, August 13, 1974).

A series of announcements soon followed to inform about another Central Bank measure and debunk rumors; in this case, the question was a foreign bond payable in dollars and available to local investors. *La Nación* ran a cover story, noting that the new bond "aims to put an end to speculative maneuvering on the parallel market in recent months" (*La Nación*, August 14, 1974). That same day, *La Opinión* noted that the measure "will deliver a death blow to the black market for dollars." According to this paper's analyst, the bond was the brainchild of Central Bank president Alfredo Gómez Morales, who considered the black market a "small gambling ring run by underground operators, to maximum psychological effect."

*El Economista* also cited the rumors circulating about this "special bond in dollars." In line with the critiques by other news outlets, the paper characterized the measure as "astonishing," since it allowed people to acquire dollars in a context characterized by "rigorous exchange control measures." A few days later, the same columnist noted the "psychological" repercussions of the "black" market. Despite the fact that fewer transactions were taking place on the "parallel" market, its effect on the public made it a "barometer" for people's perceptions and opinions of the economic situation (*El Economista*, September 10, 1974). Another publication specializing in the business community, *Economic Survey*, ran a new story on "the scandal bonds." It attributed the project to the minister of economy, Jose Ber Gelbard,[4] and stated that Gómez Morales, who would resign a few days later, in fact had opposed the bond. According to the weekly, the new bond was a "disgrace": "Never before have bonds been issued in such a disconcerting fashion, sparking a sort of capital flight with enormous initial profits guaranteed" (*Economic Survey*, September 10, 1974).

In summary, in September 1974, the forex market was far from "discouraging speculation," as the Peronist administration had promised a year earlier. In a context of exchange controls, every transaction on the parallel market was illegal, while the fluctuations of the "black dollar" exchange rate had taken on special public meaning. For observers and analysts, but also for the authorities, these transactions had "psychological" repercussions, causing "negative outlooks" on the economy. Yet unable to admit defeat, the government continued introducing new measures to combat exchange "speculation."

In previous decades, the tourist market had been the first to use the dollar as a benchmark when promoting airfare and package tours to global destinations. In the 1970s, especially at moments when the peso was strongly overvalued, ads for tourist services often used the greenback as the reference unit. In those days, agencies published trip and tour options in dollars. Exprinter advertised a cruise starting at US$175, while Braniff International offered a payment plan for a trip to Europe consisting of a down payment followed by twenty-four installments of US$41. Airlines followed suit; Cruzeiro offered flights to Brazil for US$54.56, while passengers could fly to South Africa on the country's flagship airlines for US$650. This type of advertisement would continue in the years to come, making the costs of tickets, tours, and cruises in US dollars the norm.

The so-called tourist dollar—or a special currency exchange rate for trips abroad—linked the tourist sector with the illegal market for foreign currency. Those privileged enough to travel abroad actively sought out currency on the parallel market. On the one hand, a portion of the currencies that changed hands on this market came from travelers who seized on the opportunity an airline ticket provided to acquire dollars at a preferential rate and then sell them for higher on the parallel market. On the other hand, during time of more extreme forex restrictions—when, for example, each passenger could buy only a limited amount of "tourist" dollars—it was assumed that a portion of the demand on the parallel market could be attributed to travelers.

By the start of September 1974, the gap between the exchange rate for "tourist" dollars and the rate on the parallel market had reached AR$600. According to the banking authorities and the media, this fostered speculation among travelers. In August 1973, US$395,000 had been sold to travelers at aboveboard exchange offices; a year later, the monthly total for August was notably higher, reaching US$18,315,000 (*Clarín*, September 19, 1974). Besides setting a "record," reported *Clarín*, the stunning rise revealed that the public was milking the enormous gap between the official and the parallel exchange rates. Until then, the Central Bank's efforts to audit traveler's demand for foreign currency were limited; there was no comparison of the amount of currency purchased and the number of days spent outside the country, for example. Due to the lack of controls of this sort, travelers would often buy more dollars than they actually needed and then sell the extra on the parallel market. These transactions, noted *Clarín*, were causing "an enormous drain on dollars, the demand for which is evidently speculative" (September 28, 1974). In the face of this glaring evidence, the Central Bank opted not to increase the limits on the amounts travelers could request; the original plan had been to raise the limit from US$300 to US$450 for trips to neighboring countries and US$900 to US$1,500 for trips to other countries.

New regulations would be introduced in June 1975, although at that point, the biggest news was the new economic plan of the third minister of economy of the Peronist administration. This minister, Celestino Rodrigo,[5] had been appointed by Perón's successor and widow, the former vice president María Estela Martínez de Perón. Shortly after being sworn in, Rodrigo had emphasized the need to do away with "speculators" who profited from "illicit earnings" and sent them to "financial markets abroad." In his description, speculators were associated with "violence and terrorism," making them not only "enemies" but also part and parcel of the current economic malaise (*Clarín*, June 5, 1975). As Argentine historian Marina Franco has noted, the government, press, and military had already recognized the need to wage "war against the subversion" that was undermining "the Argentine people and nation" (Franco 2012).[6] The new minister's economic policy was designed around a war metaphor: the forex market was another target to be retaken. The "battle against speculation" by the administration meant establishing the conditions for well-being that would prevent "terrorism." Besides leaving the problem of inflation unresolved, "price controls" had led to a "black market" that fostered "speculation." While international reserves continued to fall, explained the minister, "illegal currency transactions surged." In order to address the problem, Rodrigo outlined an "austerity plan," calling on "the people to avoid spending in excess" (*Clarín*, June 5, 1975).

A short time after Celestino Rodrigo was sworn in, *Clarín* noted that the "official exchange rates for dollars (AR$10 for the trade dollar, AR$13.06 for the mixed dollar, AR$15.10 for the financial dollar, AR$25 for the tourist dollar) fall short of satisfying the needs of those engaged in foreign trade or contributing to a trade surplus." The parallel market was depicted as the key indicator of the real value of the US currency. "Despite the underground nature of the parallel forex market, the prices it offers show that the official exchange rates are entirely fictitious." The paper added, "The enormous distance between the legal dollar and the parallel dollar is an automatic guarantee against contraband imports, but it encourages contraband exports" (*Clarín*, June 2, 1975).

Ultimately, Rodrigo announced an economic plan based on a "drastic" devaluation combined with a hike in fuel and utility taxes. Analysts characterized this as a "shock" for the economy and as the "largest" devaluation in Argentine history (Dellatorre and Restivo 2016). The newly established exchange rate meant that the trade dollar was 160 percent higher, while the financial dollar rose 100 percent. At the same time, the price of fuels rose 181 percent, electricity by 75 percent, and other utilities, by between 40 and 75 percent. As a result, the cost of bus and train fare rose as well. The government defended the devaluation, arguing it was a necessary in order for the "country to export like it used to, and import less" (*La Nación*, June 5, 1975). With regard to foreign currency for tourism—"one of the most sensitive items of the national economy," according to *La Nación*—the administration admitted it "was entirely aware that there must be some limit on funding for recreation." Rodrigo shared his thoughts on this with the press: "I call upon Argentines to consume less. All men worthy of the name should produce and set aside a little for savings. Up until now, we've been accustomed to producing as little as possible, consuming, and accruing debt. Starting now, whoever wants to travel [abroad] must have the money to do so" (*La Opinión*, June 6, 1975).

According to a chronicle in *La Opinión* the following day, the devaluation the administration had announced was indicative of the "drastic" rise in the US currency. A piece entitled "The City watches as seven million economists passionately debate"[7] notes the knowledge and interest of an increasingly diverse public in economic affairs. In every home across the country, explains the journalist, family members awoke wondering about the new exchange rates and taxes. "So, gas is at 1500 and the tourist dollar's at 4500, what do you think?" went the imagined family dialogue the morning after the economic plan was announced. Across the city, similar conversations were taking place, as depicted in the chronicle. When a passenger opened the door to a cab, the driver hissed, "No! How can I take you anywhere, when I'd have to charge you 1,200 pesos just to start the meter, and then a hundred more every few blocks! And we're not authorized." During a walk through the capital city's financial district, the journalist described the bulletin board outside the offices of *La Nación*, where some 500 people were crowding to get a peek. At a downtown tourist agency, the information on new ticket prices left no one smiling. Potential travelers who came in asking for a price departed "glum," according to agency reps consulted by the journalist. He then continued down San Martín Street, where employees at one exchange office after the next informed them that "we've got no dollars to sell." In the home of the journalist—despite the fact that he himself "never left Villa Dominico," a working-class neighborhood outside the capital city— the tourist dollar was a benchmark, obliging everyone to predict what a hike in the exchange rate would mean. This chronicle thus presented the buck as a touchstone that allowed people to make decisions in the new economic context.

Papers like *La Opinión* evoked historic tragedies to describe the offshoots of the "drastic devaluation." A special supplement titled "Requiem for the middle class" discussed the effect of the economic policy "shocks" on this particular social group. According to the supplement, June 4, 1975—the date Minister Rodrigo put his economic plan into action—"would open a dark chapter in middle class history, a holocaust." All the privileges this social class had accumulated for decades had "vanished into thin air": automobiles, the coveted trip to Europe, the home of one's own, appliances, furniture, literature, tickets to performances featuring international stars, etc. A few paragraphs later, the piece is categorical: "The tidal wave of economic measures has also drawn a very clear line between the haves and the have-nots." The "dramatic devaluation" had myriad repercussions; until just a short time ago, middle-class salary workers and professionals had been able to save and then draw on their savings to purchase a trip or a luxury item. Now all of that "had been ended with the stroke of a pen" (*La Opinión*, June 10, 1975). According to analysts from this period, the "rodrigazo," as the economic measures launched by Minister Rodrigo became known, marked a turning point. The "Requiem" supplement in *La Opinión* examines the various ways in which the "drastic devaluation" had affected the middle classes. The rodrigazo had limited the participation of these sectors in the first markets to be dollarized (like international tourism) while also reducing their ability to save and acquire foreign currencies. Yet it is important to note that in the list of consumptions and expenditures, the dollar is not mentioned.

In the middle of the 1970s, although the dollar's integration to the financial repertoires of the middle classes was far from complete, the US currency had become a touchstone for the country's economic reality. It was an accessible benchmark for the public, as noted by the sustained interest in its fluctuations among "seven million economists." The same could be said with regard to the "black" dollar: the "parallel" market had been clearly established as a "psychological barometer" of the economy. The fact that a chronicle like "Requiem for the middle class" overlooked the dollar reveals that the integration of the US currency in people's financial repertoires developed separately from its meaning as an interpretation device. This would change after the economic policy shock of June 1975; in the period that followed, the dollar's public meanings would increasingly evolve in step with its incorporation to the financial repertoires of more and more social sectors.

At the end of 1975, the musical *Los verdes están en el Maipo* (The dollars are at the Maipo) premiered at one of the oldest and most emblematic Buenos Aires theaters on Corrientes Avenue. The show was written and directed by Gerardo Sofovich, who would create some of the biggest hits on Argentine television in the decades to come. Starring some of the biggest names in theater of the time—their faces featured on dollar bills on the show poster—the musical revue promised to throw around "the beauty dollars of our breeding females for export" combined with the "highly valued 'greenbacks' of laughter." While in 1973, the humor in *Polémica en el bar* stemmed from a character who sold off his dollars to adapt to a new status quo, less than three years later, the US currency had become the leitmotif of a theater musical. The aim was to get the audience to smile knowingly, leveraging the dollar's public role as a barometer of current affairs. In the aftermath of the rodrigazo, and just weeks before the military coup d'état that would seize power in March 1976, the musical was designed for a city whose inhabitants had become "seven million economists": interested, preoccupied, and largely affected by the dollar-peso exchange rates.

## The Dictatorship: A New Mindset

A little over a year after the military coup,[8] in the context of the first liberalization of the exchange market since 1971, the daily *Clarín* ran an editorial entitled "Currency and sovereignty" that summarized what is referred to herein as the "popularization of the dollar." "It is true that rapid, persisting inflation has led a small part of the population to carry out its transactions in foreign banknotes," notes the editorial. "But the vast majority continues dealing in the country's own currency, a behavior that the public sector should safeguard and encourage." The text questioned why civil servants would use the greenback as a unit of account in official communications. These numbers, the author argued, ran afoul of the day-to-day economics of the "average citizen" who "earns, spends, and does calculations in pesos." Nothing was wrong if a "merchant" made "calculations in foreign currency, as vendors rely on it to draft price lists for customers." Yet it was unacceptable for them to be used in "public announcements by officials." Perhaps, the editorial conceded, the problem could be attributed to "confusing informal language with the language of public speaking," but undoubtedly, such talk promoted the disintegration of national symbols. In particular, this could lead to the "abandoning of our national currency as an expression of value" and a "financial policy that seeks to avoid national investments in currencies other than the peso." (*Clarín*, May 9, 1975). This *Clarín* editorial thus revealed the contradiction between the stated objectives of the recently announced financial reform and the language employed by the military regime when discussing certain economic numbers.

Two years after the great devaluation commonly known as "rodrigazo"—in which the peso lost more than half its value—the economic landscape had seen a great transformation, but politics had changed even more drastically. The coup d'état that took place on March 24, 1976, ushered in the most violent dictatorship in the country's history (Novaro and Palermo 2003; Pucciarelli 2004; Canelo 2008). The regime's political aim was to crush all organizations that had taken up arms, but also unions, political parties, and any type of activism that challenged the social order. In an authoritarian climate marked by repression and censorship, the military set out to transform the country's economic structure (Canitrot 1980). In line with the transformation spearheaded by Augusto Pinochet's regime in Chile since 1973, the regime's first minister of economy, Martínez de Hoz, took a strongly monetarist approach (Fourcade and Babb 2002). As sociologist Daniel Fridman has noted, the regime was after a "change in mindset," and its ad campaigns called on citizens to see themselves fundamentally as "consumers" and "investors" (Fridman 2010). In 1977, in pursuit of these objectives, a series of new regulations on the denationalization and decentralization of deposits were introduced, along with a new legal regimen for financial entities. Under these financial reforms, banking was subject to far less control and fewer restrictions; capital inflow and outflow were encouraged without limitations; and a system that had been working for decades, which the regime dubbed "financial repression," was dismantled. For those enacting the reforms, the state's monopoly on loans, and the nationalization of credit, had consistently yielded negative interest rates (i.e., interest rates unable to outpace inflation), thus dissuading investment. Now financial entities were free to compete for deposits and no longer bound by government-controlled interest rates. Part of the goals of reengineering the system in this manner was to discourage investors and savers from choosing foreign currencies, especially the dollar. From the perspective of the economic authorities, the financial reform was also a moral reform that would stop savers from getting "robbed" (i.e., seeing negative interest on their deposits). As a result of these measures, between 1977 and 1979, bank deposits skyrocketed 500 percent, and the number of banks rose from 119 to 219. The new institutions transformed the landscape of "la City" and expanded its reach across society. New banks were constructed, and aggressive ad campaigns were launched in those years.

Media coverage and ads from this period—in which the "small saver" was an oft-cited figure—are indicative of the "multiple options" available to anyone looking to invest. Founded at the end of 1976, the daily *Ámbito Financiero* played a key role in creating a standard layout for reporting on different interest rates (Ruiz 2005). The aim was to guide "investors and steer them clear of 'speculation,'" a term increasingly reserved for the sale and purchase of dollars. Other newspapers referred to the "beleaguered character" of the small saver, forced to defend his "feeble pesos" from inflation. The variety of proposals from the "finance sector" could be overwhelming to such a "novice." At the same time, countless press articles set out to explain these proposals and thus let the "small saver" decide. Ads abounded: "The best interest rate for demanding investors," promised COSMOS S.A. "We know how to preserve your money's value—put it in a C.D.," urged Banco Provincia. "There are serious institutions that have accumulated prestige over the years. Trust us with your deposits," exhorted Banco Crédito Argentino.

Below a photograph of a group of people studying a bank board listing interest rates, one newspaper explained: "The offices where financial companies operate are just part of the landscape for Buenos Aires residents walking around 'la City.' The public's interest is reflected in kind on the glass windows." The same article includes another photograph, this one a close-up of a teller waiting on a client. The caption reads, "In recent times, driven by the need to defend their savings from a further drop in value, a growing number of investors is resorting to financial firms." The third photograph shows the facade of an office whose sign reads "Exchange, Tourism, Bonds" and the board out front. The caption reads, "Potential investors stand before the boards of banks, financial firms, and exchange offices, searching for information that will help them decide where to put their money" (*Clarín*, April 29, 1977).

Trading desks handled a good portion of the rising volume of financial transactions. Journalistic accounts from the period sought to provide an insider's look at how they worked and convey their role on the market. *Clarín* published a double-page spread that included a picture showing two men in ties, their shirt-sleeves rolled up, and talking on the phone on a switchboard; it was entitled "The rising pulse of trading desks" (April 29, 1977). The article provides a clear explanation of the desk's workings and its role during the "boom of financial transactions." Trading desks, explained the article, functioned like a "kidney," "compensating" for the gap between the deposit and allocation of funds. According to the article, a single trading desk could have up to eleven phone lines and be in touch with 1,000 companies. At the touch of a button, it was possible to discover who needed money and who had money to spare. The funds, explains the journalist, came from companies, financiers, banks, and even the state.

In the revamped landscape of "la City" at the beginning of May 1977, all restrictions on the purchase and sale of foreign currency were struck from the books. For the first time in six years, Argentines could buy as many dollars as they wanted. The measure aimed to reduce the obsession with the "parallel" market. The concern with these under-the-table transactions was similar to that expressed in prior decades: "Economically, it [the parallel market] has no impact, but its psychological effects are daunting" (*El Cronista Comercial*, May 9, 1977). The level of the country's reserves at the time—around US$2.5 billion—made this measure possible.

Although an editorial (*Clarín*, May 9, 1975) in *Clarín* underlined that the "average citizen" had no relationship to the dollar, the accounts of the first days of the free exchange rate showed that in 1977, the dollar was much more popular than the papers let on. In its May 13 edition, *El Cronista Comercial* ran a story on the first day of unlimited access to the foreign exchange market entitled "The liberalization of the dollar." The "long lines" that formed even before the exchange offices or banks opened were, at the very least, "curious," noted the journalist. "The virtual looting of all they had" also struck his attention. There was only one explanation: the "taboo" surrounding the purchase of dollars, a transaction that "has been banned" for nearly "40 years." Although Argentines associated dollars with the criminal world ("speculation," "big business and bankruptcies in equal measure"), they also represented a "haven" ("during times of high inflation and interest rates not high enough to offset inflation"). For the editorial writer, these precedents revealed that the purchase of dollars was "an ingrained habit of an almost cultural sort." Therefore, the "people's reaction" during the first days of the free market should "cause no surprise." "Ordinary people" purchased some two million dollars in those frenetic days.

The magazine *Mercado* also reported on the demand at exchange offices, noting the sales on May 9, the first day of the liberalization of the exchange market. Casa Velox had sold US$200,000 in two hours; Casa Piano, US$130,000 in three hours; and Agencia Baires, US$230,000 in five hours. *Clarín* reported an "awe-struck" and "eager" public engaged in the "adventure" of buying dollars, "with broad freedom." The journalist argued that "many probably decided to buy dollars based on the usual speculative calculations." Now that the exchange market was subject to no restrictions, the "parallel" market had been reduced "to a trickle," thus liberating "the public of a weighty psychological factor." The journalist concluded that the "dollar segment still appeals to investors despite the sophisticated options available now that generally positive interest rates have been established" (*Clarín*, May 9, 1977).

The high demand for dollars on the first day of the free exchange market was the topic of another *Clarín* article entitled "Tension surrounding inflation affects exchange market liberalization" (*Clarín*, May 9, 1977). According to this article, the Central Bank aimed to put an end to the "black market" that "worked against its forecasts," though the financial institution had been unable to foresee the immense demand for greenbacks that would accompany the liberalization. This confirmed "that our inflation rate continues to be excessive in comparison to the rest of the world's." The paper here returned to the argument presented earlier in its editorial days: in a country "where officials often cited prices in dollars," the rush to buy US legal tender once all restrictions were lifted came as no surprise. Yet this was also because the "most attractive and assuring options for investments in pesos" did not suffice for those with "modest savings," looking for a "certain protection against inflation."

Days after the opening of the forex market, it became possible to make bank deposits in foreign currency. According to the daily *La Nación*, which reported on the change on May 17, the government's latest decision clearly demonstrated its will to open up the economy. In the past, as the article inside the paper noted, "foreign currency accounts" had been allowed, at least until 1964, when "balances were translated into pesos at the official exchange rate" by decree. This had put an end to all such accounts. However, the article points out that other "legitimate" options for investing in foreign currency had appeared, such as foreign bonds, issued during the 1960s, or in 1975, when "forex offices were allowed to sell foreign bonds." The aim of the measure, the article concluded, was "to avoid the exodus of foreign currencies that has characterized many prolonged periods in recent decades."

Chapter Three

# From "I'll Take Two" to "Betting on the Dollar Is a Loser's Wager"

Controlling inflation was top of mind for the military administration's economic team. However, the anti-inflation policies introduced by the military regime boasted little success in the first years of the administration. By keeping real salaries low, freezing prices, and reducing import tariffs (Schvarzer 1986), the regime had lowered inflation from 444 percent in 1976 to 176 percent in 1977 and 175 percent in 1978. However, the Economic Ministry led by Martínez de Hoz was still unable to keep a lid on prices. In December 1978, the regime decided to control the currency rate through an instrument based on a predefined schedule for the gradual depreciation of the Argentine peso. The famous *tablita* (little chart) constituted a major innovation in the process of popularizing the US currency. The dollar now had a new meaning and a new use: it had become a bellwether for inflation estimates. According to the government's new scheme—a "forex focus within the balance of payments"—the tablita would govern financial reform (Heredia 2014). Economic officials promised that the new measures would bring domestic prices and interest rates in step with international trends. In her book on the rise of economists in Argentine political life, the Argentine sociologist Mariana Heredia (2014) describes the tablita as an experiment to control widespread price hikes, while giving a new generation of economists authority in public debates. This is a critical moment in the popularization of the dollar, one in which the expert opinions of economists, the struggle against inflation, and the meanings of the dollar would come together in a way the author considers "as convoluted as it was enduring."

Two women sip tea at a café in Barrio Norte while debating which world city is most expensive. These "ladies of around fifty" concur that "Cape Town is much more expensive than Buenos Aires." This is the opening scene in the *Clarín* article "Travel abroad is booming," from December 14, 1978. Despite 160 percent annual inflation and depressed wages, an "astounding phenomenon" was underway: "It is hard to find a seat on a flight to any international destination." The article explored the socioeconomic profile of those making these trips. One source, a tourist agent, tells the journalist that travelers abroad are members of "the upper-middle class," those able to pay tours costing between US$1,500 and US$2,000. Yet there were also "infiltrators" on these tours, people who were not "the national jet-set per se," but "middle class folks": "Considering that two people can get a meal at a Miami restaurant for US$10–12 and that a solo traveler can get a room in a respectable hotel for the same amount, it is logical for there to be many 'infiltrators' in this group."

In 1979, a lag in the real exchange rate caused by the tablita further exacerbated the tourism boom. In January 1979, a piece in *El Cronista Comercial* noted "long lines outside the U.S. Embassy of people seeking a visa." Most international flights were booked, the article clarifies, and ads for businesses in Miami, Paris, or Rio de Janeiro frequently ran in Argentine newspapers, a curious fact in a "country that is not exactly awash in prosperity." The columnist is also surprised that the upscale Uruguayan beach destination Punta del Este has become "the second Mar del Plata." At the same time, the comparison with the foreign tourism boom in 1974 and 1975 revealed what was different about the two contexts on the forex market. In the final years of Perón's third administration, the journalist explained, trips abroad by "great numbers of Argentines" could be explained by the "difference between the official and the black market exchange rate." The sale on the "parallel" market of dollars legally purchased to pay for trips abroad was "an open secret." In contrast, the exodus of travelers of 1979 could be attributed to the opening of the economy and the "end to the taboo" created by exchange rate controls: "Argentines seem to have finally discovered the freedom of spending the money set aside to vacation to destinations of their choosing and are taking full advantage of the new option available." This "discovery" was that they could access as many cheap dollars as they wanted both to travel and to acquire goods abroad.

The economic opening, the liberalization of the forex market, and a cheap dollar were critical to getting travelers abroad to fully engage in the consumer experience, which is collectively remembered as a trend known as "I'll take two." In the film *Plata Dulce*, one of the biggest box-office hits of 1982, this experience is captured in a memorable scene. One of the characters, Carlos Bonifatti, flies into Ezeiza airport with his family. They fill two luggage carts with what they have purchased abroad: home appliances, televisions, tennis rackets, and sports attire by well-known brands. Bonifatti's brother-in-law is there to pick them up. He knows something about imported goods himself because he runs a window *kiosko* where he sells products acquired on shopping tours to the Brazilian city of Uruguayana, located across the Uruguay River from the town Paso de los Libres in the province of Corrientes.

The "I'll take two" and the tourism boom would both end with the 1981 devaluation. Financial reform, the liberalization of the foreign exchange market, and the tablita had been implemented to "eliminate the use of foreign currencies as a savings method" and encourage people "to forget the continual references to foreign currency by virtually everyone" as noted by an analyst in the magazine *Mercado* (March 26, 1981). Things would change drastically that year.

As Italian economists Massimo Amato and Luca Fantacci have shown, the new global financial architecture based on high international liquidity encouraged both the state and the private sector to go into debt (Amato and Fantacci 2012). For the state, debt guaranteed it had the reserves it needed to sustain an overvalued exchange rate and finance its loans. For companies, going into debt was the first move in a game of extreme financial speculation. Companies would take out loans abroad at low interest rights, invest the money locally at higher interest rates, and launder the difference by purchasing dollars (Basualdo 2017). When the interest rate on foreign loans skyrocketed, capital from abroad no longer flowed into the country. However, most importantly, the interest rates on the debts of both the private and public sector rose. The government found itself with a rising foreign debt and a drop in the reserves it had used to keep the exchange rate unnaturally high.

Between 1976 and 1982, Argentina's foreign debt increased fivefold, going from US$8.3 billion to US$43.6 billion. The country's reserves during this same period fell from US$7.7 billion in 1980 to US$3.2 billion two years later. Capital flight nearly tripled between 1979 and 1982, going from US$11.2 billion to US$30.2 billion. While Argentina had boasted a trade surplus between 1976 and 1979, it now suffered from a trade deficit, which reached US$2.5 million in 1980 but spiraled to US$287 million in 1981. In addition to the problems plaguing foreign trade, a banking crisis unfolded in 1980. Since 1977, financial expansion had been achieved by granting loans with real positive rates and little control by the Central Bank, which provided a guarantee on deposits but left banks responsible for deciding whom to lend to without any type of supervision.

The system left ample room for unfair lending, including bankers approving their own loans. Inevitably, it led to high-risk transactions. When the number of such transactions came to light, instead of introducing new mechanisms of control, the Central Bank simply withdrew the official guarantee on deposits. Yet even this did not suffice. The crisis came to a head in March 1980 when the Banco de Intercambio Regional (BIR) went belly-up. The bankruptcy had enormous repercussions. The popular Channel 13 news program *Realidad 80* did special coverage on the day that BIR depositors began receiving the payback of their checking account balances. On a Buenos Aires corner where a BIR branch had operated, the program host interviewed two elderly women: "Ladies, are you here to make a withdrawal?" They responded: "We had certificates of deposit. Mine expired on the eleventh but the newspaper says the bank will announce when we can pick up the money. Probably on the fourteenth. Today is reserved for people with checking accounts." The women—probably both retirees—were two of some 350,000 customers of the bank, which held 21 percent of all deposits in the country's banking system. After the BIR went bankrupt, distrust of the banking system grew, toppling an additional forty banks. Although the Central Bank reinstated its guarantee of deposits and raised interest rates, the deposit drain continued.

The banking crisis was a clear sign that the economic policy introduced by Martínez de Hoz was up against the ropes. In order to ameliorate the situation, a few days into February 1981, the government announced new changes to the tablita. Observers noted that the new measure represented the "first mega-devaluation" since March 1976 and that the new tablita, which included a 10 percent currency devaluation, interrupted the "continuity established on December 20, 1978" (*La*

*Nación*, February 3, 1981). The daily *Clarín* attributed the joint decision to address the "repressed inflation" to an agreement between the Martín de Hoz team and that of Lorenzo Sigaut, who would replace the minister of economy under a new military-appointed president, General Roberto Viola. The cover of *La Nación* highlighted "public interest in the currency exchange measure," explaining that although "there has not been a run . . . there were many customers at currency exchange offices." Sources from "la City" cited in the article attributed the crowds to the "expectations sparked by the forex measures" (*La Nación*, February 4, 1981).

The more changes were introduced, the more opinions by economists the papers published. At the same time, as at other times of crisis, information on the foreign exchange market went beyond the opinion of economists. All the major national papers set aside pages to present information on the economy in a more reader-friendly way, using plain language that clearly targeted readers outside the world of finance. This coverage was not daily, but it was regular, generally delivered weekly. These articles harken back to the first accounts of the forex market of the 1960s in several ways: they use a "folksy" tone, prioritize the archetypal spaces and people involved on the market, and depict "la City" as the privileged setting of financial life. At the same time, beyond these common features, each media outlet had now clearly defined its journalistic style.

In *La Nación*, the best example of such pieces are the "Dialogues in la City" by D. Home—a pseudonym of David Casas—published every Sunday that continued into the 1990s. The principal aspect of the "Dialogues" was that they offered an insider's perspective: in a colloquial tone with plenty of humor, Casas shares fictionalized conversations in which a series of regulars who frequent "la City" discuss the state of the economy, government measures, and investment decisions. Though written in layman's terms, the "Dialogues" are clearly for knowledgeable readers: the familiar formulas, clever nicknames, and winks toward the reader are combined with economic jargon like interest rates, monetary base, and call money. The imaginary exchanges between these typical characters allow the author to present diverging opinions on certain measures but also provide a roundabout lesson in economics.

In response to the decision to modify the schedule laid out in the tablita, the characters in-the-know in "Dialogues in la City" are both surprised and incensed.

"*Che*, Lucho, you could have warned us."

"But Gordo, I mentioned the possibility of a 10% devaluation to all of you last Friday. If you didn't take me seriously, that's not my problem."

"And did you exchange your pesos for dollars on Monday?" asked el Gordo.

"Of course I did! . . . No, Gordo, I'm just messing with you."

## Chapter Three

In a colloquial tone, the conversation reiterated some of the arguments common to economists and businesspeople. The tablita had led to an overvaluation of the peso and was responsible for the loss of AR$400 million at the beginning of January. But the cure was worse than the disease. After the devaluation, US$100 million "evaporated" in just a day. The overview of what would happen to the price of different assets (real estate, land) serves as an excuse in this next dialogue to pose the question about what to do with one's investments.

> "But cutting to the chase," El Gordo insisted. "Do I pull out of the carry trading and take my dollars out of the CDs or do I keep them in?"
> "That all depends on whether you believe in the *tablita*."
> "I want to know what you all think. And what the market will actually believe."
> "But Gordo . . . You want to have your cake and eat it too!"

Despite the fact that Martínez de Hoz defended the continuity of his economic policy and argued that the "exchange rate adjustment" only aimed to dissipate doubts about the new military-appointed president taking office on April 2, it was not enough to quench the "thirst for the dollar." On February 11, US$100 million were sold and the most established exchange offices ran out of money. "The long lines that form every morning at the exchange offices are a reflection of a growing uncertainty that blights the country" (*Clarín*, February 12, 1981). The photograph included in the article showed some older women and a few men waiting at the counter of an exchange office. In the following days, besides covering "the struggle to buy foreign currency" (*Clarín*, February 13, 1981), media outlets noted rumors that the government planned to impose a new holiday on foreign exchange.

A growing concern, especially for the regime, was to stop the flight of dollars. In this context, the demand for dollars began to exceed the capacity of "la City." National media outlets ran stories on Mendoza, Córdoba, and La Plata that contributed to a narrative on the "intense demand for dollars." Just a month before leaving the ministry, Martínez de Hoz publicly explained that the "drop in foreign currency reserves" was a natural part of the transition; he also complained that the "calculations of the private sector on an artificially low exchange rate [were] simplistic and erred" (*Clarín*, February 18, 1981). However, as *La Nación* reported, the modification of the tablita had a "boomerang" effect. In just a few weeks, the run had drained US$2 billion from the economy. In an editorial on March 1, the daily demanded that the "market" establish the "real" worth of the peso in order to temper "expectations of a devaluation." With a similar argument a few days later, the paper noted that the "run" on the peso had occurred because the public was convinced that the "fictional" dollar-peso exchange rate could not last long. Finally, the paper clamored for a drop in public spending as a principal measure to address inflation.

In the middle of March, the covers of the major papers were reporting on the dollar's rise on the exchange market and the ebbing foreign reserves. *Ámbito Financiero* published a running commentary of these feverish days. Inside the crowded exchange offices, pushing and "pardon me" had become the norm. Following a rumor, people hurried from one office to another. An elderly woman with a "little bundle" of dollars "wandered here and there, incredulous at the low offers." Testimonies were included in the article, including that of a man, his brow furrowed, who "didn't understand why people are so worked up when the schedule is still in place." One office employee added, "They think it's the end of the world or the country is finished. Everyone comes in to buy—we even see government officials." Like other play-by-play accounts (and their accompanying images), the text noted not only the presence of both older men and woman in "la City" but that of some young women as well. In a twist on the stories and images from previous decades, women had now become regulars in "la City."

By the end of the month, as reserves plummeted, the government made a financial affidavit mandatory for anyone looking to purchase foreign currency. The new norm led to the sudden emergence of a "fringe market." In "la City," many speculated that the measure would precede "real, comprehensive foreign exchange control." In *La Nación*, the "regulars" in the "Dialogues in la City" column scoffed at the financial affidavit requirement:

"The affidavit is a form of exchange control."

"But because of it, fewer dollars were sold today."

"Sure, maybe today . . . But wait until Monday. Customers will be back with a vengeance."

"Some guy wrote on the form that he intended to use the dollars to wallpaper a room. Isn't that illegal?"

The financial affidavit requirement did not staunch the demand for dollars. On March 24, *Clarín* noted that the requirement had caused some "jitters" and that the largest exchange offices had handed out piles of them due to the great number of people. At the same time, the paper observed that a parallel market was already flourishing. The photograph included in the article showed busy employees are on one side of the counter, with their calculators and typewriters. Two older women stand across from them.

The Argentine writer Jorge Asís worked as a journalist at *Clarín* during those years. Using the pseudonym Oberdán Rocamora, he published the article "Opportunity Street" on March 24, 1981. The piece describes the typical characters on the streets of "la City" during those nerve-wracking days brought on by mandatory financial affidavits and the resurgence of the parallel market. From the corner of Sarmiento and San Martín streets, the journalist observed the "downtrodden looking for salvation," who carried with them "a little bag with maybe one grand" to brave the "collapse." In "la City," "the spectacle of desperation" was being staged, and desperate characters crowd together in the author's description. There is "shorty" who doesn't have "enough to pay his way to Chacarita [cemetery]" but pulled "ten million pesos from a C.D. with the idea of turning them into four thousand greenbacks," but who, "like all *porteños*," was terrified "of the financial affidavit." The journalist could hear the "moaning" that was an "exemplification of our lifestyle." While a "[man] tanned from bike riding" complained "nothing doing with the dollar," calling it "a lucrative opportunity for four guys in-the-know," a woman

> from an outlying neighborhood, the kind you'd see at the market or cooking up a fine stew, says, "If they're offering high rates, you can bet a devaluation is coming: the real price of the dollar should be 3,500 pesos" as if she grasped the subtleties of an economy that leaves even the experts scratching their heads. (*Clarín*, March 24, 1981)

Another character was the "fortune-seeker with the air of a rich boy." And in this "exhilarating" city, where "no one knows what will happen tomorrow," all that was left was to "dance the collapse conga and shoot streamers up toward the heavens to see if God remembers us."

Asís's narrative brought back exchange market figures who had been absent in prior decades. The characters of this piece are "desperate," a far cry from the "curious onlookers" or "two-bit speculators" that appeared at the end of the 1950s and beginning of the 1960s. Besides serving the narrative figure, these characters also represent a locus of enunciation on the forex market (Telechea 2006). The people who held certificates of deposits in dollars at the BIR, the bank that declared bankruptcy in 1980, are perhaps the best example of this. When the BIR went belly-up, the Central Bank had committed to returning deposits of up to one million pesos to all customers. However, around 40,000 customers with foreign currency deposits of less than US$10,000 were excluded from the measure.

A paid ad run in April 1981 and addressing the military regime noted that it had not kept its promises to "savers in dollars"—promises made just a year earlier. The ad was signed by a group of "people of ordinary means: retirees, housewives, etc." Their decision to save in dollars, the ad explains, responded to the need to "defend our meager savings, the fruits of our hard work," from inflation. The ad posed the question as to whether they too were "victims of the system" and whether it was fair that a different policy should apply to them only because their savings bore "a different currency symbol." "Is it possible to believe that savers with deposits of US$1,000-$5,000 contributed or are responsible for the system's collapse?" The situation affects the "peace and serenity of homes" and "endangers our health," they warned, as already seen in certain "tragic outcomes." The ad was signed by the B.I.R. Savers Committee.

The paid ad ran not long after Lorenzo Sigaut was sworn in as economic minister and made the oft-remembered quip, "Betting on the dollar is a loser's wager" (Clarín, June 20, 1981). As if to make good on his words, the minister's first measures included doing away with the tablita, overhauling the forex market, and ordering a 30 percent devaluation. This new context made the "B.I.R. savers" an oddity; paradoxically, their situation confirmed Sigaut's affirmation. They were the only ones who really lost despite having "bet" on the dollar.

## The Dollar Becomes the Currency of Choice on Other Markets

In 1981, the popularization of the dollar could be seen in settings and events far beyond the economy and politics. The echo of six-figure contracts in the world of soccer and show biz further increased the public's interest in the US dollar, an interest that went far beyond the boundaries of the forex market. The transfer to Club Atlético Boca Juniors of soccer player Diego Armando Maradona—who would later go on to become the idol of the multitudes—was not the first in US dollars to make headlines. In January 1979, River Plate had acquired the Uruguayan player Juan Ramón Carrasco for a half million dollars. And a few days earlier, the same club had announced that its team captain, Daniel Alberto Passarella, had been sold for US$1.5 million. Nor was this the first local team transfer paid in greenbacks. The Boca Juniors payment in American currency to Argentinos Juniors for Maradona was part of a process already underway on Argentina's soccer market.

As on other markets, the sale and purchase of soccer players had begun using the US dollar as the unit account—to establish the value of the transfer—and sometimes as the payment method as well. When the future world champion Leopoldo Jacinto Luque came to River in September 1975, the transfer fee paid to Club Unión de Santa Fe was AR$7.5 million. Thus, while Luque played for River, all the contracts signed were stated in the national currency. However, when the scorer returned to Unión de Santa Fe in February 1981, it cost US$122,000. That same year, Oscar Ortiz was transferred to Club Atlético Huracán for US$200,000, using the midway point between the commercial and financial exchange rates as of November 5, 1981. However, US currency was not used for all player transfers. In September 1981, Américo Gallego went to River Plate for AR$3.3 million.

Maradona's transfer from Argentinos Juniors to Boca Juniors reverberated far beyond soccer stadiums. On February 12, 1981, *Clarín* ran the following headline: "Boca pays nine million dollars for Maradona." The sports magazine *El Gráfico* put a picture of Maradona holding the Boca jersey in his hand on the cover with the title "The transfer of the century: Maradona costs Boca over US$10 million." The news also hit celebrity publications. When the magazine *Gente*, which advertised heavily in national papers, put Maradona's girlfriend Claudia Villafañe on its cover, the headline read: "The 10-million-dollar girlfriend." Until that date, no local club had put out quite so much for a player. However, the announcement coincided with a drop in value of the peso, and thus the public's obsession with the dollar can explain why the news about a player who had risen from the lower divisions of Argentinos Juniors had resonated outside of sports.

For comic strip artists of the period, Maradona's sale was excellent fodder for humor. One by Viuti, the pseudonym of comic strip artist Roberto López, shows a crowd that appears to be gathered to cheer on Maradona but is in fact waiting outside his house to buy dollars from him (*Clarín*, February 12, 1981). In a vignette published in *Clarín*, a man atop a stretcher is loaded onto an ambulance. He has fainted after learning just how many pesos Maradona's transfer was worth (*Clarín*, February 12, 1981). In *Clemente*, a comic strip by Caloi that would become a classic on the back cover of *Clarín*, the character compared the "confetti by the millions" that accompanied Maradona's first match at Boca with the "green bills by the millions" that the player had received. During the months to follow, as new devaluations chipped away at the peso's value and Maradona scored more and more goals for Boca, comic strip artists continued to make use of the soccer star as part of broader commentary on the US currency. There was, for example, a new kind of dollar, the "Maradollar," that calculated the worth in dollars of each goal scored by the man with the 10 on his jersey.

In August 1981, crooner Frank Sinatra arrived for his one and only visit to the country (Mancusi and Grandi 2018). Sinatra was a beloved celebrity of Argentines, and his stay in Buenos Aires attracted ample press coverage. In February of that year, the cover of *Clarín* announced the signing of a contract to bring Sinatra to Argentina for two concerts at Luna Park stadium and four dinner shows at the exclusive Sheraton hotel. In the picture, "The Voice" is seen posing with Argentine producers Ricardo Finkel and Ramón "Palito" Ortega. The dinner show cost US$1,000, or, as stated on the ticket, "Amount in pesos equivalent to US$1,000 using the Banco Nación selling rate of the day prior to purchase." Audience wise, the dinner shows were a flop. The coverage of Sinatra's days in Argentina noted the controversy over the amount of dollars spent to bring him to Argentina and the millions lost by the producers, especially popular singer "Palito" Ortega. *Gente* magazine, for example, dedicated a sixteen-page spread to the crooner's visit (*Gente*, August 13, 1981).

Included in the coverage was an opinion piece by the former economic minister Álvaro Alsogaray entitled, "If Palito had asked me . . ." In the piece, the man who would go on to start the Unión de Centro Democrático (UCD) party noted that Sinatra's visit was perfectly understandable. After all, "cheap foreign currency" had allowed more than one million Argentines to travel abroad, purchase color TVs, and "splurge" on many other things, thanks to the government generously keeping the exchange rate so low. Yet it could not last; at some point, the dollar would get expensive again. Alsogaray was "sorry that Ortega hadn't asked him whether the contract in dollars was a savvy investment" before adding that Ortega was not the only one to face losses: "Many businessmen have suffered similarly by blindly trusting in the government's promises."

Right around the time of Sinatra's visit, on August 13, 1981, the acclaimed visual artist Marta Minujín organized the *Fiesta del dólar* (Dollar party) at the nightclub Regine's. On the invitation, guests were asked to use "their imagination to create an outfit that goes with the theme or otherwise [accessorize] with something green." Guests were also encouraged to bring one dollar in order to participate in the raffle at the end of the night. Ms. Minujín welcomed the guests—actors, artists, theater stars, models—in a dress consisting simply of two giant twenty-dollar "bills." Journalists and celebrities who didn't make the list were left vying for a spot outside of the fete organized to honor the US currency. Only those wearing dollar-inspired costumes were allowed into Regine's, including women draped in green tunics, overalls, miniskirts, pants, and shorts. Green bills—or sometimes coins—adorned waists, hairdos, shoulders, and necks.

At an "exchange office" on the upper level of the club, partygoers could exchange their dollar for a ticket for the four-hundred-dollar raffle. The Bach choir sang "Hallelujah to the dollar," and four designers created a "little dress" inspired by the greenback. In the view of the partygoers, Mary Tapia's "black dollar" was the most ingenious costume. The painter Santiago appeared inside a mug made out of cloth—a word play on *taza/tasa* (mug/rate)—to evoke the relationship between interest rates and the dollar. A montage of scenes featuring the dollar from different well-known films was screened. Two "Baby Dollars" dressed in green bodysuits and stockings, models Paula Domínguez and Pata Villanueva, kissed the raffle winner. The newspapers and magazines that covered the event noted that Marta Minujín was the first artist to pay homage to the dollar in a year in which the US currency was the "starlet," as *Tal Cual* magazine referred to it.

The artist herself told the press that she had organized the party to celebrate "the person of the year." Partygoers had "sung the dollar's praises" and "gone off about the devaluation and its consequences" (*Tal Cual*, August 14, 1981). "No one refrained from laughing at the expense—literally—of the devaluation" (*Vosotras*, August 14, 1981). Minujín's gathering of artists and celebrities staged a "true ritual," as if the dollar "were a ghost to be exorcised" (*La Nación*, August 14, 1981). In the magazine that accompanied *Convicción*, the newspaper owned by one of the members of the 1976 military junta, critic Hugo Beccacece noted that Marta Minujín had admittedly organized "the most entertaining gathering of the year, but also the most caustic and corrosive." Beccacece concluded that it represented "the first hyperrealist party in Argentina," that allowed people to mock and be cynical about a certain level of Argentine decadence (*Convicción*, August 15, 1981).

At the beginning of the 1980s, the social groups that relied on the dollar were expanding, as seen in the use of this currency in contracts and other transactions. In this regard, one particular milestone was the gradual dollarization of the local real estate market. The first real estate ads that state prices in dollars appeared in July 1977 in *La Nación*. Originally located in the capital's most expensive enclaves, the dollar was gradually used in price listings for homes in other Buenos Aires neighborhoods, though it was initially more prevalent in upper-class and upper-middle-class areas (Gaggero and Nemiña 2022). Chart 1 clearly conveys the spatial and class logic of dollarizing the real estate market.

During the 1960s, in an economy with negative interest rates and a strongly regulated, scarcely developed financial market, real estate investment had become a savvy way for the well-to-do to protect their savings and watch them grow. The military regime that seized power in 1976, sociologists Alejandro Gaggero and Pablo Nemiña explain, enacted laws to undo rent controls and cut taxes on the construction of rental apartments in an attempt to drive real estate investment. In 1977, classified ads listed property prices in dollars for the first time. In 1981, a real estate analyst explained why the US dollar was being used for transactions in this sector. Inflation had been "raging" since 1974, leading homeowners to sign sales contracts with real estate agents for only two or three days. "In this context," the analyst explains, "Making a sale proved impossible." As a result, real estate firms decided to "propose listings in dollars in order for owners to agree to a 30-day sales contract and give the realtor some leeway" (*Ámbito Financiero*, February 27, 1981).

In 1981, the expanded use of the US currency was put on hold when the military regime did away with the tablita and ordered a devaluation of the peso. This meant sudden obstacles for transactions in dollars and led some to question its use on the real estate market. Yet before the collapse of Minister Martínez de Hoz's economic plan impacted real estate market transactions, a new regulation required that all prices be listed in the national currency, causing an immediate drop in the appraisals of properties in US legal tender. The argument was that market transparency depended on avoiding the proliferation of prices in dollars, which made property comparisons exceedingly difficult.

In 1981, the same agents who had pushed for the use of the dollar in order to facilitate transactions on the real estate market now considered the solution

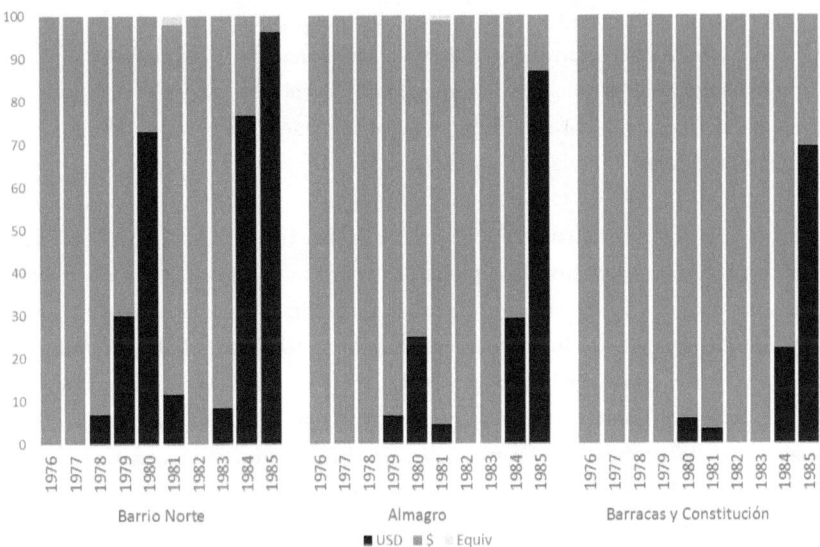

Chart 1. Properties for sale in Barrio Norte, Almagro, and Barracas-Constitución (Buenos Aires). Distribution based on currency of price listing. 1976–1985. Source: Gaggero and Nemiña (2022).

problematic. The media echoed their concerns regarding dollarization. In *Ámbito Financiero*, Abraham Astekolschik, head of a local company, noted that two years earlier "everyone started selling dollars" in order to preserve the value of their money. However, in the new context, "money has been lost to these transactions" since "the dollar has risen due to the *tablita* but not nearly as much" as prices. The businessman added that "even people with no knowledge of what a transaction of this sorts involves" purchased and sold properties in dollars. "Appraisals in dollars are pure habit, not a form of speculation," he noted (*Ámbito Financiero*, March 15, 1981).

A journalist from *Ámbito Financiero* spoke to several people from the real estate sector to get their opinions on the matter. "Just as we were blindsided by this devaluation (February 1981), the same could occur in a not-so-distant future. Therefore, properties cannot maintain their prices at current levels . . . as regards the dollar," explained architect Eduardo Lavaque. Another source from the sector had the following proposal: "Forget about appraisals in dollars from now on and set prices in pesos with a fixed schedule for adjustments." Finally, in the view of real estate executive Armando Pepe, "Buyers today don't dare wager on the dollar because they no longer trust the economic plan. So no buyer is going to make a down payment and agree to pay the rest—in dollars—when closing. Right now, 90% [of home sales] are in pesos." In addition, Pepe recommended that people from the "upper-middle class who have savings and want to protect them" should go for "bricks":

> Property never loses its value. Brick is the country's only currency—
> let's treat it like a currency—that never let anyone down. It has a
> constant value, a constant currency, and is a real asset that you can
> touch, have, and feel and it's mine because come what may, I hold the
> deed. (*Ámbito Financiero*, March 15, 1981)

After the 30 percent devaluation announced at the beginning of April, the Real Estate Chamber recommended, first, that properties priced in pesos not be subject to more than a 10 percent hike and, second, that the prices of real estate appraised in dollars be reduced by 15 percent. In this context, then, the use of pesos in transactions was necessary for real estate agents. The preference for pesos would not last long, however.

Yet the real estate market was not the only one whose transactions were increasingly dollarized: cars and works of art also began to be appraised, bought, and sold in dollars. In 1960, the newspaper *Clarín* published a survey it had conducted with a group of gallerists to gauge, among other things, the prices of some of the most sought-after works of art (Andrada 2018). The reconstruction of the aesthetic and monetary hierarchy not only provides insight into how gallerists evaluate an artist's prestige but also reveal that at that moment in time, works were still priced in pesos. Paintings done in oil or mixed technique by artists from the 1920s generation and earlier artists such as Emilio Pettorutti, Pedro Figari, Cesáreo Bernaldo de Quirós, Fernando Fader, and Lino Enea Spillimbergo went for somewhere between AR$100,000 and AR$500,000, depending on their dimensions. The cost of works by renowned middle-aged artists such as Leopoldo Presas, Sarah Grilo, José Antonio Fernández-Muro, Luis Seoane, Raúl Russo, and Vicente Forte was between AR$80,000 and AR$150,000, again depending on the size. Finally, the value of similar works by artists of around the age of thirty who had already been featured in several shows was placed at between AR$20,000 and AR$50,000.

Along a similar vein, an article published in the weekly news magazine *Panorama* in January 1964 quoted the well-known gallerist Guillermo Whitelow, the manager at Bonino, as saying that a Figari painting had sold the previous year for the record-breaking sum of AR$500,000. As these stories reveal, during the first stage of the dollar's popularization, it was neither a benchmark for prices nor the currency of choice among local artists making a sale.

The panorama had changed drastically at the end of the following decade. An opinion piece included in the first issue of the art magazine *Plaza de Arte*, published in 1979, announced a new era for the sale of art in Argentina. Like *Ámbito Financiero*, which provided its readers with organized information on financial market numbers, the magazine promoted the purchase of art as a safe "investment," hinting at this type of transaction's niche within the financial universe. For that reason, the magazine published the prices of works based on information from "galleries, auctions, artists, and dealers." Going through pages from the 1979 issues, the prices for the works of Argentine artists are listed in dollars. For example, according to the prices on pages 10 and 11, a self-portrait in acrylic by Carlos Alonso is listed for US$2,500; an Antonio Berni pastel on paper portrait from 1955 has fetched US$5,000; and a Fernando Fader oil painting dating back to the beginning of the century is worth US$15,000. The use of the greenback in art market transactions continued in the following years. In August 1981, for example, *Ámbito Financiero* provided information on an Emilio Pettoruti and Joaquín Torres García show at the Rubbers gallery. After a brief review of the show, it informs readers that the value of the works included in the exhibit "ranges between US$18,000 and 400,000."

Car imports grew briefly during the first two quarters of 1980. Despite limits imposed as part of a special imports regimen for vehicles, inflation—combined with an undervalued dollar tied to the tablita—sparked a veritable boom in imports. For high-income consumers able to afford brands like Buick, Volvo, Subaru, Mercedes-Benz, and Citroën, prices were published in dollars (or, on occasion, in both dollars and pesos) in the country's major newspapers. This phenomenon led insurance companies to propose new policies for assets appraised in foreign currencies, in a context where everyone expected the exchange rate to shift at any time. In order to accompany the sale of the imported vehicles, then, policy coverage amounts were listed in dollars but with premiums in pesos.

After the 30 percent devaluation in April 1981, a few things changed. Some companies started running ads to reassure the public that the new exchange rate would not affect price tags. An ad for Citroën, for example, offered: "Imports free from devaluation: the dollar didn't go up, it's worth AR$2,400." Others resorted to discounts: with the caption "Alfa Romeo: Worth More, Costs Less," an advertisement promises between US$3,000 and 5,000 off the final prices of its Italian cars. At the same time, ads for locally manufactured cars emphasized the advantages of buying national vehicles priced in pesos. The Fiat Mirafiori, for example, was advertised with an image of a car alongside a dollar bill. The text read, "Now there are 30% more reasons for you to enjoy the pleasure of having it all."

Finally, high-income consumers—those able to buy a work of art or a foreign car priced in dollars—also found other opportunities to invest both in Argentina and abroad. In 1981, ads promoting parking spaces, farms, and properties on Argentina's Atlantic coast and in the United States and Brazil listed prices in dollars. "Extraordinary deals on lots for houses in Marion Oaks, Florida, USA. Try to buy a lot like this one in Argentina for just US$5,895," preached one ad, which ran in one of the largest newspapers. Another read as follows: "Here's to an investment that doesn't depend on a finicky dollar." By investing in a property in the coastal city of Buzios, Brazil, in Brazilian cruzeiros, "You can earn an average of US$120 per day renting it out. It's similar to prices in Cancun or Acapulco, Mexico, but costs three to five times less per square meter."

Chapter Three

# The Foreign Debt Crisis

> Carlos Bonifatti and his brother-in-law Rubén Molinuevo are getting into a car parked on a quiet neighborhood street. They are discussing the disastrous economic situation of their little factory.
> The mother-in-law of both men, Doña Hortensia, comes running out of a house across the street.
> Doña Hortensia: Are you headed downtown?
> Carlos: Yes. Where are you going?
> Doña Hortensia: To buy dollars. You see, I got my pension check today and I need to get my hands on some. Don't you invest? What do you two do with your money?
> Minutes later, Doña Hortensia is standing outside the board of the exchange office in the heart of "la City." She jots down numbers in a notebook. Other women her age are milling around, doing the same.

The Fernando Ayala comedy *Plata Dulce* (Sweet cash) took third place at the box office in 1982. It attracted nearly one million spectators, doubling the audiences of two movies starring Los Parchís, a band that sang hit tunes in Spanish. The only two films that outranked it in ticket sales included the Hollywood blockbuster *On Golden Pond* and the bawdy *Los Fierecillos indomables* (The wild scoundrels), starring the comic duo Alberto Olmedo and Jorge Porcel. *Los Fierecillos indomables* attracted 1.3 million viewers.

*Plata Dulce* is set in the days after Argentina hosted (and won) the 1978 Soccer World Cup, during the dictatorship. The influence of the economic policies of the regime's first economic minister, José Alfredo Martínez de Hoz, is evident in both the plot and the characters' actions. In an exceedingly folksy tone, the film describes the dilemmas and conflicts of a middle-class family whose business has gone belly-up; at the same time, it reveals the opportunities that came with liberalization, the basis for the economic reforms introduced under dictatorship.

Before the film's premiere, the director had considered other titles, including *Qué verde era mi dólar* (How green was my dollar) in a wink toward John Ford. Besides making an appearance in the scene described above, the US currency comes up several times in the film. Doña Hortensia's sons-in-law, who own an ailing factory that produces medicine cabinets, resent the progress of their neighbors. Their mother-in-law knows the best way to "invest": heading downtown to exchange the pesos she receives from her pension for dollars.

As film critic Marcela Visconti (2017) has shown, *Plata Dulce* is one of a series of films to home in on the dollar during the period. Others include *Tiempo de Revancha* (Time for revenge, 1981), *Últimos Días de la Victima* (Last days of the victim, 1982), and *Noches sin lunas ni soles* (Nights without moons or suns, 1984). However, Ayala's film occupies a singular place in this series. Its smashing success at the box office reveals just how popular the dollar had become as an intelligible reference for a mass public. The daily financial repertoires of social groups that had already assimilated the dollar as a currency for "investment" are reconstructed in the film. According to the critics, as well as the film's director and producers, what made *Plata Dulce* such a hit was its portrayal of the daily realities of Argentines and the impact of Martínez de Hoz's economic policies. For the many viewers who saw *Plata Dulce* at theaters in 1982, Doña Hortensia was a character to whom they could relate: an older woman with a pension who lives in the suburbs but is accustomed to heading into Buenos Aires and visiting the exchange offices of "la City" every month. Purchasing dollars was a fact of life, just one financial strategy, for Doña Hortensia, as it was for so many of those who saw the film.

> Virtually nothing remains of that avid Argentine consumer, the one who bragged of dining better than anyone in the world, who watched as a national automobile industry rivaling that of more developed latitudes thrived, who got dressed up, took summer vacations, and outfitted his home while the country expanded with virtually no debt. Today, this Argentine is poorer and spends in a different way: when not forced to worry about what's for dinner, he talks of the dollar and the lottery almost obsessively. (*Clarín*, October 31, 1982)

The "sweet cash" party had ended toward the end of 1982, as captured in this description from *Clarín*'s economic supplement. Trips abroad and imported goods had also vanished. Besides suffering a crushing defeat in the Malvinas War against the United Kingdom in 1982, the country had seen its economy collapse. There was only one thing it could not forget: "That each and every one of us owes the world US$1483.40, an amount that can only be paid if all of us can generate around US$2,000 per year" (*Clarín*, September 13, 1982). As with many other Latin American countries, foreign debt would become a millstone in the years to come.

Amid growing economic and political turbulence that would culminate in a call for open elections in 1983, the dollar was no longer just the currency for trips, investments abroad, luxury goods, and time deposits. Above all, as a *Clarín* journalist noted, it was a source of concern. Persisting inflation and frequent devaluations had led "an increasingly wary public," as one magazine columnist noted, to cling to the dollar "like a talisman offering true protection" (*Mercado*, November 11, 1982). This went beyond the theoretical arguments that analysts in "la City" put forth to justify growing exchange rate speculation: "protecting oneself" in the face of the peso's depreciation had become of the essence. And advertising made the most of this situation. Banco Palmares, for example, turned it into a slogan to appeal to customers: "Dollar deposits: protection against devaluation."

Strict exchange controls had been in place since the war with the United Kingdom, limiting the purchase of dollars for savings. Therefore, devaluation drove people to exchange their pesos for dollars on the parallel market, leading to an ever-increasing gap between the value of the black market dollar and the official exchange rate during the second half of the year, as amply covered in the daily papers. In addition, reports of fraud—the under-invoicing of exports and the over-invoicing of imports—were rampant. In response, Jorge Wehbe, the last minister of economy under the dictatorship, set out to eliminate the parallel market, "which has unfortunately served as an incentive for immoral and even criminal activities that undermine our national economy" (*Clarín*, October 30, 1982). Harsher penalties for violations of the foreign exchange regimen, however, hardly made a dent in the sprawling parallel market.

In any case, the more or less ordinary investors who sought refuge "in an asset that never loses its value" were not the true problem. The real time bomb, whose clock was already ticking, was private foreign debt. Finally, after two successive quarters in which exchange rate insurance had begun providing some relief for many companies with debt abroad, the Central Bank announced the nationalization of all private debt. For the dictatorship, it marked the beginning of the end. And, for the Argentine economy, it was karma that would come back to haunt it.

Over the course of the country's last military dictatorship, the Argentine economy entered an inflationary spiral unlike any other in its past, triggering a prolonged high inflation regime. As in many other Latin American countries during those years, the first structural reforms were introduced in an attempt to change the matrix of accumulation. By opening up the economy and deregulating the financial system, the military government sought to lay the groundwork for a new economy. The unprecedented growth in capital flows toward developing countries (Amato and Fantacci 2012), which had begun in the mid-1970s, was also part of this process. Like other administrations across the region, the military regime of Argentina sought to capture its portion of the newly globalized capital market.

The government's idea was for the state to abandon the active market interventions so common in the past. Yet at the same time, during the years of the regime, the foreign exchange constraints that had plagued the country in previous decades persisted. These three factors—a high inflation regime, economic opening, and foreign exchange constraints—are the ones most commonly mentioned when explaining the importance of the US currency in Argentine society and the economy. For this reason, experts often note that these dynamics date back to the 1970s.

The previous two chapters have presented arguments for an alternate timeline. Based on a hypothesis focused on the popularization of the US dollar as a category, the previous chapters have traced this process back to the end of the 1950s, reconstructing the sociocultural dynamics that enabled the greenback to become both a topic of public discussion and part of the financial repertoire of increasingly broader social groups. As shown here, the popularization of the dollar was a slow and gradual process. This interpretation does not overlook the other factors commonly cited in this process (high inflation, the opening of the economy, a new cycle of foreign exchange constraints), but it does underscore one fact that often goes unnoticed: as part of larger macroeconomic dynamics, these economic trends did not provoke spontaneous reactions or occur in a vacuum. Instead, they were part of an underlying process in which meanings and practices associated with the dollar had already taken hold.

In any case, in the 1970s and 1980s, even more social groups developed a relationship with US currency and the dollar itself became even more widespread, with more markets incorporating it as the benchmark currency for transactions. Its popularity had also risen, with an increasing number of people fixated on its ups and downs. Besides adding to the existing meanings and practices associated with the dollar until that date, the dollar's popularization was entering a new phase. Still largely overlooked in international literature, this chapter of the dollar's popularization is part of the financial globalization that unfolded between the late 1970s and early 1980s. Macroeconomic transformations were a key part of this process, but so were changes in the ordinary practices of economic agents, both in the core capitalist nations and in peripheral countries.

In the next chapter, we shall see how this process—which combined macroeconomic transformations, institutional dynamics, and daily practices—continued to develop in the years to come, while a spike in inflation causes one of the country's worst economic crises in the twentieth century.

*Chapter Four*

# STRONG DOLLAR, WEAK DEMOCRACY

# (1983–1989)

In the first days of 1983, before the military regime had announced that elections would be held, the state of the economy was making headlines almost daily. This could be attributed in great part to a package of financial measures introduced in December 1982 by Economic Minister Jorge Wehbe and rumors of a new upcoming devaluation of the Argentine peso.

In *Clarín*, a cartoon from the beginning of January offered a humorous take on the state of affairs. A man in a suit and top hat, a classic character of comic strip artist Landrú, is heading toward the door. The caption reads "The Planner." In the background, a radio host announces, "It's just been confirmed: there will be no devaluation." At the bottom of the cartoon, the man has a single line of dialogue: "I'm going out to buy dollars—just in case." The cartoon captures two trends that had become the norm over the past decade: the practice of buying dollars in response to devaluation of the Argentine currency, and news reporting on the economy that helped average men and women navigate an increasingly turbulent economy.

A page turned on a new chapter in this history when democracy was reinstated in December 1983. Economic reports had reached the evening news, a source of information for the vast majority of Argentines with no formal training in economics. At the beginning, the evening news simply ran brief clips of journalists reporting from "la City" or the trading floor of the Buenos Aires stock market. Soon, however, this coverage would evolve into a regular segment that relayed economic news in more innovative ways. When the news programs focused on the dollar, reporting went beyond expert commentary and instead aimed at a much broader and diverse public than newspaper readers. At the end of the program, an on-screen chart provided the day's closing exchange rates. Like the weather, the worth of the dollar had become relevant for audiences of all ages, genders, and backgrounds—it was key information for day-to-day living. It has reached what is referred to in the social sciences as a "public number" (Daniel 2013; Neiburg 2010), providing audiences with valuable information and guidance but also helping build the world vis-à-vis this number.

In the 1980s, in addition to the exchange rate, there was another key statistic for daily life: the consumer price index, which provided insight into inflation (Daniel 2013; Heredia and Daniel 2019; Neiburg 2007, 2010). This index was inextricably tied to the US currency: despite historical statements by public officials to the contrary, a spike in the peso-dollar exchange rate inevitably led to a rise in inflation. In terms of their history, however, the two indicators have their own identity.

This chapter describes the popularization of the dollar across Argentine society during the first democratic administration that followed the country's last military dictatorship (1976–1983). As occurred in other Latin American countries, the decade of the 1980s ushered in a challenging process that became known in the social sciences as the "democratic transition" (O'Donnell, Schmitter, and Whitehead 1986). In Argentina, the issues associated with the return to democracy were not only political but also economic, and, though relatively recent, these troubles had compounded. While developed nations had kept inflation in check, often through strict neoliberal economics, Argentina would be plagued by a staggering level of inflation over the course of the 1980s, the worst in the country's history (Gerchunoff and Llach 2018; Damill and Frenkel 1990; Frenkel 1979, 1990). To start, the "debt crisis" at the start of the decade would oblige the Argentine government to continually negotiate with foreign creditors and submit to supervision by international organizations like the International Monetary Fund (IMF) and the World Bank (Devlin and French-Davis 1994; Nemiña and Larralde 2018).

The new democratically elected leader of the traditional Unión Cívica Radical (Radical party), President Raúl Alfonsín, faced the political issue of maintaining a fragile democracy. On the economic end of things, inflation was persistently high, and the country's foreign debt was staggering. Over his years in office, the social and political sway of the dollar becomes increasingly evident, despite the administration's best efforts to build a stable democracy and mend a floundering economy.

## The Legacy of Dictatorship

On Sunday, October 16, 1983, two weeks before the first presidential elections since a decade prior, *La Nación* addressed the question of whether the IMF would in fact send the financial assistance planned for the third quarter, US$500 million. The main topic of the article was not the economy but who would win the elections; the writer speculated it would be the Peronist candidate, Ítalo Argentino Luder.

Would Luder, the journalist wondered, be capable of building the trust necessary for Argentines to bring their investments abroad back into the country? The article builds its argument through a dialogue of fictional characters who argue that the IMF funds will ameliorate the country's reputation abroad, provided, of course, the funding does not "all end up in the *schwarz*" (the Yiddish term for the black market). The problem, the journalist added, was "accepting the reality that Argentina's economy is dollarized. The M2 in dollars is higher than it is in pesos. According to calculations by the Federal Reserve, there are some US$3 billion in cash, not to mention US$600 million in bank deposits and US$2.5 billion in Bonex [foreign bonds]: a total of US$6.1 billion, while the M2 in pesos is AR$480 million. Admitting this is easy since the seigniorage has already been paid. Refusing to admit this, in contrast, is akin to having a country without a currency."

Economic policy in general, especially in relation to the country's currency, would be two major topics of debate during the brief period between the elections and the swearing in of Raúl Alfonsín on December 10. The buzz surrounding these topics would continue throughout 1984 as the government faced myriad challenges beyond the economic arena. While rumors spread about what the dollar would be worth—and official announcements aimed to assuage the public—the gap between the official and parallel market exchange rates widened, exceeding 70 percent in November 1983.

Argentines, particularly those with accounts denominated in US dollars, were preoccupied by many economic indicators. In the weeks before the election, Banco Mercantil Argentino ran an advertisement in an attempt to reassure these savers: "We inform all customers who have deposited foreign currency in our institution that our bank will return all deposits on their respective maturity date, paying both capital and interest in U.S. dollars." The ad was a response to a postponement ordered by the military regime on the maturity date of all certificates of deposit in dollars; certain financial institutions apparently lacked the foreign currency required for mass repayment on these deposits.

A series of contradictory statements by market officials and in the media, combined with continued advertising of investment opportunities, belied widespread uncertainty regarding the economic policies of the new administration. The closer the elections, the more advertisements banks ran on their most popular product: deposits in pesos with a cost-of-living adjustment or with a dollar clause. The greatest risk, however, was spiraling inflation (that year, the annual inflation reached 433.7 percent) or a devaluation of the peso. The banking system wanted investors to breathe easy, knowing that the savings instruments banks provided could protect them from any of these catastrophes. Banco Mercantil, for example, set out to capture jittery investors in a full-page ad: "To keep your money up to pace, invest in the adjustable deposits of Banco Mercantil Argentino. Make sure your money is adjusted to the times" (*Clarín*, October 1983). For deposits adjusted according to the consumer price index, the minimum period was 120 days with an interest rate of 3.5 percent. For deposits relying on the dollar clause, the minimum was 90 days with an interest rate of 1.5 percent. All deposits were backed by the Central Bank.

Foreign banks operating in Argentina did not stand out from national banks in their account promotions. Citibank attempted to attract customers with the following message:

> Invest in adjustable deposits today and you will already have earned 33.9%. In what is left of October, your investment will yield a monthly interest rate of 17.2%. In the following 30 days, you'll be assured 21.4%, equal to the rise in the cost of living in September, for a yield of approximately 33.9%. Don't let another day go by. Come to Citibank and make an excellent investment in deposits with a cost-of-living adjustment. Because in addition to one of the highest rates on the market, you'll have the assurance of banking with Citibank. (*Clarín*, October 17, 1983)

A stopwatch was featured in the ad. A second ad, part of the same campaign, showed a light bulb with a peso sign instead of the filament to promote deposits with the dollar clause adjustment. This, the ad promised, was "today's investment": "That's intelligent . . . Invest in pesos and adjust your peace of mind to the dollar's value +1.5%."

At the end of 1983, a plethora of public and private banks, credit unions, and financial companies actively promoted such products. Naturally, despite what they promised, the interest offered on these products was no higher than the now-customary investment of a seven-day certificate of deposit in dollars: at Banco del Interior y Buenos Aires, these deposits offered a 13 percent annual yield on a minimum deposit of US$3,000 but were not backed by the Central Bank.

Once Alfonsín was sworn in, the Central Bank kept good on a promise it had made in the press a month earlier to continue allowing dollar deposits. The goal was to recapture a portion of the savings stored outside the domestic financial system. An ad by Banco del Oeste eloquently captures how financial promotions aligned with economic policy. In black boldface type, the ad called on the public to "Nationalize the dollar" (*Clarín*, January 4, 1984):

> Dollars in safe deposit boxes or savings accounts abroad represent an old country model of uncertainty and gridlock.
> 
> Like everyone else, you voted for another Argentina, a country of freedom and growth.
> 
> Investing your dollars in an Argentine bank is more than a financial decision.

> It's exercising your freedom to earn international interest rates on foreign currencies while your savings stimulate the nation's growth.
> Foreign currency deposits at Banco del Oeste. A solid decision for Argentine investors.
> YOU AND THE COUNTRY WILL REAP THE BENEFITS.

A democratic era was dawning, under a new administration whose president had called on Argentines to lay the groundwork for a prosperous nation and where national and foreign banks alike leveraged the opportunity to invoke national development as an incentive for potential customers. In just two months, Citibank abandoned the argument of beating inflation through adjustable deposits and instead appealed to classic investors looking for the biggest bang for their buck. "Get your dollars working with the assurance Citibank provides," reads one ad where the face of George Washington on a dollar bill has been replaced by a man in a suit and tie, smiling from his armchair. The text beneath the image reads, "Certificates of deposit in dollars. Choose Citibank. A prestigious, solid, efficient bank that has been doing business in Argentina and contributing to the country's development since 1914" (*Clarín*, January 1984).

While the question as to whether the new administration would continue allowing foreign currency deposits still worried customers and, more broadly, the financial system, the future of the parallel market received even more attention. What would happen to this market? Would the official forex market merge with the parallel one? Would the government assure that the gap between the exchange rates on these markets remained low? Would the parallel market be legalized? Much had happened since the days when the black market was subject to legal persecution and moral condemnation. Citizens instantly understood what *el paralelo* referred to, with no need to mention either the market or the dollar. In fact, information on the peso-dollar exchange rate on this gray market had become a daily piece of information while the "gap" between this and the official exchange rate was now a key economic indicator. A question that had persisted at every turn of forex controls now resurfaced: What was one dollar actually worth?

In an interview with *Ámbito Financiero*, former Central Bank president Domingo Cavallo—who would become the minister of economy less than a decade later—gave his opinion on the topic:

> The best thing to do is legalize the parallel dollar market, creating a free market or tourist market for all transactions not authorized by the Central Bank. This would have a favorable effect since whatever happens on this market would no longer be seen as abnormal or mysterious; it would be just another variable. Plus, by creating a free

market for the dollar, its rise would attract capital that is currently abroad for the purchase of physical goods or other types of investment [in Argentina]. (*Ámbito Financiero*, January 1984)

A columnist from the same daily was even more categorical in his assessment:

> The gray market, a market covered by both the print media and radio, is an absurd hindrance. The fact that foreign currency cannot be legally purchased for obvious needs such as a trip abroad or remittances to help a family member, among others, merits an immediate solution. (*Ámbito Financiero*, January 1984)

The new economic team, however, did not appear to be of the same mind. Bernardo Grinspun, a month after taking office as Alfonsín's minister of economy, was asked about the preoccupying rise in the parallel dollar, In statements to the press, he minimized its importance: "The parallel dollar doesn't worry me because that's not what we base our decisions on. If it goes up, the rise can probably be attributed to the pressure caused by too many Argentines in Punta del Este." He then added, "The rise in the parallel dollar should only be a concern to those buying dollars on that market because they're going to have to shell out more for the same quantity" (*Ámbito Financiero*, January 1984). However, as had occurred at other moments in the country's history, the expansion of the parallel market was a simple fact, as was its impact (albeit superficial) on the economic practices of many Argentines. This can be seen in a print news story about a man accused of selling counterfeit dollars at the beginning of December 1983. The transaction that led to the discovery of the counterfeit bills, a purchase of US$700, had taken place far from "la City," at a pizzeria in Lanús, a suburb south of the capital.

The now firmly established trend of stating electronic equipment, trips abroad, and other key prices in the Argentine economy in dollars was one of the clearest signs of an even greater "dollarization of the economy" that could no longer be denied by the time President Alfonsín took office. On the real estate market, property prices in dollars were going for record prices (between US$500,000 and US$800,000) in the most exclusive Buenos Aires neighborhoods.

In the urban landscape and in popular culture, the dollar's image had become so familiar that the bill could be identified even with artistic interventions. In July 1984, a party flyer for a discotheque in the posh Buenos Aires neighborhood of Recoleta showed a dollar bill with music idol Michael Jackson's face replacing that of George Washington. The other side of the flyer said, "Enough of dollars already! Don't invest in foreign currency. Don't speculate: spend on fun! Don't miss the best party of the year."

Chapter Four

# Dollars on the Street, in the House, at the Square

In March 1985, there had been changes at the Ministry of Economy. The first minister of the new democratic era, Bernardo Grinspun, had failed in his attempts to increase real salaries, lower inflation, and recover a national industry hard hit by the elimination of trade barriers under dictatorship. Price controls had always been a controversial method to fight inflation, especially in a context of rising market concentration domestically. Negotiations with foreign creditors required that the country adapt its fiscal and monetary policies in ways that further exacerbated the country's preoccupying inflation. In fact, 1984 had ended with what would remain, until 1989, the highest annual inflation that decade, 688 percent. Overall, the Radical administration had been unable to address the issues that had plagued the country a year earlier, especially inflation, which continued to worry Argentines of all backgrounds. Dollar-related anxiety came in myriad forms: the exchange rate, the options it offered as an alternative form of investment, and in relation to the existence of the parallel market.

When Juan Vital Sourrouille was sworn in as the new minister of economy, a joke went around "la City":

"Did you hear Alfonsín is going to the United States?"
"No, what for?"
"To ask Reagan to start printing dollars on black paper: that way, he can legalize Argentina's exchange market."

The joke revealed that the parallel market was still news, while the usual crowds in "la City" (along with some new arrivals) sought options for the day's most pressing problem: beating inflation.

As had occurred during other times of economic and financial imbroglio, newspapers and magazines ran chronicles with play-by-play accounts of the city's financial district. Who were the people responsible for driving exchange rates up from one day to the next? Who was waiting in line or pushing to get a look at the boards in "la City"? And, perhaps most importantly, what were their motivations? In the middle of April that year, *Clarín* described the type of people at a Buenos Aires bank in an article entitled "Stories of money."

> Most of the people come in or out in trench coats or heavy jackets, "just in case." There are also crowds outside the boards or blocking narrow sidewalks. Inside a corner building covered in glass, the air is cool and dry inside the branch of this powerful and renowned banking institutions, where many are interested in fifteen or thirty-day CDs. "I

want to breathe easy, at least until May. I couldn't continue with the bonds, not even the foreign bonds. What can I say . . . I don't think they're going up." The man looks a little passé in his smooth, pearl gray suit, sky blue shirt, and red tie. He doesn't say how much he's pulled from his bonds or how much he intends to deposit when he reaches the teller. But he does clarify, "My accounts are paid in full. I don't owe my people even two weeks' back pay and I've got no merchandise to pay for. I'm not going to buy anything big from here until the end of May. So I'm putting my money into the real legal tender, the greenback, to rest easy."

Just a few weeks earlier, the news magazine *Somos* ran a report entitled "The dollar, legal tender." After a description of the real estate and automobile market, the journalist notes,

Housewives, students, and employees of all sorts now convert their meager savings into dollars. Like the illegal gambling dens that were raided when the state-run lottery was introduced, small-time dollar vendors in all the city's neighborhoods offer their nontraditional wares at supermarkets, fairs, even delicatessens. "Some buy fifteen, twenty, thirty-five dollars. Others, but not many, buy two or three hundred," explained one of these unofficial forex agents who works the streets of Almagro to *Somos* magazine. (March 1985)

The concern over what to do with one's money was the subject of expert analysis, daily conversations, graphic humor, and advertising campaigns. For example, a cartoon by the artist Ian in mid-1985 shows a long-haired, curvaceous woman twice as tall as the man on her arm. Despite being in such good company, he is calling out his investment suggestions: "Dollars, Bonex, CDs, stocks." That same year, Banco del Oeste launched an advertising campaign on TV. Though it would be dissolved two years later, Banco del Oeste was ranked forty-fifth on the list of national banks at the time. The commercial opens with a close-up of a pair of hands counting dollar bills as a voice-over calmly repeats, "Dollars, dollars, dollars." The camera advances down a hallway with doors both left and right. Now the voice-over shifts gear: "Like many Argentines, you may have some dollars. So where should you put them? The mattress, the safe deposit box, an investment abroad?" The doors in the hallways opens to reveal a man hiding dollars beneath the bed, a wall of safe-deposit boxes, a woman on a plane gesturing toward the camera. Now a light appears at the end of the hallway. "We have now entered a new phase with renewed assurances. And in this phase," the voice-over continues as a sun rises over an industrial landscape, "your dollars can contribute to the country's development. Invest them in an Argentine bank. For you, it's profitable. For the country, it's vital. Dollar deposits at Banco del Oeste."

In just one minute, the ad not only promoted a specific product but also provided advice to help consumers choose. A few shots conveyed the basic options available to anyone with savings in dollars. And the final message relays the best choice for viewers. What is interesting about this advertisement is not the arguments used for the ad but the fact that it explains both the options available and the criteria for selecting among them. Instead of targeting a savvy investor who closely followed financial news, comparing return on investment (ROI) and risk, the ad appealed to people interested in making money on their money but who, like as good citizens, also wanted to contribute to national development. At the same time, these citizens needed more knowledge to maneuver the world of finance.

Radio stations and television channels alike had launched their own economic segments since Channel 13 news in Buenos Aires had introduced the first of its kind in 1983. This reporting combined news with expert tips: "Who were you talking to? Who do you think I was talking to [on the news]? To everyone. Not to businessmen or economists . . . To my mother-in-law, Porota. Listen, Porota, let me explain what's going on: This, that, the other, that's the story," remembered journalist Osvaldo Granados,[1] describing the target of these news segments.

The economic news offered stories and reports that made audiences familiar with the settings, roles, devices, and languages of the world of finance. When the press and media reported on the financial strategies of the "average Joe," they conveyed the growing significance and breadth of the world of finance. At the same time, they held up a mirror to readers and viewers, giving them a model to emulate. The *Clarín* story "Small-time savers also wheel and deal," from the first days of May 1985, reported on a government decision to increase regulated interest rates by 4 percent. The chronicle described the scene at several coffee shops in downtown Buenos Aires, where women around the age of fifty were meeting up with friends at lunchtime to crunch the numbers. "We've got enough for three treasury bills," says one. Others waved their checkbooks or pulled bills from wallets, pooling their money to invest in Central Bank treasury bills, which yield 32 percent monthly. "We don't want the risks that come with other types of investments: we want something sure," they explain.

> Most of us know each other from waiting in lines at banks and finance agencies so we decided to get together once a week and exchange tips. Along the way, we became friends: thanks to the investments. Now we've formed . . . Why, it's practically a club. Sometimes we even go to the movies, because it's not all about money. (*Clarín*, May 3, 1985)

By that time, the world of finance had become much more extensive and diversified than anyone would have imagined just a decade earlier. In the imagination of journalists, older women were the paradigmatic example of the average audience, lacking economic expertise and knowledge. Yet in the mid-1980s, older women were frequently checking the boards outside financial institutions of "la City," and defending their investments at the Florida Garden café, in the heart of downtown. Though still a minority, they were also a sign of the times, as widely captured in the comics. In 1985, artists Maicas and Fortín ran a comic strip in *Humor* magazine entitled "Not your grandmother! Grannies of yesteryear and grannies today." The comic strip contrasts the housewife of yesterday, always comparing prices at the market and scolding the grocers for raising their prices, with the 1980s housewife, a downtown regular who admonishes the bank teller, "Oh, no you don't! If you can't up that rate one point, I'll withdraw all my money and buy dollars. What kind of country do you think this is, young man?"

## Runs

In the 1980s, two types of newspaper stories caught the eye of small-time savers: the folksy chronicles of "la City" whenever the exchange rate spiked and the liquidation of private banks. In the first two years of the Radical administration, both occurred. On May 10, 1985, it was announced that Banco de Italia y del Río de la Plata would be liquidated. This was no small financial institution that had gone on to become a bank when the dictatorship deregulated the sector; it was an institution founded in 1872 that boasted eighty branches and Argentine peso deposits worth US$180 million. When the bank's customers heard the news, they crowded the sidewalks outside its headquarters.

Those with foreign currency accounts, which represented US$80 million of the bank's portfolio, were especially agitated, as Argentina's Central Bank offered no guarantees on these deposits. Many regretted not having accepted the offer the bank had made in the days prior to the announcement, when rumors about its collapse had begun to circulate. Now that they had refused a payment in Argentine pesos or a check drawn on a foreign bank that could be cashed at forex offices, they were at risk of losing all their savings. "I should have kept those dollars in the can buried in the garden out back," one woman interviewed on television on her way out of the bank quipped. The news of the bank going under came as no surprise to financial news outlets, as the institution's financial troubles were an open secret.

As had occurred in the past, the crisis at Banco de Italia set off tremors across the financial system. In the weeks that followed, people withdrew their dollar deposits from other banks, especially in Argentina's interior. Fearful that the funds available would end up in dollars on the "marginal" market (another euphemism for the black market) and thus drive inflation, the Central Bank jacked the interest rates of treasury bonds and government-backed deposits. Even with the spike in interest rates, deposits continued to fall. The artist Basurto captured the absurd climate in a cartoon in *La Nación*. A customer is standing at the teller window, about to withdraw a stack of bills. Another customer inquires, "Where are you taking those? Dollars, a CD, Bonex . . . ?" The response: "To the mattress!" (*La Nación*, June 1985). Finally, a few weeks after Banco de Italia collapsed, the Central Bank froze all dollar deposits for six months. Holders of these accounts could exchange these deposits for foreign bonds at face value. At the same time, the banking authority suspended all new investment opportunities in foreign currency and obliged banks to transfer all their US currency to the Central Bank.

Overnight, two types of advertisements appeared in the papers: ads by financial agents offering to buy Bonex, and ads by attorneys for anyone willing to go to court to access their foreign currency deposits. At the same time, journalists continued their daily beat on San Martín Street, though at times this obliged them to leave "la City" and head to the neighborhood of Ciudad Vieja in Montevideo. There, they covered—and, unwillingly or not, gave tips on—the most popular offshore options among Argentine investors:

> Nowadays, the Argentines who cross the Rio de la Plata in one of six daily flights out of Aeroparque airport from 7:30am to 9pm are flying to safeguard their foreign currency, precious metal, or Argentine dollar bonds: all can be converted into actual dollars in Montevideo. However, those who embark on this experience should know that foreign currency buffs specializing in capital flight prefer the 9am and the 1:30pm flights. . . . Uruguayan banks serve the public between 1 and 5pm. In the morning, they are open exclusively for forex offices and stock traders, but what would they do without the informal Argentine traders? Who would handle their dollar transactions? The trading of Argentina's foreign bonds has become so common in Montevideo that any day now, the Montevideo Stock Market will have them up on the board. (*Clarín*, May 19, 1985)

At the same time, arguments and discussions from times past made a comeback in the media. The media was again asking questions such as: What does the dollar mean for Argentines? Is it a profit-making instrument or a safeguard against a government incapable of maintaining the national currency's value? Business columnists seem to favor the latter argument. At the beginning of May, the economic daily *Ámbito Financiero* published a monthly overview of different financial instruments available (deposits with floating vs. fixed interest rates, the purchase of dollars on the parallel market, bonds, stocks) and the best investments with an eye toward the future. Despite the fact that the current state of affairs seemed to favor peso deposits ("May is the month for the peso"), "there are political variables that are closely linked to a strong currency that has become a haven for investors" (*Ámbito Financiero*, May 5, 1985). At the end of that month, the business magazine *Mercado* published a lengthy article on the crisis that was openly critical:

> Perhaps it is time to admit that those who opt to buy dollars are not sellouts or traitors, as some simple-minded arguments of late would have it. These people choose the dollar because they are looking for a safeguard against the scandalous inflation Argentina is experiencing. That—and that alone—is responsible for destroying the Argentine economy and swindling all of the country's inhabitants. (*Mercado*, May 30, 1985)

Outside the financial world, the dollar also appears as a tool to avoid uncertainty. As had occurred in the past, comic strips poked fun at the situation. In *Juan y el preguntón* (Juan and Mr. Inquisitive), artist Juan Broccoli sketched the comic's main character writing in his diary. In the first three panels, Juan writes, "I have faith in the future again . . . There is promise on the horizon . . . Things no longer seem so uncertain." In the fourth panel, the reason for this change of heart is revealed: "I found the dollar I had lost."

As the months passed, the economic situation worsened. When the numbers came out for April 1985, monthly inflation was almost 30 percent, and it looked like May would be even higher. The government continued its negotiations with the IMF, which had laid out a series of monetary and fiscal goals the country had to meet before signing. As part of these obligations, the government announced an 18 percent devaluation on June 12, the highest since 1983. The devaluation was followed by other measures designed to reduce the fiscal deficit: hikes in export and import duties, and in fuel and transportation costs. Rumors ran rife about a new economic plan that would abandon gradualism in favor of shock therapy. Though the government had yet to confirm the news, *Ámbito Financiero* announced the advent of the new plan on its June 13 cover. That same day, the cost of buying one dollar on the parallel (or "marginal" or "free") market exceeded AR$1,000. One day later, news of the plan was on the cover of every newspaper, and the government announced a mandatory bank holiday until June 19. That evening, President Alfonsín and Juan Vital Sourrouille announced the Austral Plan on a nationwide broadcast.[2]

Wearing a gray suit and blue tie, his hands folded over a large desk with a double inkwell, a somber Alfonsín spoke to the country for twenty minutes:

On April 26th, I told you that we found ourselves in a war economy. . . .
Tonight I am here to describe a battle plan that will allow all of us
to turn the page on this chapter of national decline together. I have
already mentioned that we Argentines have a battle to fight: the enemy
is poverty, stagnation, and also a certain chronic incapacity to find
concrete, efficient solutions.

A bit later in the talk, the president notes that the priority of the first stage of his plan for reforms is the fight against inflation, which has become "the origin of all social uncertainties." More specifically, he clarifies, "First off, we have decided to address inertial inflation because if we cannot put an end to expectations of inflation, it will never end." Minister Sourrouille then spoke about the specific measures that the press would later describe as "a drastic shift" in the country's economic policy: a price and salary freeze, the elimination of automatic price and contract adjustment clauses, cutbacks in public spending, and higher tariffs. When the topic turned to the dollar, the administration's second economic minister defended the current exchange rate, arguing that it "suffices to promote the country's exports." The recent devaluation, then, was necessary to return to an exchange rate "compatible with a policy to fight inflation" (Alfonsín and Sourrouille 1985). Starting June 15, a new exchange rate was introduced: each dollar would be worth eighty cents of the austral, currency symbol ARA. A new currency had been born, and the government was determined it would remain stable.

As part of the set of strategies adopted to fight inertial inflation, the government now required that all assets—including real estate—be stated in the national currency. The measure was effective for a limited time; within two years, the majority of the classified ads for homes would be listing prices in dollars once again. In terms of foreign currency investments, the banks stuck to the schedule originally established to return foreign currency deposits starting in August. Thanks to the trust this instilled, many let their deposits renew. Despite the myriad restrictions, the government decided to authorize banks to again accept dollar deposits (though the minimum term was extended from seven to sixty days). These new deposits were guaranteed by the Central Bank.

The Austral Plan represented a heterodox economic policy pursued by several countries in Latin America seeking stability, including Brazil and Peru. These initiatives were based on the idea that inertial inflation represented one of the country's biggest challenges and aimed to bring inflation under control without any shock measures.

While the economic team was wagering on the austral's power to slow inflation, Argentines could not wait to unload their precarious pesos—and have the promised australs in their hands.[3] "It's official: the austral note will be the same size as the dollar. An almost magical format for a new symbol that some eccentrics attribute to whimsical origins," reported Clarín in August 1985 in an article in which fortune tellers, tarot card readers, and other psychics offered a genealogy of the new currency's symbol, a letter A crossed twice. Magical or not, the specter of the dollar continued to haunt Argentina's currency.

## 1989: A Year of Danger

The so-called Spring Plan was the last systematic attempt on the part of President Raúl Alfonsín's administration to stem inflation. Due to a series of failures following the Austral Plan, a new strategy was needed to stabilize the economy. In September 1988, a set of measures were announced, including price agreements with large companies, higher official exchange rates, a hike in tariffs and interest rates, and a new division of the forex market with a gap between the official and "floating" exchange rate that would not exceed 25 percent. Yet by the end of that year, it was patently clear that the new strategy had failed. The exchange rate was between 20 percent and 25 percent lower than what it should have been, according to some observers. The plan might have worked with assistance from foreign creditors, but a delayed interest payment on the country's financial obligations abroad that predated the administration had given them cold feet: it was not at all clear that the Alfonsín administration would be able to keep the exchange rate stable.

As the media assessed the state of affairs at the end of 1988 and the beginning of 1989, comparisons with the summer of 1981 were frequent. As temperatures rose in January and February, everyone recalled the hot summer of 1981 when the government did away with the tablita. Some journalists even made comparisons between José Martínez de Hoz, the minister of economy under the dictatorship, and Juan Vital Sourrouille. The media was also discussing "sweet new money" in reference to Argentines vacationing abroad that summer thanks to a *dólar planchado* (dollar ironed flat)—a reference to an artificially low exchange rate (*Clarín*, January 10, 1989). The situation at the end of the decade harked back to the times of Minister of Economy Martínez de Hoz, when Argentine society had lived "the mirage of a dollarized Argentina" that had "bewitched many an Argentine." The Spring Plan created a similar situation for those who could "buy bills to spend abroad" (*Clarín*, January 10, 1989). However, the comparisons between the summer of 1989 and that of 1981 overlooked a key development as the decade ended: the election campaign to decide who would succeed Alfonsín as the nation's president.

Underdog Carlos Saúl Menem, governor of the small province of La Rioja, had won the Peronist primary against Antonio Cafiero, governor of the powerful province of Buenos Aires. As part of his campaign, Menem was crisscrossing the country. The Radical party candidate, Córdoba governor Eduardo Angeloz, had a difficult juggling act, attempting to distance himself from the largely unsuccessful economic policy of the Alfonsín administration yet defend other aspects of the Radical platform.

The enormous quantity of humorous depictions of the US dollar in 1989 belies its growing presence at this particular time. The dollar often showed up in comic strips poking fun at the election campaign and the forex market. For example, in the famous Tabaré Gómez Laborde comic *Diógenes y el Linyera* (Diogenes and the Bum), the main character, a drifter usually accompanied by his dog Diogenes, speaks with a woman in a park:

> "Hmmm! It looks like the percentages in the political surveys are changing."
> "Has there been a new survey? Are the numbers changing?" the woman asks.
> "The numbers aren't just changing: they've been overrun," responds the bum, "Overrun by the interest rates and the cost of the dollar."

During the first few months of 1989, the forex market was not only the focus of the election campaign: at times, it took precedence over the campaign. By keeping the cost of the dollar in check, the administration sought to buy time until the May 14 elections.

However, despite a hike in interest rates to attract savers and the sale of dollars by the Central Bank—some US$500 million the first week of February, and US$1.8 billion since August 1989—the administration was unable to keep the price of the dollar down: "The problem is not [the Central Bank] selling dollars, it's that it continues selling despite high interest rates"; "no matter how draconian the fiscal policy, the dollar doesn't come down." These opinions were attributed to money managers at financial institutions (*Ámbito Financiero*, February 1, 1989). In the press, at the "trading desks," and among bank executives, there was talk of a "bank run."

On February 6, banks and foreign exchange offices were unexpectedly forced to close for the day once again.[4] That day, it was announced that the Central Bank would no longer intervene on the "free" market but would create a "third market" exclusively for financial transactions, in addition to the "trade" market for agriculture exports, and the "special" market for imports. The bidding on bonds that the Central Bank had issued to control the value of the dollar on the "free" market was suspended. When the forex market reopened, the dollar—which had been selling for around ARA 18 at the end of January—climbed to ARA 23.50. In the days that followed, it rose to ARA 27. As Central Bank president José Luis Machinea denied rumors of his imminent resignation and the public grew increasingly angry with the Alfonsín administration, the tension was palpable across "la City." Scenes from the street evoked times past, with worried-looking tellers, crowds outside banks and exchange offices, and people elbowing one another for a glimpse of the boards. Forex market observers attributed the demand in recent weeks to a reversal of capital flow: foreign investors drawn by high interest rates and the artificially low dollar to invest in Argentina were now withdrawing their money.

For the opposition, the government's handling of inflation was a total fiasco. Eduardo Duhalde, Menem's running mate, said as much in statements to the press: "Thanks to this plan, we've lost two billion dollars to capital flight, a handful of government contractors, and five-star summer holidays. It's an updated version of Martín de Hoz's 'sweet money.'" Saúl Ubaldini, the secretary-general of the Confederación General del Trabajo (Argentina's workers confederation), stated that the measures "do not favor workers in the least. Every time there is a run on pesos, prices skyrocket, reducing people's real salaries." Central Bank spokespeople emphasized that the rising cost of the dollar was the result of "speculation fever," adding that "the price of the dollar has nothing to do with anything." According to an official statement, "the administration is not responsible for what happens on the free market" (*Clarín*, February 8, 1989).

On the streets of "la City," long lines began forming outside banks and exchange offices at 8:00 a.m. Employees had to deal with "shouting and shoving" by "nervous people," especially "small ill-informed investors." Some customers even demanded that certificates of deposit due to mature seven days later be translated into dollars immediately. The voices cited in the story convey people's anger with Central Bank president Machinea, who had promised that the authority would keep control over the forex market (*Clarín*, February 9, 1989). According to financial experts, people who had exchanged dollars for australs at the beginning of the Spring Plan, invested them in CDs, and then purchased dollars before February 6 had turned a 35-percent profit; those who had done the same but waited until September had earned 25 percent on their money. Those who had not exchanged their australs for dollars in time incurred losses of around 10 percent in the days after the mandatory forex holiday.

Again, the upcoming election and outsized influence of the foreign exchange market was a source of inspiration for comic strip artists. In one cartoon, a passerby smiles knowingly at a poster for the Radical party ticket, Eduardo Angeloz- Juan Manuel Casella. "You know they bought dollars at the end of the month for ARA 19.75!" (*Ámbito Financiero*, February 17, 1989). In February that year, it was difficult to imagine that the candidates of the Radical party would have other reasons to smile.

The rising dollar and its impact on prices were a headache for the administration. In addition to officials denying any connection between the "floating" dollar and rising prices, the administration went so far as to run paid ads in the papers. "There is no reason for prices to rise," begins a paid ad by the Domestic Trade Department of the Ministry of Economy.

> Foreign exchange measures recently adopted by the national government do NOT affect the products you buy . . . Why? Because the cost of imported articles depends on the official exchange market. The floating dollar is exclusively for financial transactions . . . As an alert and responsible consumer, your attitude matters. Collaborate. It's in your best interest. (*Ámbito Financiero*, February 10, 1989)

However, the fact that the exchange rate was affecting prices was not the only concerning issue: it was that the cost of a US dollar continued to skyrocket. Just a few days after the new forex market measures, the cost of produce had risen 20–40 percent, medicine had spiked 15–20 percent, and industrial inputs, 10–35 percent. Transactions on the free-floating exchange market were driving the price of the dollar higher and higher. "La City" was awash with rumors of people turning extraordinary profits. Chronicles of the trading desks described agents exhausted after ten-hour days negotiating purchase and sale prices for dollars and seeking new sources of profitable investment, all while discussing the officials who had turned in their resignation and names of potential replacements. Despite Alfonsín's public support for his minister of economy, and more denials by the Central Bank president that he planned to resign, the rumors persisted.

At this point, business organizations like the Unión Industrial Argentina (UIA), which had agreed to pitch in with government efforts as part of the Spring Plan, declared that they were "impartial" to the new measures. Representatives of the farming and livestock sector, the country's foremost exporters, were seething over the administration's broken promise to create a single foreign exchange market. As a result, they vociferously opposed the government decisions through their spokespeople and exerted pressure by postponing the currency conversion of export payments and thus the export duties owed on the transaction. During a visit to Europe, Radical party candidate Eduardo Angeloz had expressed his support for merging the two exchange rates. By the time he returned to Argentina, however, there were three different exchange rates, not two.

On February 20, as yet another mandatory forex holiday was ordered, the government introduced a new tablita that would set prices, duties, government salaries, and exchange rates starting in March. Although the new measures resulted in a more favorable exchange rate for exporters—or, as the press quickly dubbed it, the "agri-dollar"—the countryside was quick to voice its discontent. It the view of farmers, the new tablita only moved the country a step further from a single exchange rate. Export settlements were the main source of foreign currency for the country's ebbing reserves, which the Central Bank had to preserve once the World Bank announced it would postpone payment on a loan for US$350 million agreed on in October 1988.

On March 1, UIA members resigned from the Price Control Committee, effectively withdrawing their support for the administration. A few days later, the press noted that the exchange rate had doubled to around ARA 38 since the Central Bank had stopped selling dollars on the free market. Interest rates were triple that of inflation, yet there seemed to be no ceiling for the dollar. At a press conference held on March 5, Minister Sourrouille denied that the administration would be moving to introduce a single exchange rate for all transactions or a "mega-devaluation" of the austral, declaring "the dollar has nothing to do with pricing." On the streets, however, people remained unconvinced.

In those first days of March, office employees pooled their money to buy small amounts of dollars, usually somewhere between US$25–50. Financial office employees described waiting on these buyers: "People push their way to the front, totally unhinged. They'll buy no matter what the price" (*Clarín*, March 9, 1989). Those who only dabbled in the forex market, as opposed to professional investors, were the focus of chronicles such as these. *Clarín*, for example, ran a story on a group of taxi drivers exchanging tips and opinions on what would happen to the greenback (*Clarín*, March 22, 1989). One of these men, who was hoping to pay for a four-day vacation, regretted leaving his money in a CD instead of "moving" to the dollar. Another avoided mentioning the high exchange rate he had paid to purchase dollars to avoid being the butt of everyone's jokes.

The drastic rise in the dollar in February and March set off a buying "frenzy" of cars, home appliances, and nonperishables. This new run, which lasted a few weeks, revealed people's anticipation of spiraling inflation. As long as the cost of the dollar exceeded the rise in the cost of goods, this speculative consumption continued. As prices caught up, it slowed. Thus, despite Minister Sourrouille's statements and the government campaign to refute the dollar's impact on prices, reality was proving otherwise. The hard data confirmed that the Argentine economy was largely abandoning the austral. According to *La Nación*, Argentines were holding US$5.5 billion. Financial analysts were certain that the value of the US dollar was "exaggerated." A few weeks before the presidential elections, there was talk of a "psycho-dollar" in reference to the absence of "real prices" and the existence of a "psychological" value attributed to the US currency.

Comics made light of the "political uncertainty" and its effects on the foreign exchange market. The first panel of a cartoon published in *Ámbito Financiero* under the title "Psychosis 1" shows a journalist approaching Angeloz as he emerges from a foreign exchange office, his pockets overflowing with dollars: "YOU'RE buying dollars?" "Yup . . . afraid Menem might win," responds the Radical party candidate. The second panel, entitled "Psychosis 2," shows the same scene but features the Peronist candidate. When the journalist poses the same question, Menem responds, "Yup . . . afraid of Alfonsín."

After Angeloz voiced his support for the changes to the government's economic course, Minister Sourrouille and his team resigned six months before the presidential elections. The drawing that accompanies an article published in *Ámbito Financiero* to announce the minister's resignation, following by the appointment of Juan Carlos Pugliese in the post, is particularly indicative of the most common reading of this replacement. Entitled "Four years of Sourrouille: From praise for the austral to ostracism for the spring," in reference to the two economic plans overseen by the minister (the Austral Plan and the Spring Plan), it includes a cartoon featuring the minister's head resting on the guillotine above a plaque reading "Dollar." Most agreed that the dollar was responsible for the abrupt end to the minister's term.

In the meantime, businesspeople continued clamoring for an end to the multiple exchange rates, but the minister turned a deaf ear, proposing instead a 25 percent devaluation in the export exchange rate. A few days after the new minister was sworn in, the "floating" dollar surpassed ARA 50. "I spoke to them from the heart and they responded with their wallets" was Pugliese's reaction; over time, he would be quoted often. The minister also borrowed from Alfonsín's playbook in his accusations against speculators. The government had announced that the Central Bank, the General Tax Bureau, and the State Intelligence Office would investigate those responsible for the dollar's continuous upward trend. Echoing the hypothesis of members of the government and the Radical party candidate that speculators were to blame, the Argentine Chamber of Foreign Exchange Offices ran a paid ad (*Ámbito Financiero*, May 7, 1989) under the title "The dollar: Myths and realities at exchange offices." In the ad, the chamber defended these agencies as "efficient" operators handling the purchase and sale of foreign currency while denying any responsibility for "the prevailing uncertainty, which is driving the strong demand for dollars."

On April 14, the administration imposed a new foreign exchange holiday, and exporters became subject to retentions in order to protect the country's ebbing reserves. It was the fourth day in two months that the government had shut down foreign exchange. During the following seven days, the floating dollar rose 40 percent; since the new minister had taken office, it had climbed 100 percent. At the end of April, 90 percent of all certificates of deposit had a seven-day maturity, and the dollar was close to ARA 100. In response, Pugliese declared that there was "no objective reason for the dollar to reach such levels . . . The problem is that people don't trust the election process . . . We are confident that after May 14, the market will return to normal" (*Clarín*, April 26, 1989). The swearing in of President Menem would be the first democratic changing of the guard since 1952, yet also the first time a Radical party president would hand over the presidency to a Peronist, and the resulting expectations tinged both the political and economic state of affairs. In a statement that echoed Pugliese, Treasury Secretary Mario Brodersohn noted how the upcoming inauguration was affecting the forex market:

> There is a political reality here: in a nutshell, Argentina is not accustomed to the election process and so ludicrous rumors start circulating: that we're not going to pay bond holders, that we're going to declare a debt moratorium, and twenty thousand other arguments of the sort. This affects the credibility and the trust of the economic team. (*Ámbito Financiero*, March 10, 1989)

With elections two weeks away, the government announced yet another foreign exchange holiday: it was the lead-up to a unified exchange rate and an end to forex market restrictions. Under the new system, the dollar reached ARA 118, while interest rates climbed to a monthly rate of 160 percent. On Sunday, May 14, the opposition's candidate, Peronist Carlos Menem, won the elections. On Friday, May 19, the dollar hit ARA 210. In a little over four months, it had skyrocketed nearly 1,000 percent—and the run was far from over. Between February and August, the rise would reach 3,600 percent. The monthly inflation during the final months in office for Alfonsín—who resigned in July, five months before he was scheduled to leave office—was also astronomical (78.5 percent in May, 115 percent in June, and 197 percent in July). This was a period of hyperinflation that reached a 4,924 percent rise in consumer prices during 1989.

## Dollarization Runs Amok

While the tablita and the Martínez de Hoz economic policy had often been invoked when discussing the final stage of the Spring Plan, the rodrigazo was the touchstone when it came to the last months of the Alfonsín administration. A few weeks before he resigned, Minister Pugliese took it upon himself to clarify, "This is no rodrigazo" (*Clarín*, May 20, 1989). Again, graphic humor helped people understand the social and cultural shifts in the uses and meanings of the dollar over the course of 1989 that enabled this comparison.

In one cartoon, two important-looking men dressed in suits chat over drinks, probably whiskey: "Accountant, I have come around to the idea that there is a secret, profound, ancestral Argentina . . . I have heard, for example, that for certain commercial transactions, the custom of using the 'austral' still persists" (*Clarín*,

May 21, 1989). In another, a man is reading what appears to be a report while another man with a stack of files, apparently his secretary, says, "No matter what they say, I think the economy is less dollarized than ever. Two weeks ago, people were complaining about the price of the dollar. Now they're complaining they don't have an austral to their name" (*Clarín*, April 30, 1989).

Published in *Clarín*, the two cartoons offer a parody on how the uses of the dollar had expanded in unprecedented ways. Another way of analyzing the dollar's popularization is to assess the meaning of the term "dollarization" during this same period. In the past, it had been a term reserved for economists; now cartoon artists were also employing it. Comic strips and cartoons thus succinctly captured the rising drama and tension caused by the expanded uses and meanings of the dollar, in economic transactions and in personal and family life.

At the beginning of May 1989, shops across the city of Buenos Aires posted signs with messages of this sort: "Closed. We don't know the prices of the merchandise and we are too ashamed to sell. Please forgive us. Thank you." "We don't have prices" was an oft-heard phrase among businesspeople at this time. Shopkeepers would often empty shelves with the excuse of doing inventory. Given the state of affairs, consumers had to reorganize their purchase strategies based on a difficult reality characterized by missing products and totally unpredictable prices. A pioneering sociological work on Argentine inflation provides insight into the consumer practices in the households of different social classes in the tense second half of 1989:

> Before you buy, you need to walk around and compare: milk is cheaper here, eggs are cheaper there. You need to go into a shop and jot down prices, then to another ... I miss the days when I could go to the market and buy everything in the same place.
>
> When I go out shopping, I never know what I'll find. I don't make a shopping list. Instead, I see how much each product costs and only then do I think about what I'll eat that day. (Sigal and Kessler 1997)

The risk of shortages was old hat for Argentine society. The fact that the national currency had ceased to function as a unit of account and payment method, however, was novel; the austral had been increasingly replaced by the dollar, a currency whose value changed not just once a day but several times a day, even within a single hour.

Food industry reps warned that suppliers had begun charging for their products in dollars. At the end of April, an executive from a supermarket chain confirmed fears of widespread shortages: "A dollarization of the economy is underway ... Deliveries have been suspended" (April 28, 1989). A few days later, the president of the Argentine Chamber of Commerce admitted that members were drafting price lists in dollars. The Argentine Industrial Council (CAI) filed a report with the secretary of domestic commerce on sale terms specifying payment in dollars. The official's response was to send in a government team to oversee the running of the council, given that legislation prohibited vendors from soliciting payments in dollars. "There is no more credit. Merchandise must be paid in cash upon delivery and there are several product categories listing their prices in dollars," reported Federation of Commerce reps to *Clarín*. "The prices of electric light bulbs and fluorescent tubes have already been dollarized," said a representative from the Association of Hardware and Paint Stores.

This went far beyond the markets that had dealt in dollars in recent years, like real estate, cars, and art. In 1989, as inflation reached unprecedented of levels, the types of goods listed and sold in dollars included chemical products, raw materials for the food industry, plastics, vehicle parts, paper, ink, guitars, and photography supplies. Even services like plumbing (US$30 for works that required welding) and therapy (US$50 for a session of psychoanalysis) had been dollarized.

While the use of the dollar was controversial for many, some actors pushed to legalize it. Opposition members like liberal legislator José Ibarbia of the Unión de Centro Democrático (UCD) party drafted a bill that, if enacted, would allow farmers to use dollars for their transactions. The new law, according to its author, "would simply acknowledge the way things are. Today farmers pay for their supplies, seeds, and agrochemicals in dollars, and increasingly list prices for different products in U.S. dollars. Anyone knows that a ton of sunflower seed goes for US$125; a ton of corn, US$65; a ton of soybean, US$155" (*La Nación*, May 3, 1989). Yet support for these dollarization initiatives was limited among orthodox economists and well-known supporters of economic liberalism as well.

Purchase and sale transactions could be dollarized in several different ways. The most common was to use the US currency as a unit of account (to set prices) and the austral as a payment method. In order to avoid the fluctuations of the exchange rate over a single day—and potentially drastic changes from one day to the next—payments were made in dollars and in cash, though the paperwork (purchase orders, invoices, waybills) was denominated in australs in keeping with the law. In some cases, flying in the face of the law, the entire transaction was done in dollars—including all the paperwork. Financial publications like *Ámbito Financiero* ran opinion columns by attorneys who provided expert opinions on the legal aspects of transactions in dollars. Some argued that "invoicing in dollars" was legal under Argentine legislation, provided the parties clarified the type of exchange rate that applied to the transactions.

The dollar was also used when discussing any rise in prices that varied with the exchange rate. Despite its daily fluctuations, the cost of the US dollar was the benchmark for a range of everyday economic decisions. *Clarín*, for example, reported to its readers on the "Dollarization of meat," an article explaining that "in a dollarized economy, just about everything is affected. The devaluation of the austral over the weekend has impacted the cost of all goods, meat included" (*Clarín*, May 3, 1989). In the media, the term "violent dollarization" was used to refer to the drop in real salaries and the accompanying loss of purchasing power. For this reason, a "worker who is earning a [monthly] salary equivalent to US$50 is accustomed to checking the forex boards outside exchange offices to see how much he'll be shelling out for deodorant, a razor blade, a can of tomatoes, or any beef cut" (*Clarín*, May 3, 1989).

Unlike what had occurred during the rodrigazo, when the Argentine peso suffered a 100 percent devaluation overnight, the cost of the dollar rose day after day, week after week, during the hyperinflation of 1989. For that reason, a frequent practice among sales chain actors was to calculate the replacement cost by taking a guess at the dollar's future value. This *sobredolarización* (over-dollarization), to use the term coined by one analyst, consisted in hiking the price of raw materials even higher than the dollar based on the very real possibility of shortages.

While retailers could resort to this strategy to protect themselves from the reigning uncertainty of hyperinflation, the sectors hardest hit by the prices and shortages resorted to looting shops and supermarkets. At the end of May and beginning of June 1989, this was a strategy for survival among inhabitants of poor neighborhoods and slums along the outskirts of Argentina's biggest cities like Buenos Aires, Mendoza, Córdoba, and Rosario. They would storm supermarkets and local shops and make off with food, household staples, and other merchandise (Auyero 2007; Dalla Corte-Caballero 2014; Serulnikov 2017).

## Dollarized Markets during Hyperinflation

Dollarized markets were not immune to the austral's phenomenal devaluation. On the real estate market, where the dollar had been the reference currency for over a decade, there was "concern" regarding the measures introduced the first week of that month that had led to the devaluation. According to a vituperative document released by Argentina's Real Estate Federation (FIRA), "modifications to the exchange rate regime" had caused "discontent and uncertainty" given that "almost all properties in Buenos Aires, and in a great part of the interior, have been denominated in U.S dollars for some time." The text warned that while in the past, "this was an attempt to protect property value against inflation . . . it becomes a negative and distorted practice in the face of devaluations." Emphasizing the sector's discontent, the authors argued that "it is unreasonable for a property to rise 40% in value from a Sunday to a Monday," since in this case, "the cost of properties would no longer be aligned with market prices, making a sale impossible." As a result, FIRA noted that "the price of properties denominated in dollars must be reduced (provided they continue to be denominated in the foreign currency) in order to keep prices at levels that match demand." In conclusion, "merely stating the price of a property in dollars does not suffice to 'protect' its value." According to FIRA, the only way to avoid "impoverishment" was "to fight state deficit and privatize" (*Ámbito Financiero*, February 21, 1989).

According to the real estate sector, the state of affairs in 1989 was so unprecedented that it cast doubt on strategies used in the past to preserve the value of properties. As noted by the federations, stating prices in dollars—and paying in dollars—was not enough to prevent financial losses. However, unlike in 1981, when some had wondered whether it would be better to again denominate property prices in the country's own currency, any suggestion of the sort would have been preposterous during the months of hyperinflation. In April 1989, the secretary of commerce published a resolution on "price advertisements and signs," reminding vendors that, in keeping with the 1984 legislation, the price of all goods and services must be stated in "the legal currency of Argentina" (Resolution 51/89, April 3, 1989). Argentina's Real Estate Chamber immediately requested an exception, arguing that "the offer in australs of properties will prevent virtually any sale and bring an unprecedented level of legal uncertainty." The position taken by the business chamber was echoed in newspapers like *Ámbito Financiero*. One column, for example, stated that "obliging advertisers to work with a currency whose value changes by up to 20% in a single day is unrealistic, because reality cannot be modified by decree." The same column analyzed the legal validity of a growing practice on the 1989 real estate market: rental prices stated in dollars (*Ámbito Financiero*, April 1989).

In May, just days before the presidential election, the issue of the dollar reached the world of Argentine soccer. As the currency of choice to denominate player salaries, signing-on and transfer fees, and bonuses since the beginning of the decade, the US dollar had risen more than 200 percent so far that year. Although the signing-on fees stated in foreign currency had dropped for new players, the possibility of clubs reconsidering the dollar amounts for existing players set off a conflict. Clubs unable or unwilling to meet their financial obligations saw players move abroad for more lucrative opportunities. Talleres, a popular Córdoba team, had to let two players go when it became unable to pay a signing-on fee stated in dollars to one and a debt for transfer fees to another. Treasurers from institutions that were part of the Argentine Soccer Association (AFA) formed a commission to address the issue. The alternative they proposed was to set a special exchange rate for player contracts, the "soccer dollar," of around ARA 50.

Ricardo Bochini, a star midfielder, issued a statement against the soccer dollar: "When I signed my contract, it was in dollars. So I want to be paid as agreed, in dollars." While most players agreed with him, a few, like José Batista, were more understanding. "I understand that the dollar has gone through the roof and in my opinion, we can't ask the club to pay our contracts at the real value of the dollar . . .

I'm willing to negotiate. I just hope they pay me at least 50% higher than the market value" (*Clarín*, May 10, 1989).

Many team executives understood that existing agreements favoring players had to be respected. Others asked players to be understanding, noting the need to set a reasonable exchange rate for the dollar to avoid financial troubles for sporting institutions. Others, in a forward-looking approach, suggested laying out a new way of agreeing on player fees, abandoning the dollar and instead using an indexing mechanism that considered the cost of living and the price of game tickets.

## Social Humor and the Dollar

In March 1989, a print ad for the nursery Alparamis, which had recently opened a new branch in the posh Buenos Aires suburb of Olivos, featured an image of a dollar bill and the following caption: "Green won't make you happy. But it calms the nerves." It was a joke readers would appreciate, where green was both a colloquial way of referring to the dollar (*el verde*) but also to plants: "Those with green know nothing else compares: the whole world yearns for the haven it offers. In short, it makes life easier and surer." The description, an obvious nod toward the dollar, was also a seductive argument to draw new customers into its recently opened nursery, a "paradise for all those who love green."

At around the same time, an advertisement by Equitel S.A. also invoked the dollar to promote its services: "Everyone talks about the dollar. We get down to work! Exceeding expectations is how we define success. We concentrate on moving our business forward, producing state-of-the-art technology and taking our work seriously. We have the long term in mind—no speculating there." Paradoxically, the products the company offered, like its services for the state telephone company Entel, were stated in dollars.

Both advertisements revealed a shift in the dollar's public meaning. In previous decades, when advertisements had also featured references to the US dollar, the focus was on profitability or favorable interest rates; now, the dollar appeared to capture ideas relating to society as a whole. Either because "everyone yearns for" it, or because "everyone talks about it," the greenback was a way to express individual moods and/or collective attitudes in 1989. The economic side of the dollar goes unmentioned in these ads. Its advertising potential went beyond its usefulness for saving, investing, or calculating the prices of different goods: now it was a vehicle for social humor. In the context of hyperinflation, advertisers used the US dollar in both a positive and negative light. On the one hand, this meant emphasizing the happiness associated with a currency that would not lose its value; on the other, there was the speculation associated with it.

Advertising captured the spillover of the dollar's popularization, which had clearly exceeded its overt political meaning and its role in financial repertoires by 1989. As part of this process, interpretations of the dollar's connotations and uses were subject to a new psychological reading. In the past, psychological readings of the dollar had been almost exclusively tied to what was happening on the foreign exchange market. The stories related to "stress" or "nerves" associated with purchasing foreign currency on the streets of "la City" now dated back decades. Yet in 1989, the dollar had found its way into the day-to-day, personal sphere.

In a *Clarín* cartoon, a psychoanalyst poses a question to a patient during a session: "What is your existential doubt?" From the divan, the patient responds unequivocally, "Dollar or CD" (June 1989). Around the same time, a comic strip homed in on the "obsession" for the dollar in the following dialogue between an older man and younger woman: "Let me assure you that I have no recollection of a time when people were so obsessed with the economy," she says. "How old are you, Marisa?" When she responds "twenty-five," he quips, "How many of those years were in dollars?" (*Clarín*, c. June 18, 1989). This graphic humor revealed how Argentines had come to rely on the dollar, a frequent source of frustration. In an interview, a journalist asks, "As a sociologist, how do you explain this dependence on the economy, this need to constantly keep up on interest rates and the dollar?" The answer: "It's perpetual frustration: every Argentine sees himself as a potential millionaire" (*Clarín*, April 1989).

As part of the economic and social crisis that was unfolding, the dollar was also associated with the way Argentine families experienced the economic tremors:

"I was lucky today. And let me tell you, I never thought it would happen. But of course, it was always a possibility. In fact, I had a hunch this morning, right when the banks opened, when I was in the car and they had announced the dollar had jumped . . . "

"Listen, Alfredo, this may not be the right time, but I . . . "

"Let me finish. I was so excited that I turned off the radio. It was like I wanted to keep the exchange rate from changing."

"Let me say something, Alfredo. Let me get a word in. We're through."

"And overnight, I made twenty thousand australs! When you know what you're doing, it makes all the difference. Just like I told you! What was it you wanted to say?"

For the *Clarín* journalist who replicated the dialogue, the scene could have taken place at a café in "la City" or virtually anywhere: on a square, in a greasy spoon in the suburbs. The topic could be a couple breaking up, children, health. The lack of dialogue sabotages communication, argued the journalist, when a party to the conversation always thinks and says the same things. The couple's inability to hear one another because Alfredo is so worried about his dollar transaction is depicted as something that "happens to all of us." The photograph accompanying the article was the now typical image of a group of people studying the board outside an exchange office in "la City." The question in the picture caption, however, was novel: "As these citizens contemplate a board in la City, what might they be discussing? Poetry? The latest Woody Allen film? Love? Racing Soccer Club? Problems in China? None of these things, right? We're all in the same boat." The focus was now on the psychological effects of the dollar and its impact on personal lives.

The intensity of the dollar's popularization at this time brought new kinds of experts to weigh in on the ungovernable foreign exchange market. In 1989, psychoanalysts, psychiatrists, and even sex therapists chimed in, building new meanings around the dollar and its influence on subjective experiences. *Clarín* provided a summary of these professional opinions in an article entitled "The crisis is a killer" on the emotional disorders associated with the economic crisis. Combined with inflation, the *dolarazo* (dollar spike) was identified as a cause of "anxiety, psychological issues, and even sexual problems." Once again, the article included a photograph of a crowd outside a forex office. The caption read: "'For the past two months, it's been one calamity after another. This is hell: anyone who isn't sick yet is about to be,' say people on the verge of a nervous breakdown in 'la City.'" "Dollar fever" was presented as one of the "vital elements" of every conversation; the "greenback's fluctuations" led to "unhealthy" obsessions. In order to explore the psychological repercussions of topics like these—topics that captured "the attention of all Argentines"—journalism needed the opinion of experts from the world of psychology and psychiatry, two fields that had been flourishing in recent decades (*Clarín*, April 15, 1989).

Guillermo Rinaldi, a member of the Argentine Association of Psychoanalysis, offered his thoughts on how the "ups and downs of an unstable economy" contributed to the "onset of emotional disorders." "People put their energy into something superfluous" and "are disorganized and unable to concentrate due to exhaustion and mental fatigue." After sharing the psychoanalyst's opinion, the journalist offers an example: the crowds glued to the boards of "la City" for three or four hours at a time—as if it were a site of worship whose faithful engage in terse dialogues: "Did you see? It's going down. Down, down, way down. I told you. I'm never listening to your advice again" (*Clarín*, April 15, 1989).

León Gindin, a sex therapist and director of the Center for Sex Education, Therapy, and Research, told *Clarín* that he had seen an uptick in the number of financial workers seeking help. "Sexual dysfunction and a lack of desire" were what motivated them to come in, Gindin explained. "Having sex doesn't even cross their minds. It may sound strange, but they swear off sex in order to dedicate more energy to their work." In order to illustrate how these workers had been affected "by the pressure of the crisis," and "sacrificed their sex drive for it," the sex therapist describes a typical day of a forex office worker.

On Thursday, explains the patient, the day started out with the dollar at ARA 55 and annual interest rates at 100 percent. The day ended with the dollar at ARA 50 and interest rates somewhere between 350 percent and 370 percent. Plus, a client who used to call in for advice once a day was now calling in five times a day to ask the same question. The adrenaline can work for or against you, depending on the accuracy of the answers. There is a point where you do not even believe what you are saying.

According to the sex therapist, "once the worker is suffering from the dysfunction, success or failure on the job is no longer relevant, and his or her partner also begins to have symptoms. It's 'contagious'" (*Clarín*, April 15, 1989).

While the end of the 1980s brought the collapse of the Berlin Wall and a profound crisis of the Socialist Bloc, neoliberalism—especially the reforms introduced by the conservative governments of the United States and the United Kingdom—was being consolidated in the Western hemisphere. In Latin America, however, things had unfolded differently that decade. At the political level, a great number of countries governed by dictatorships had successfully returned to democratic rule. Economically, however, many had succumbed to instability, with unprecedented levels of inflation and even bouts of hyperinflation that wreaked social havoc. Countries like Argentina, Venezuela, Peru, Bolivia, and Brazil all suffered extreme devaluations of their national currencies and tense relations between society and state. This left states weak and fostered extreme levels of social violence, as seen in the lootings that took place in the second quarter of 1989 in Argentina.

Any assessment of the expansion and growing intensity of the dollar's popularization during the final stages of Argentina's first democratic regime must consider this economic havoc, especially the hyperinflation of 1989. The US dollar played a key role in public life and in private life as well. It affected politics and economics at its most basic level: daily transactions. It left Argentines sleepless and even sapped their sex drive. As never before—and, it would turn out, never again—the popularization of the dollar had become a "total social fact." This was the term coined by French sociologist Marcel Mauss to discuss extraordinary social phenomena, ones in which every aspect of collective life converged (Mauss 1967). During 1989, the popularization of the dollar reigned supreme in Argentina.

This chapter covered the third stage of the dollar's popularization in Argentina, the enormous crisis in which the economic uses of the dollar proliferated like never before, and the expanded public presence of the US currency from casual conversations on the streets to confessions from the divan. As in the prior stages, it was a piece of information everyone had to have, and its importance in the local economy expanded in step with deteriorating macroeconomic conditions. Yet it also experienced autonomous growth associated with its clear position in the financial repertoires of large swaths of the population. There were two important innovations during this phase: the first was the widespread use of the dollar in daily transactions, even those involving basic consumer goods. The second was not economic—despite hyperinflation—but political. For the first time in nearly forty years, there would be a democratic changing of the guard in 1989. Argentines were voting in a new presidential election, and the uncertainties surrounding the process could be seen not only in opinion surveys but also up on the currency exchange boards. In 1989, the forex market had emerged as another arena for national politics. As we shall see in the following chapters, this will later become one of the most salient traits of democratic life in Argentina.

*Chapter Five*

# LEGAL TENDER

# A NEOLIBERAL EXPERIMENT IN DOLLARS

# (1991–2002)

> Late in the city, dollars
> People coming and going, dollars
> I bought them at 7,000, dollars
> Because they were about to go up . . .
> And since I was never a fool, dollars,
> I said: it's going up to 15,000!, dollars
> When I purchased in February, dollars
> Oh, Lord, what a fool . . . [1]

The late show *Tato, la leyenda continúa* launched a new program season in May 1991 with this song. Along with the traditional stand-up routine by the show's celebrated host, Tato Bores, it also featured song-and-dance numbers in which the comedian poked fun at the state of affairs. The year had started with an extraordinary run on foreign currency and the lyrics echoed the word on everyone's lips: dollars.

When Raúl Alfonsín left office early and Carlos Menem took over as president,[2] the country was still wallowing in an economic crisis characterized by hyperinflation. During the first two years of the Menem administration, there would be two spikes in inflation that, though lower than the hyperinflation of 1989 (2,314 percent in 1990), were equally dire (Bulmer Thomas 1994). This was the political and economic backdrop to the ongoing popularization of the US dollar, which continued to occupy the daily lives of Argentines in myriad ways. There was the information on the forex market and the increasingly varied clientele shopping for dollars; its role as a currency, used as payment for certain goods; and finally, its mention in small talk and jokes, or as a source of concern. These growing references to the dollar led certain journalists at the beginning of 1991 to report on a "culture of the dollar" that, in their telling, had originated to the 1970s. As an article in *Clarín* noted, the dollar had "branded the economy" since that decade, eliciting "ceaseless devotion" among Argentines, as seen in the dollarization of prices—from wholesale goods to therapy sessions—and the proliferation of amateur forex trade, even children's savings. In the view of the journalist and certain sources cited by the paper, "an erratic, unpredictable economy" was not enough to explain a phenomenon that would require "psychological insight" to understand (*Clarín*, February 17, 1991). For that reason, when Economic Minister Domingo Cavallo began putting together a plan to peg Argentina's currency to the US dollar in 1991, experts cited in the press and columnists alike concurred that it was a strategy that meant "accepting the reality of daily life."

In a book that reconstructs the introduction of the dollar peg, French-Argentine sociologist Alexandre Roig (Roig 2016) shows how the government attempted to end the inflation that had plagued the Argentine economy for decades. Drawing on interviews with those directly involved in this plan (Domingo Cavallo, Horacio Liendo, and Juan Carlos Llach), the author analyzes the drafting of the Convertibility Act, the system of monetary regulations that would become popularly known as the *uno a uno* (one to one).[3]

A full dollarization of the economy would have meant replacing the national currency for the US dollar entirely. Under Cavallo's plan, the dollar became legal tender, and the printing of pesos was limited to the amount of the reserves held in the Central Bank.[4] In this regard, some came out against the new policy, considering it an affront to national sovereignty. The men putting the convertibility together defended their plan, arguing that "the dollar is already in people's heads" (*La Nación*, March 31, 1991; Roig 2016), a thought echoed by the experts and by other voices in the media.

This chapter describes the evolution of the dollar's popularization in Argentine society, starting with the convertibility enacted in 1991. It discusses the intent of the law to "domesticate" the existing monetary culture by changing the rules, leading to innovations in terms of the ubiquity of the US currency but also its daily uses and meanings. For a time, having a stable currency reduced people's focus on the fluctuations of the exchange market, yet the peg also expanded the dollar's prevalence within the financial repertoires of the Argentines. The profound economic, political, and social crisis of 2001 marked the end of the pegged exchange rate and brought the dollar back into the spotlight, as preoccupying as ever before. Yet this was not a mere winding back of the clock; the ten years of currency stability and a fixed exchange rate had transformed Argentines' relationship to the dollar beyond the "one to one."

Legal Tender

## "If People Prefer Dollars instead of Australs, Dollars It Is"

In March 1991, a month after being sworn in as minister of economy, Domingo Cavallo had put together the master plan that Congress would pass as the Currency Board Act. In a new edition of the *Clarín* comic strip "De la crónica diaria" (From the daily chronicle) entitled "The expert," a lion in the jungle asks a tiger, "What was the dollar going for at day's end?" Gesturing toward an approaching kangaroo, the tiger replies: "I'm not sure . . . But the guy back there with the *bolsa* should know!"[5] (*Clarín*, March 1991). The humor echoes that of a cartoon published around the same time in *La Nación* under the title "A critical topic." The setting here is not the jungle but a family home where an astonished father looks up from the paper as his young son asks, "Daddy . . . how much did the dollar close?" From allegorical to "realistic" representations, Argentines' concern with the exchange rate permeated all levels of society. Interestingly, as the second cartoon shows, even children are interested in currency and capable of learning about it on their own, hinting at a generation that receives an early "education" in economy.

The fixation of these fictional characters is no exaggeration. Two months before Cavallo introduced his economic plan, the dollar had jumped from ARA 5,800 to ARA 9,800. Following this run, the minister of economy and the head of the Central Bank had resigned. After keeping the forex market and banks closed for two days, a new economic team took office on January 31. The next day, the new exchange rates made the cover of *La Nación*. Newspapers had modernized their designs: the traditional exchange rate tables dating back to the 1950s had been substituted by an eye-appealing infographic. The information in the paper now exceeded the exchange rate at closing time and instead charted it at half-hour intervals over the course of the business day. Asking about the dollar close at the end of trading—and trying to guess what it would happen the following business day—had become as common as discussing the weather.

The paper's readers recalled the worst moments of hyperinflation of 1989 and 1990; many believed the sudden rise in the cost of the dollar could portend a new crisis and thus considered it important to stay up on the exchange rate. Yet there were other more practical reasons to check the boards daily. Hyperinflation had not only left Argentines with traumatic memories: it had transformed their everyday economic practices, including the habit of stating prices of both domestically produced and imported goods in dollars.

On the Larrea Street between Viamonte and Tucumán, in the heart of the Buenos Aires wholesale district, a meter of fleece cost US$8.50. A cotton-polyester blend went for US$10.50, while children's shirts and pants (wholesale) cost less than US$5. Color televisions, VCRs, refrigerators, and microwaves could be purchased at the city's major home appliance stores in six installments in dollars. A gas-powered lawnmower cost US$365, while guns sold at a traditional hunting and fishing store downtown were on sale in three monthly installments of between US$69 and US$89, depending on the model. The prices of many services were also in dollars; a company that needed to rent a switchboard could do so for US$19 (or its equivalent in australs). Construction materials and home supplies like toilets, faucets, carpets, and furniture were also stated in dollars. The time when pricing in dollars was limited to apartments, vehicles, and trips abroad had passed. At the beginning of the 1990s, prices for an enormous variety of consumer goods and industrial supplies were stated in the US currency on both advertisements and in-store price tags. The exchange rate was thus a key piece of information when pushing the numbers on sales and purchases of all sorts.

Eduardo Bonelli, a well-known economic journalist with *La Nación*, conveyed this idea a few days after the law was passed: "This orthodox economic plan is conservative and rigorous, grounded in simple solutions: first, the state should not spend more than it collects and second, if people want to use dollars instead of australs, dollars it is" (*La Nación*, March 24, 1991). In other words, by allowing the dollar to circulate as a legal payment method for domestic transactions, the economic authorities—and Congress—were not encouraging new behaviors. They were merely providing legal recognition of "a practice common in our society," as noted in an editorial in the same paper (*La Nación*, March 24, 1991). The true innovation was that the most basic rules of economic administration had changed. First, the Convertibility Act limited the government's ability to print money, a prerogative of political power; second, it put an end to adjusting contract prices based on inflation.

The chapter of the law that applied to transactions between individuals in Argentina had only an indirect relationship to the dollar. When it was enacted, the public had another concern: the fact that price adjustment provisions would be eliminated. When the austral-dollar peg officially went into effect on April 1, 1991, newspaper covers made no mention of the dollar but instead focused on services. In articles and infographics, the paper informed readers of how the prices of apartment rentals, parking garage spaces, private school tuition, private medical insurance, mortgages, and saving circles—all previously subject to price adjustment provisions—would now be set. Even the business paper *Ámbito Financiero* forwent its usual coverage of "la City," focusing instead on people's concern that no rental properties were available, given that homeowners were unwilling to sign a contract without adjustment clauses.

In any case, there was no commotion whatsoever on San Martín Street, nor were people pushing to get a look at the boards of the forex offices. The week before the law went into effect, banks and foreign exchange offices operated normally. The implementation of the new plan generated none of the expectations that had accompanied economic measures in the past, when announcements were made only after imposing "holidays" for all financial activity. Now, if the economic team's calculations were correct, the value of the currency would no longer be tied to the volume of daily transactions on the forex market. In the weeks leading up to the enactment, that exchange rate had been holding steady (as part of the "forex rescue tubes" that Cavallo and the new Central Bank president Roque Fernández had introduced two months earlier), but now the law would provide an additional guarantee by fixing the exchange rate.

This set of measures to support convertibility, like other lofty plans of the past aimed at stabilizing the economy, represented a systematic response to a critical situation. In this case, a crisis that unfolded several months earlier and peaked in January, when the austral suffered a devaluation of over 40 percent, led to the law's implementation in April 1991. Yet by the time the dollar peg was introduced, the crisis no longer seemed particularly urgent; it comes as no surprise, then, that people's first response to the new measures focused on other variables, not the currency.

## Economic Narratives during the "One to One"

On January 16, 1991, the military coalition led by the United States and the United Kingdom bombed Iraq in retaliation for the Saddam Hussein regime's violent occupation of Kuwait. The conflict would evolve into the Gulf War. On the same day the bombs began falling, the Argentine Foreign Ministry under Domingo Cavallo announced it would not remain neutral in the Middle Eastern conflict. Two weeks after this announcement, Cavallo would leave the Foreign Ministry to take his post as minister of economy.

A few days into the war, newspaper covers began prioritizing the state of the local economy over what would become of Saddam Hussein. The cost of transportation was rising, public sector employees were being laid off, chambers representing farmers were saying they would refuse to pay taxes, and the cost of the dollar had skyrocketed. On January 29, the Gulf War did not even make the cover of *Clarín*, which instead headlined the resignation of Minister of Economy Erman González and the news that Foreign Minister Cavallo had been named to replace him. A photograph on the *Clarín* cover shows a tired-looking man staring at the board of a forex office; on the top line is the dollar exchange rate, ARA 8,450. To the left of the picture, the newspaper announces a mandatory two-day banking and forex "holiday." On January 31, the market was open for business again, and Cavallo had been sworn in as the new minister. Once again, the forex boards made the cover of *Clarín*: that day, the peso-dollar exchange rate hit 9,500 australs, and a picture showed two women of different ages, perhaps mother and daughter, staring at the board with furrowed brows.

Although it would not have been possible to imagine it at the time, many years would pass until the movements of the forex market would make headlines again. Over the course of thirty years, as part of other media transformations, the vicissitudes of the US dollar had been critical to the economic narrative of Argentine journalism. Once a key indicator, the exchange rate appeared in the familiar graphics associated with economic news (currency rate charts and, when relevant, graphs showing its fluctuations over time), though also in chronicles and photographs. Readers thus learned to associate these numbers with particular places (forex offices, trading desks, San Martín Street, and, more generally, "la City") and its emblematic characters (usual market operators as well as mere onlookers). This type of coverage was not daily but did have a certain regularity. It was employed—to use the phrase of one journalist in 1991—"in response to the slightest tremor of the sort that abound in our national economy" (*Clarín*, March 22, 1991).

In other words, educational reporting resumed whenever the press needed to make brusque market fluctuations comprehensible for a broad public. Photographs, a resource rarely used in economic reporting, had been an important component of journalistic coverage at these critical junctures for decades. The shots by newspaper photographers helped shape the storytelling of this financial world in which the greenback played a leading role. There were photographs of the boards advertising exchange rates; the counters and windows of forex offices, banks, and other financial institutions, and the crowds outside them; the curious "onlookers" on the streets of "la City"; and people's faces, denoting expectation, worry, or even desperation. Over time, some of these details—details that had originally served to inform on a set of practices, actors, and settings that once seemed foreign to the average reader—had faded. Therefore, when there was a run on the austral in January 1991, close-ups of the faces no longer seemed necessary, nor did mentions of the financial offices, or wide shots capturing the crowds on San Martín Street. Glancing at the photograph of the board with the numbers in two columns (the buy and sell price), readers instantly knew that this was an exchange office—and that the number was concerning for everyone. "The board" no longer merely described: it had become a symbol.

The intent to educate readers was a central component of this journalistic endeavor in which folksy chronicles and photographs return during times of crisis on the exchange market, and the economy in general. As noted in chapters 2 and 3, this educational style of reporting first appeared as a push to educate readers between the end of the 1960s and the beginning of the 1970s as part of a broader set of changes to the work of journalists and, more broadly, the print press. During this transition—one more evident in certain media outlets—modifying the tone and language of economic information had proven critical. In an interview, one career journalist specializing in economic news summarized this as follows:

Up until thirty or forty years ago, the economy section was written by economists. And you know who they were writing for? For themselves. They used the same terminology they had learned in college. In other words, they had no interest in people. So when I got asked to join the paper, the first thing the editor said to me was, "Listen: write for people. Forget about the journalists. Take what they tell you and make it understandable."

This role of the economic journalist as a translator of complex topics in the mass media—first in the print press, and later in radio and television—applied to more than just forex coverage. However, the tremors that affected that market proved the perfect opportunity for this type of informative reporting. During times of crisis, which were synonymous with devaluation for years, journalists and their ability to grasp the situation and interpret it for "the people" would be put to the test.

Starting in 1991, and for the ten years the dollar peg lasted, the fluctuations of the forex market ceased to be a priority for economic journalism. Nonetheless, economic journalists continued to make economic affairs intelligible and guide readers. The universe of finance was one of the areas where the reference to the dollar and its possible uses would continue playing a central, though not necessarily predominant, role. In any case, technical vocabulary and information persisted in coverage of the economy, even in general publications. As in the past, the national papers published lists of exchange rates, stock values, and indicators hard to comprehend for readers outside the world of business. Commentary by experts who used erudite language also persisted. Yet *La Nación*, *Clarín*, and *Ámbito Financiero* also presented economic information in a more reader-friendly way, employing plain language that clearly targeted readers outside the world of finance. Though not daily, this coverage was generally done on a weekly basis, and generally on weekends—or more frequently in times of crisis. In these columns, journalists worked to show readers the "behind the scenes" of the world of finance, providing detailed explanations on speculation or play-by-play breakdowns of how financial agents operated. At the beginning of 1991, this led them to switch the focus from the small world of investors to the Central Bank, "the mother of all trading desks" (*Clarín*, March 17, 1991).

One Sunday in March, *Clarín* reserved a double-page spread for the trading desk at the Central Bank, "where currency enters and exits without anyone seeing a single bill, and where up to two billion equally invisible australs are exchanged for treasury bonds." The article, which relied on two career bank employees as sources and was illustrated with photographs, drew attention to activities the public could not see; at the same time, it explained the specific practices behind that piece of information—the value of the dollar—that so captivated public opinion. In order to achieve this, it returned to typical elements of the chronicles of the San Martín Street universe: the description of settings, the presentation of characters, and accounts of usual scenes. Resources such as these allow the journalist to present the hazy financial world to readers with little understanding of the economy:

> He is wearing a classic gray suit, with a thin-striped shirt and matching tie. This gives office 308 on the fourth floor of the [Central Bank] building at Reconquista 266 an air of discretion, a nearly religious austerity. Even the most fanciful imaginations would find it hard to imagine that this is where government decisions to drive the dollar or interest rates up or down are made minute by minute. (*Clarín*, March 17, 1991)

For an understanding of this milieu, where millions change hands out of the public's eye, the reference to technology proved indispensable, as it had in the past when attempting to make sense of "the parallel." Readers of the article were informed that even at the Central Bank, a trading desk is

> just a room with six consoles covered with geometrically distributed red buttons. Starting at ten each morning, it is connected with the top fifty-five banks, fifteen exchange offices, and ten financial companies, all sites where the bills and coins that nourish the national economy (or let it go hungry) circulate. (*Clarín*, March 17, 1991)

In order to give readers an understanding of the modus operandi of Central Bank trading desk, *Clarín* offered an account of a feverish run. It was a day when the demand for dollars grew by the minute and monetary officials worked to rein it in without the exchange rate spiking or liquidating its reserves. At the time the article was published, the memory of the most recent run on the dollar was still fresh in people's minds. Just two months earlier, the government officials interviewed by *Clarín* had described being quick on their feet on that difficult day. In January, when the dollar hit ARA 8,300, one recalled,

> He [the Central Bank president] gave the order to sell US$50 million to bring it back down to AR$7,500. There were two directors and a high-ranking official with us, both desperate, and as the market begged for more, we hit the buttons to offer the 50 mil at AR$8,300. Not a single taker. We dropped to AR$8,200. Not a one. Evidently, talk of the rising austral was just that. Finally we sold them at AR$7,500 and we were done, as requested. When we turned around, the officials had left the room. Apparently, they couldn't take the heat. (*Clarín*, March 17, 1991)

In this chronicle, the newspaper no longer put a face to the speculators both small and large working to turn a profit in "la City": it set out instead to describe the day-to-day operations of the Central Bank and its attempts to control the financial market. Ironically, just two weeks after the article was published, a law would dictate the exchange rate, and the adrenaline of these financial maneuverings would become just a memory for Central Bank employees.

## Romancing the Markets

In the 1980s, a series of commercials for cream cheese instilled a new catchphrase in Argentines' unique rendition of the Spanish language. In all the ads, two women are doing housework (hanging up clothes, giving the kids a bath) while one shares with the other a new recipe that includes the product. All the ads end with the same exclamation; after hearing her friend's new recipe, the second woman turns to the camera with an envious look on her face and wonders, "*Cómo no se me ocurrió!*" (How come I didn't think of that?) In April 1991, *Ámbito Financiero* published a cartoon that accurately captured the reaction to the dollar peg among economists. The catchphrase from the commercial would appear here as well, only this time, the envious ones were economic experts from years past. Ministers and secretaries of economy from the past three decades, the former president of the Central Bank, and even former president Raúl Alfonsín are posing for a group picture in the cartoon. Together they exclaim, "How come I didn't think of that?"

Though it was too early for any conclusions on convertibility, the administration had convinced Congress to make it law, and "the markets" had reacted positively. These were two signs of a lull that had none of the government officials captured in the cartoon—or even Cavallo, at least to date—had ever enjoyed. In February 1991, *La Nación* reported on the "cautious market reaction" to the shake-up at the Ministry of Economy (*La Nación*, February 5, 1991), while *Ámbito Financiero* noted that "the markets suspect the plan lacks fiscal efficiency." For that reason, when that same paper ran a story entitled "The market believes in the new plan" on April 2, it was indeed possible to imagine the envy it could have sparked among officials of the past.

There was nothing new about the expectations surrounding the launch of an ambitious economic reform program, one involving an overhaul of the forex market and measures to control inflation. Since the announcements of President Arturo Frondizi's Stabilization Plan toward the end of 1958, every administration had anxiously awaited how its new economic plan would be received. Historically, press and experts alike had relied on two different indicators. The first was the reaction of different actors in the world of business and politics—business chambers, company executives, esteemed economists, leading figures of the ruling party and opposition, etc. The second was the dollar exchange rate, a benchmark for the success or failure of any new plan. For years, both of these indicators had been closely tied to one another, and a spike or drop in the demand for dollars led relatively identifiable figures (grain exporters, industrial importers, large public banks, "two-bit speculators," etc.) to act accordingly. By the beginning of the 1990s, however, this association was no longer possible. The entity that would now determine the success or failure of economic policy (e.g., "the markets") was much more otherworldly.

This growing reference to "the market" and the at times desperate need to gain its trust is one way of expressing how the relationship between politics and economics had been reconfigured in those years. As Argentine sociologist Mariana Heredia revealed in her book on the growing power of economists in Argentine politics (2014), since inflation became Argentina's albatross in the 1970s, economics has been increasingly seen as separate from politics. Something similar can be said of the growing division between the expanding universe of experts—considered, over time, the only worthy sources of opinions in economic affairs—and the lay world, which encompasses both average citizens and professional politicians. This building of a domain among economists and their triumph over politics is the result of a lengthy and gradual process worldwide (Fourcade 2010; Dezalay and Garth 2010). In the case of Argentina, however, it would reach its peak during the years of the dollar peg.

The relationship between Minister Cavallo and President Menem is indicative of this process. During the final months of the 1995 campaign for reelection, the president, who was comfortably ahead in the polls, quipped to the minister: "I promised you four years of politics at the service of the economy; now all I ask of you is one month of the economy at the service of politics" (*Ámbito Financiero*, April 17, 1995). When Menem came out victorious in the first round of the May 1995 election, political analysts across the board cited the importance of convertibility. Menem's own party had incorporated it into the campaign: while in 1989, one of the future president's promises had been a "revolution in production," the posters hung across the capital city to celebrate his reelection read, "We voted for stability once again."

## From the Mattress to the Teller Window

> When my father died three years back, he left us US$120,000 in savings, the hardware store, and our house. My mother got half the money and Mariano and I split the remaining US$60,000. We sold the house in Wilde[6] and used the money to buy three apartments downtown, one for each of us. We rented the hardware store to some people

from the interior who were gradually expanding their business toward the capital.

Mariano worked to multiply his share of the inheritance, wagering on speculation and reinvestment. He bought and sold shares, land, bonds, licenses for foreign companies. He partnered with a few others and opened up a restaurant downtown.

My mom had invested half of her money in peer-to-peer mortgage loans and she earned monthly interest on that. Plus, she got the monthly rent on the hardware store and owns her apartment.

In my case, I'm just sitting back and watching my US$30,000 disappear. I study law and I don't have a job. I opened a bank account and I like to watch my money gradually running out, day after day, unable to do anything about it. (Rejtman 1996, 75)

In this excerpt from a story by Argentine writer and filmmaker Martín Rejtman (1996), the detailed description of a father's inheritance shines a light on a repertoire of monetary and financial practices of a relatively prosperous urban middle-class family during the years of the dollar peg in Argentina. As in the story, savings and properties are stated in dollars, which is also the currency used for divvying up funds and calculating all related transactions (sales, purchases, rentals). For those "wagering on speculation and reinvestment," like the narrator's brother, myriad options are available: from shares in commercial enterprises to the purchase and sale of financial instruments like stocks or bonds. Those with less investment savvy—and less interest in profits—are not entirely absent from the financial system, however. The bank accounts of families and individuals are part of a landscape largely presented as run-of-the-mill among middle-class urban sectors and involving older, more informal types of financial intermediation, like peer-to-peer mortgages signed in the presence of notaries.

The dollar peg and its conditions contributed to shaping this financial repertoire. While the real estate market had been dealing in dollars for over a decade, the launch of a new forex regimen had reactivated the sector, especially by enabling mortgage loans in dollars. Similarly, the combination of exchange rate stability and financial system reforms had brought Argentine money back into the banks and fostered a more diverse offering of credit, including personal loans (in pesos and dollars), car loans, and mortgages with longer terms (in dollars).

After two decades of high inflation, the return to bank financing in the 1990s was a cause for celebration. One day after the dollar peg was implemented, long lines crisscrossed the hall of the *Caja Nacional de Ahorro*'s main office in Buenos Aires. These potential customers were eager to learn about the new loans denominated in dollars; private banks would soon be offering the same. The dollarization of bank deposits and loans proved key to the rebuilding of the financial system after hyperinflation and its progressive expansion over the following decade. In November 1989, just months after Carlos Menem had taken office, Congress passed a law allowing both sight deposits and certificates of deposit in foreign currency. Banks could use these deposits to offer loans in dollars to all Argentine residents. The law also established that deposits, loans, and all related interest would be returned or paid out in the same currency in which the account was denominated. This last clause eliminated any doubts about a possible mandatory conversion to pesos of the financial obligations. As a result of the new law and the stable exchange rate, dollar deposits represented 45 percent of all deposits in the system in 1994 (the rate was slightly higher in the case of CDs), while 55 percent of all bank loans were denominated in dollars. Over time, this trend expanded: by the end of 2000, foreign currency deposits would reach 56 percent of all deposits, while bank loans in dollars would be even higher (64 percent of the total) (Luzzi 2012).

This relatively quick recovery of the financial system would suffer something akin to an earthquake in 1995. The first tremor came in 1994 when the US federal government under President Bill Clinton hiked interest rates, leading to a sudden and drastic drop in foreign investment in Argentina; until that year, capital from abroad had been one of the keys to the success of convertibility. Second, toward the end of the year, the Mexican devaluation under President Eduardo Zedillo set off a capital flight that affected all the so-called developing countries, sparking a crisis across the region that would become known as the Tequila effect.

Published at the beginning of 1995 in *Clarín* was a comic featuring two women, both looking carefree, walking down a street. One says to the other, "During times of crisis, you can't rest on your laurels . . . " "What will you do, Clarita?" her friend asks, to which Clara replies, "Many are now resting on their dollars." This comic offered a humorous take on the initial aftereffects of the international crisis, which hit the banking system particularly hard. No further written descriptions or visual markers were needed for Argentines to read between the lines: people were putting their dollars beneath the mattress for safekeeping once again, and thus many "rested" on them. It was indicative of a trend that had captured the attention of the experts and become a prominent topic during the candidates' debates in the first months of 1995: the mass withdrawal of bank savings. Between December 1994 and May 1995 when Menem won reelection, bank deposits overall fell 19 percent, and dollar deposits dropped by 23 percent.

Thus, in 1995, a bank run made headline news once again, though with certain differences: the threat of devaluation did not translate into a spike in the demand for dollars that could push the peso's value higher. Instead, it resulted in mass bank withdrawals. Though different, this jeopardized the country's economy in a way similar to the runs on the national currency in the recent past. During the first months of the year, both public discussion and campaign debates were focused on the drop in deposits and subsequent decrease in Central Bank reserves. Though the situation was nowhere near as critical as it had been during hyperinflation, the crisis threatened the dollar peg and brought back memories of the late-1980s malaise. With elections around the corner, keeping the situation under control was a priority for the government. Cavallo responded with a series of measures that reduced public spending and established a new system for bank deposit guarantees to help stem the flow of bank withdrawals. The minister also approved an issue of a bond in dollars targeting local businesspeople to compensate for the drop in foreign investments. Finally, a new agreement with the International Monetary Fund helped the country emerge from the crisis.

The approval of the Deposits Guarantee Fund was announced a month before the elections, along with several measures aimed at buttressing the financial system, closing down financial entities with liquidity issues and allowing part of their customer portfolio and/or branches to be absorbed by "healthy" banks. The provinces were part of these efforts, privatizing ailing public banks in exchange for assistance to help them weather the crisis. The aim was not just to signal to savers that the system was reliable: it was about a profound restructuring of the financial system, though its main effect would be fewer—and increasingly foreign-owned—banks (Rozenwurcel, Bleger, and Kampel 1997). In fact, of the 168 banking institutions operating in Argentina as of December 1994, only 135 made it to August 1995. The difference can mainly be attributed to the number of cooperative banks, which went from thirty-eight to twelve in the same period; the majority were shut down or absorbed by larger entities. Similarly, private national banks went from sixty-six to fifty-nine. At the same time, in a context of growing capital mobility across the globe, the dollarization of deposits became a solid response to the crisis (Rozenwurcel, Bleger, and Kampel 1997).

Once again, comic strip artists captured the essence of the process underway. The same day the announcements were made, *Clarín* published a comic in which a caricatured Cavallo is smiling and waving as he announces, "Happy Easter: the banks are in order." The one-liner brought back memories of Easter week 1987 when the still fledgling democracy under President Raúl Alfonsín faced a military uprising that threatened to topple the government. Argentina was on tenterhooks until the president appeared on the balcony of the Casa Rosada and pronounced, "Happy Easter. The house is in order."

The truth of the matter, however, was that the guarantee on bank deposits Cavallo had announced covered only a small portion of the money deposited in banks: up to AR$ or US$10,000 deposited in savings or checking accounts or ninety-day CDs, and up to US$ or AR$20,000 in certificates of deposit with longer terms. Though nominally deposits of this sort represented 80 percent of all bank accounts, less than 25 percent of the money in banks was actually covered. For the press, the crucial question about what to do with the money in banks represented the perfect opportunity for the kind of economic instruction they had been giving readers for three decades.

> "So if most of the deposits are not covered by the guarantee, it doesn't seem like this will do much to rebuild trust," I said.
> "No, you're missing the idea. Remember: if you split your deposits between several banks, you can multiply the guarantee, which can easily go up to fifty or a hundred thousand if you put it in for ninety days," Lucho replied. (*La Nación*, April 16, 1995)

In a return to the now classic form of fiction he had introduced in his fictitious *Diálogos en la City*, David Casas (writing under the pseudonym David Home) advised readers on how to make the most of the new guarantee a day before it entered into effect. The advice was echoed in another daily; less than a week later, a chronicle noted, "Small savers want to keep their money safe. Many with deposits of over AR$10,000 have divided them into several accounts in the names of friends and relatives to ensure all their funds are guaranteed" (*Clarín*, April 19, 1995).

However, not all journalists were of the same mind. In an opinion column in *Ámbito Financiero*, a well-known economist and financial advisor stood out from his colleagues when he noted, "The best guarantee of all is choosing the right bank for deposits, as opposed to splitting deposits in smaller banks or several banks, and ploys of the sort" (*Ámbito Financiero*, April 24, 1995). Even the magazine *Humor* made an effort to guide readers in a section called "The great economy coach" (a reference to a popular game where people played at coaching a major-league soccer team).

> If you've got savings, keep the cash or deposit them in the best banks. What matters right now is protecting your capital, not speculating with one percentage point more. Should you leave the money in pesos or exchange them for dollars? That is up to you. But you'll earn more interest on the peso and devaluation is highly unlikely. But if you can't trust the peso, exchange them for dollars. (*Humor*, March 1995)

During the lead-up to the elections, no candidate who hoped to have a chance at the polls dared to question the dollar peg. Yet besides the international crisis afflicting Argentina, there was uncertainty surrounding this presidential election—again, only the second of its kind since the end of the dictatorship—and the mass withdrawals of savings from banks had become a bellwether for this uncertainty. In the same way that at other times, the media homed in on the forex boards, the focus now was on the amount of deposits that banks had gained or lost during the past week. Since the dollar peg had stabilized Argentina's currency, bank deposits had become the litmus test for the economy. Hopes and fears, success and failure: all now depended on the observed (and imagined) behaviors of bank customers.

A new stage in the popularization of the dollar had begun, one in which questions and references to the greenback merged with the ever-increasing presence of families in the financial system. In the middle of the 1990s, the mention of banks no longer brought to mind companies and investors but instead "small savers" (i.e., individuals with accounts, credit cards, loans, or mutual funds). Economic analysts were catering to these bank customers, who were profiled in the media. In April 1995, for example, the *Clarín* Economy section ran a full-page article on the recently launched Deposits Guarantee Fund entitled "What did savers do?" In addition to photographs of the individuals cited in the article—a male retiree, a male administrative employee, a male hairdresser, a female yoga instructor, a female employee, and three people out of work—it described what each did with their deposits.

In an article on what motivated Argentine voters to reelect Menem, one daily described this as a move "from the mattress to the teller window" (*La Nación*, May 17, 1995). This metaphor on deposits returning to banks indicates the growing emphasis on the behaviors of less sophisticated bank customers, the people for whom banks represented no more than a place to keep household cash safe. At the same time, it puts these customers on par with other bank depositors, making the withdrawal of money from local banks synonymous with capital flight (especially to Uruguay, where tax regulations have traditionally been more relaxed than in Argentina).

The deposits the banking system recovered were in both pesos and dollars, reaffirming the connection between an expanded financial system and the dollarization of accounts and loans since the introduction of the dollar peg. Following the country's comeback from the "Tequila effect," Argentina's financial system would be characterized by three converging processes. First, new financial stability measures in the face of the crisis meant fewer banks (i.e., larger, private banks, the majority headquartered abroad). Second, these institutions continued a trend that began years earlier, expanding on the offer of products in dollars—especially loans—to the detriment of the peso. Finally, during the second half of the 1990s, many companies began paying employee salaries via direct deposits into banking accounts, bringing into the financial fold a set of households that had previously forgone banking or visited banks only occasionally.

## 1995: The Vote Installment (in Dollars)

The 1990s brought changes for those involved in foreign exchange as well. The dollar peg made certain types of existing businesses inviable, but other new ones surfaced to take their place. For example, some traditional forex offices became banks where customers could deposit their savings and access a wide range of financial services. For one businessman who spent a lifetime in foreign exchange, the 1990s was its own unique chapter in the history of this sector. In an interview at his company's headquarters, he remembered the variety of services they had incorporated during the 1990s after years of exclusively handling currency exchange. Most of the new customers were employees as well as other freelance and informal workers drawn to banks in the mid-1990s not by any special offers or advertisements but because of requirements by their employer or mutual fund. "Here we help retirees weather financial difficulties," he explained, pointing to a sign for loans.[7]

Besides these personal loans, purchasing on installments was a widespread practice during this period. At the end of 1995, for example, home appliance store Frávega promised "a color TV for every Argentine" to promote the financing it offered customers. By simply presenting a pay stub, an employee with at least one-year seniority could purchase a twenty-one-inch television with stereo sound in sixty "mini-installments" of US$26.90. In order to make the offer even more tantalizing, the first installment did not fall due until two months after the purchase. In a practice that had become common for home appliance stores, the Frávega ad did not bother clarifying the (lower) price of items if paid in full at purchase, as virtually everyone paid in installments. Shoppers could opt to pay in either dollars (up to sixty monthly installments) or pesos (only eighteen monthly installments). Nearly five years after its introduction, the dollar peg had fulfilled its objective of legalizing the dollar for Argentines. Not only were contracts drafted and paid in dollars, but also at least a portion of local consumer accounts were also denominated in US currency: prices, especially those of durable consumer goods, were stated in dollars. The same went for bank heists, other high-profile robberies, and investments both formal (regulated by the Central Bank) and informal.

> You know Father Casas? Yeah, that's the one, brother Fabián . . . Well, he's a fake. He says he sinned before he found Jesus: let me tell you, he's a swindler. He didn't find Jesus. He found the way to rip off the Evangelicals. The cop ratted him out because, turns out, some cops are straight shooters—when they're off the clock, that is. I don't know how Father Casas does it but he steals money from the Evangelists and deposits the dollars to earn interest with a notary public in Berazategui and in the real estate office of that Englishman, the one they beat up. (Fogwill 1998, 114)

In this Rodolfo Fogwill novel, two characters are planning how to blackmail a priest, Father Casas.[8] In those years, notary public offices often ran newspaper ads in major cities, either offering mortgage loans with approval in as little as forty-eight hours or attracting investors in "tier-1 mortgages" with "maximum security and a minimum of US$10,000." For several decades, these offices played a key role on a financial circuit that ran parallel to that of banks, where those who had properties to put down as collateral could get the cash they needed to finance a project or cover emergency expenses. In addition, these offices, often working directly with real estate agents, increasingly became a path to homeownership for Argentines who could not meet the bank requirements for a mortgage. On the financing side of these loans were individuals looking for an investment with higher returns than those offered by the banking system and a way to profit on their savings without any questions about the origins of their funds.

Besides the stability that characterized the financial landscape of the 1990s, it had also become highly diverse. Argentine families had gained access to a growing selection of short- and long-term bank loans, credit cards, and other lending options on the part of notary public offices, real estate companies, and even retail chains. Though their costs and conditions varied, these lending options had one thing in common: the vast majority were in dollars.

A few weeks before the presidential elections of 1995, a cartoon by artist and writer Roberto Fontanarrosa emphasized the financial system's outsized effect on politics and its connection to the spike in domestic consumption after hyperinflation. A speaker at a podium stands in the background of the cartoon. His hand held high and with a fiery look in his eyes, he calls out to an audience that the viewer does not see, "And our movement is guided and led by George Washington, whose image is as alive as ever!" In the foreground, a man explains, "It's the Debtors in Dollars Party." The fictional party name hints at a motivation for reelecting President Menem that many analysts echoed in 1995: people had voted according to their own economic interest—interest in dollars, that is. The "installment vote" overlooked any political or ideological consideration, especially if the voter owed money in dollars. Only a continuation of the dollar peg, currently inseparable from the administration that had created it, would allow them to pay back their loan in installments. The government's own party understood the importance of this thinking and turned it into a successful campaign argument. A memorable campaign ad looked back on Menem's achievements during his first term, writing them out in golden letters on black: "He's eliminated inflation. Brought back credit. And modernized the country. He did more than anyone. And he'll do even more."

It would take six years for the crisis to turn Fontanarrosa's cartoon into a reality, when those with debt in dollars became an organized group that took to the streets (Luzzi 2017). The group that worried over whether to leave its money in the banks in 1995 would later turn the label "savers" into a protest movement. Yet in the mid-1990s, the dollar peg had made one thing clear: while forex offices and trading desks had been the settings par excellence of financial life—and the dollar's popularization—in the 1980s, a decade later, the banks had replaced them. When street demonstrations of savers and debtors began in summer 2002 (Luzzi 2012; 2016), it was a corollary to a slow and gradual process that had begun years earlier.

## 2001: Trapped inside the Pen

The economic recovery that followed the Tequila effect was short-lived. The influx of foreign capital that nourished the dollar peg had ebbed; there were no more state-owned firms to privatize,[9] and Argentine exports did not suffice to maintain the trade balance. For the economic team, increasing Argentina's foreign debt proved the only way to sustain a system that had allowed them to nip inflation in the bud at the beginning of the decade. The years of economic growth came to a halt in 1998. The recession further deteriorated the living conditions of Argentina (after peaking during the 1995 crisis, unemployment had stabilized at around 14 percent of the economically active population[10]) and also impacted at the state level, as tax collection fell and foreign financial obligations increased (Schvarzer 2006).

The changing of the guard at the end of 1999 further exacerbated the problem. An obstinate defender of the dollar peg, President Fernando de la Rúa found his administration in a pinch just a year after taking office. Toward the end of 2000, the Radical party president addressed the nation:

> My dear Argentines: all our hard work this year paid off. I have announced an international *blindaje* (shield) that will minimize our risk and create an extraordinary platform for growth. It comes after a difficult year: difficult for you, as you've born a crisis that has not let up for nearly four years. But we're ending this year with a big success: the 2001 *blindaje*. This is what we were working on while some said we weren't doing a thing. . . . This represents a success for me, as president, and for all the people who will benefit, because this extraordinary economic transaction will allow us to grow by leaps and bounds and create the jobs we need. The *blindaje* is an unprecedented economic, political, and financial transaction that will create a guarantee fund for the country so large that any threat or doubt about the future of Argentina will dissipate. (*Clarín*, December 19, 2000)

The speech ended with a promise that 2001 "will be a great year for all." Yet before that year ended, de La Rúa would be forced to flee Casa Rosada, the presidential office, in a helicopter, as protests raged across the city.

What the president referred to as the *blindaje*, a large advance payment on a loan from international credit organizations, was a poor financial decision on the part of the government. Since the end of 2000, people had again been withdrawing their bank deposits out of fear of a country default, and just a few months into 2001, the Deposits Guarantee Fund had evaporated in efforts to stem the losses. Foreign investors were the first to go: between December 2000 and April 2001, foreign currency deposits among nonresidents fell by 35 percent. At the end of January 2001, *Clarín* published a photograph of an enormous bank lobby with just a few customers. The caption read: "Will the customers return?"

In March, the administration reappointed Cavallo as minister of the economy. The floundering de la Rúa administration trusted in the "father" of convertibility to overcome the crisis. Yet over the course of 2001, the situation only worsened: between February and May, deposits continued their downward spiral, falling by 8 percent. During this same period, Uruguayan banks saw a spectacular rise in deposits by nonresidents (the vast majority, Argentines): over US$300 million in just three months. The mass withdrawal of deposits brought attention to capital flight, and, once again, Montevideo was the chosen destination of the Argentines.

During Cavallo's months as minister under President de la Rúa, the country continued to negotiate postponements on its foreign debt payments, and some of the money withdrawn from banks came back into the financial system. In April, the press closely followed the level of deposits from week to week, with statistics and photographs. *Clarín* published a picture showing three people at automatic tellers; the caption reads, "Savers are putting their money back into the banks." At that moment, it was difficult to anticipate how that image would become emblematic of the end to the dollar peg.

The cost of getting deposits back into the system was an even more profound dollarization: accounts in dollars went from 61 percent of all deposits in February 2001 to 70 percent in October. Yet by July, the situation was unsustainable. Cavallo decided to cut back on state spending, ordering a 13 percent reduction on all government payments, including social security, salaries for all public service personnel, and suppliers. It was the first time in the country's history that the government had cut back salaries. In August alone, deposits fell by 11 percent. At the end of that month, Congress passed a law making bank deposits intangible assets and affirming they could not be withheld or subject to embargo. The law, however, did little to ebb the flow.

In the interior, the situation was even worse, particularly in the country's most populated province, Buenos Aires,[11] and home to the largest economy in the interior. In the face of the fiscal crisis and with no aid coming from the federal government, Governor Carlos Ruckauf introduced *patacones*, treasury bonds that would soon begin circulating as legal tender. Public service employees and retirees in the province began receiving part of their income in this quasi-currency. Other provinces would follow suit in the following months until fourteen provinces had their own fiat money. In November, the federal government issued the Lecop, a provincial debt bond, the only quasi-currency to be accepted nationwide.[12]

With the crisis as a backdrop, the midterm elections in October 2001 delivered a major blow to the ruling party. The discontent among voters clearly exceeded the government coalition: despite mandatory voting in Argentina, more than one-fourth of the electorate stayed home on election day, while another 20 percent who did go cast a blank or spoiled ballot. Since democracy had been restored in 1983, no election had had such a poor turnout, an indication of the profound crisis in political representation (Torre 2005; Levitsky and Murillo 2005).

As the bank run continued, legislative candidates critical of the dollar peg now dared to raise their voices. While virtually none had spoken out against the system while campaigning in 1999, the climate had changed drastically by 2001. The question was no longer how to keep convertibility afloat but how to end it; in the view of some experts, a full dollarization of the economy (that is, the elimination of the peso and use of the dollar for all transactions) was the only viable option. Others believed that devaluating the peso was the sole solution to the three-year recession (Castellani and Szkolnik 2011). Despite the severity of the crisis, however, Argentines did not necessarily agree. According to a survey conducted a few weeks before the election, more than six out of ten Argentines continued to support the dollar peg, with even higher percentages among the lower-middle and middle classes (*Clarín*, October 27, 2001). In the view of the president, dollarization was a moot point. In an interview with the weekly *The Economist* a few days before the election, President de la Rúa quipped, "To a great extent, the economy is already dollarized. If you look at bank transactions, the majority are in dollars. If a worker wants his salary in dollars, he can request that. So dollarization today is voluntary and entirely possible: there would be no reason to make it mandatory" (*Clarín*, October 20, 2001).

In the meantime, the crisis advanced: urban employment had surpassed 18 percent and bank deposits continued to drain. In desperate attempts to attract consumers, retail stores unveiled new strategies: while one large supermarket chain continued offering installments in dollars, customers at its branches in the province of Buenos Aires could now pay for their purchases entirely in the fiat currency patacones. A message by Minister Cavallo on the first day of December 2001 marked the beginning of the end. The president had just signed a blanket decree limiting all bank withdrawals to US$/AR$250 per week starting Monday, December 3.[13] The decree also prohibited all wire transfers abroad not associated with foreign commerce and forbade individuals from leaving the country with more than US$10,000. The government had finally reacted to the alarm bells of a bank run that had been ringing since February, but it was too late. Despite Cavallo's statement to the press a day after the announcement—"This should put to rest any conjectures of a devaluation" (*Clarín*, December 2, 2001)—the dollar peg would end just a month later.

While the emblematic image of the economy during the first months of the year had been deserted banks, the scene in December was exactly the opposite: lines outside bank branches in every city and every neighborhood. In a country where more than 86 percent of household purchases were paid for in cash (INDEC 2022), there was simply not enough cash in automatic teller machines for all bank customers to withdraw their weekly limit: after long waits, many customers got up to the machine only to discover it was empty. Cash dried up, and bank account holders were forced to accept the minister's "boost in banking penetration" (*Clarín*, December 23, 2001). The debit card, used in the past for little more than withdrawing cash from ATMs, now became a payment method. A few weeks after the measures were introduced, the philosopher and political analyst Oscar Landi described the state of affairs:

> Far from politics, with great mistrust in their elected officials and in the judicial branch, the masses of those directly and indirectly affected by the disappearance of the money go from bank to bank, attempting to gain access to a portion of what belongs to them. . . . Those who wish to depict the imposition of banking products as the country's introduction to the first-world culture of money management have failed in their attempts, given that most people have no experience in bank transactions and institutions have struggled to meet the abrupt surge in demand. . . . These roaming customers turn teller windows into confessionals, where employees are privy to personal dilemmas and dramas, turning the bank into an impromptu school of finance and a makeshift accounting firm for vendors and companies. (*Clarín*, December 23, 2001)

In neighborhoods far from the financial districts, the lack of cash proved equally problematic: How could workers doing odd jobs get paid? As had occurred during the hyperinflation of 1989, hungry Argentines went out to loot supermarkets and retail stores. At the same time, other lawful strategies to weather the crisis also appeared (Auyero 2007). For example, toward the end of 2001 and the beginning of 2002, bartering clubs sprung up across the country. Founded in the 1990s as a response to rising unemployment, these self-managed networks for the exchange of goods and services relied not on legal tender but on a newly created social currency (Luzzi 2005; González Bombal and Luzzi 2006; Gómez 2015); in the country of the legal dollar, currency creativity was one of the first responses to the crisis.

In response to the lootings, de la Rúa announced a state of siege on national radio and television. In large cities across the countries, people took to the streets. The slogan Que se vayan todos ("All of them must go," in reference to politicians) marked the start of a series of protests that continued for nearly two years (Dinerstein 2003; Svampa and Pereyra 2003; Epstein and Pion-Berlin 2006; Svampa 2014); that same night, Minister Cavallo and President de la Rúa would both hand in their resignations.

## The End of the Currency Board and the Return of the Forex Boards

A few days after restrictions on bank withdrawals had been announced, the press began employing a catchy term for the measure that most Argentines had already heard. The *corralito* or "little pen" (i.e., a small place of confinement) became the slang term for the withholding of bank savings. In its coverage of the measures introduced on December 3, *Ámbito Financiero* focused on a different aspect of the restrictions. The lede to the article, entitled "Argentina's parallel market is reborn," noted that the possibility of buying currency under the table "will quench the thirst for dollars of many an Argentine now unable to drink from the Central Bank reserves" (*Ámbito Financiero*, December 3, 2001). The paper was prescient in emphasizing this aspect of the story, as forex offices would once again become a central setting in the country's financial lives. On January 6, 2002, Congress passed a law formally ending the dollar peg.

Twenty days passed between de la Rúa's resignation and the reopening of forex trading in 2002. During that three-week period following Fernando de la Rúa's departure from the presidential palace in a helicopter, three presidents took office and quickly resigned: Senate majority leader Ramón Puerta, San Luis governor Adolfo Rodríguez Saá, and House of Representatives majority leader Eduardo Camaño. Ultimately, Senator Eduardo Duhalde was sworn in as president and would remain in office until Argentina held new elections in April 2003. During those feverish days of January 2002, the country announced it would cease payment on the foreign debt and end convertibility; further restrictions on bank deposit withdrawals had also been mandated, and CD maturities were rescheduled. This became popularly known as the *corralón*, or "big pen."

The exchange market reopened on January 10. In the next day's edition, *La Nación* ran a current-day picture of América, a forex office in "la City," where dozens of people are in line, waiting for the "free dollar to resurface." Below that picture is a similar shot outside the same building in April 1989. The caption reads,

> Eleven years in the blink of an eye: history repeats itself today in downtown Buenos Aires in a familiar scene from nearly eleven years ago—specifically, Friday March 29, 1991. That was the last day of the

floating dollar-peso before a fixed one-to-one exchange rate was set. Yesterday, the forex office boards again drew all eyes of "la City." (*La Nación*, January 11, 2002)

The full-page story included a series of questions and answers in a column entitled "Tips for trading on the exchange market." The reader who remembered the photograph from 1989 would surely be surprised to read the following question: "What are, who are the *arbolitos*?"[14] Yet now, eleven years later, young people walking down Florida Street could indeed be surprised to hear the men at the entryway of shop galleries and storefronts calling out, in both Spanish and English, "*Cambio, cambio.* Exchange, exchange."

Besides ending the dollar peg, the government introduced a dual exchange rate, setting a fixed exchange rate of AR$1.40 on the dollar for certain transactions while leaving a floating exchange rate for others. In a period of heated negotiations between the government and different sectors affected by the recent measures—including private companies and large companies with foreign debt—the difference between the floating and fixed exchange rate continued to grow. A lack of clarity on whether Argentina would resume payments on its foreign debt made it impossible for the Central Bank to maintain the fixed exchange rate, which was abandoned at the beginning of February. The press again looked to the past in its coverage of the current-day measures:

> Nearly eleven years have passed. The forex boards again display a single, floating exchange market after a decade-long dollar peg and a month of dual exchange rates. After reaching AR$2.50 and topping out at AR$2.70, the dollar came back down. Finally, after a torrential downpour that drove off many curious onlookers and potential customers an hour before markets closed, the day ended with a dollar at AR$1.90 (ask) and AR$2.10 (bid). (*La Nación*, February 12, 2002)

The brief text was illustrated by a series of four color pictures of moments on the exchange market as captured by decades of media coverage of "la City": the crowds on San Martín Street, the *arbolitos*, the customers counting greenbacks, onlookers rising on tiptoe to get a look at the boards and commenting on the prices, television cameras waiting for a story. Other novel elements had been added to the coverage at the start of the new century, including new characters on the streets known as the *coleros*.[15]

With the devaluation, the daily chronicle of what was happening in "la City" had made a comeback, and the dollar-peso exchange rate, often shown as an image of a foreign exchange board with the bid-ask spread, was again a critical piece of information in all journalistic coverage. In addition, a series of practices that had disappeared—or transformed—during convertibility had now returned: forex board watching, the purchase of dollars in small amounts to "protect" a portion of one's income from devaluation, and the dollar as a safeguard "because no one knows what will happen." Once again, US currency was circulating in hard cash, from the forex office to the mattress or the safe-deposit box, from the check cashed at a shady financial service outlet to people's pockets.

Among journalists and citizens of a certain age, this new crisis revived memories of others from the past: their own personal hardships along with the multiple strategies that had allowed them to weather the crisis, make it to the next paycheck, and continue doing business.

## The Middle Classes Take to the Streets

> The line stretches on endlessly: it starts on Talcahuano Street, turns onto Tucumán and then Uruguay before wrapping around on Lavalle. At a glance, it is impossible to estimate how many people are waiting to file a writ of amparo[16] at the Palace of Justice. According to police sources, at 11am yesterday, more than 5,000 people were outside the building. The line stretches more than twelve blocks.

*La Nación* published this chronicle on February 21, 2002. It was the final day to petition the courts demanding the return of funds held in the corralito, and a multitude of savers did not want to miss the opportunity. Some savers themselves spent hours in line while others had attorneys or law firm employees wait for them. The flood of petitions at the administrative courts led the Supreme Court to order all courts in the capital, regardless of their jurisdiction, to process them. It even assigned Supreme Court employees to aid with the filings. Between December 2001 and February 2002, hundreds of thousands of petitions had been presented, and the courts would spend years resolving them. Nearly a decade later, the Central Bank would report that since the introduction of the corralito, 405,550 payments had been made to savers as a result of court sentences or injunctions. Eighty percent of these payments were made between 2002 and 2004 (BCRA 2010; Smulovitz 2006).

Besides these court efforts, the battle against the banks was also waged on the street: starting in January, hundreds of bank customers took to the streets of "la City" every week, banging on bank doors and windows and covering them with graffiti. These protests, which altered the landscape of downtown Buenos Aires, stretched on into 2006. The demands expressed on protest signs were the same as those filing for writs of amparo: "We deposited dollars, we want dollars back." While the banks were the target of anger—rotten eggs, spray paint, and banging—the state was the party accused in court of violating bank customer rights. Naturally, not everyone who petitioned the court joined the street protests, attended meetings, or identified as "savers." However, behind every "saver"—a new category that encompassed retirees, housewives, young people out of work, small business owners, or freelancers who took out their anger on the banks—there was, indeed, a plaintiff. The latest news from the courts and legal advice were part of the discussions at the protests and at saver meetings (Luzzi 2008; 2012).

The savers' protest was the culmination of a process that had begun years earlier with the gradual integration of families in the banking system. Though it had started in the early 1990s, it intensified in 1997 when new legislation obliged companies to pay employees exclusively through direct deposit. While the law initially applied to large organizations, it later extended to all formal employees in 2001, expanding the percentage of the population with a bank account. The second part of this process was the growing dollarization of deposits in the years following the Tequila effect and redoubled during the second half of 2001. Finally, but equally important, the third aspect of this process was how the banking crisis affected different social groups in different ways. Not all bank customers had been affected by the rescheduling and mandatory translation into dollars of CDs, popularly known as the corralón. Investigations by legislative commissions in both the Argentine Senate and House of Representatives showed that companies were mainly responsible for the run on banks in 2001, particularly between July and December. In fact, 87 percent of all international wire transfers during that year were done by companies versus 13 percent by individuals. At the same time, not all companies had participated equally: 70 percent of those wire transfers were made by the country's top 200 companies (Comisión Especial Investigadora 2005). A similar trend occurred among the individuals making wire transfers: the ten individuals who transferred the most money abroad sent, on average, US$22 million each. In short, those with more access to economic information and a better understanding of the dynamic of financial institutions were largely unaffected by the presidential decree signed on December 1, 2001. It was mainly families and small businesses whose money got trapped in the corralito; and the savers' protests, either on the streets or at courts, was a faithful expression of this group.

> I remembered the horrible stories dad tells when he's drunk, when he feels lonely and starts reminiscing about his supposed friends, ignoring the fact that he's talking about the very people who ripped him off. As my mom said yesterday afternoon when we talked on the balcony, those "friends" are the ones who took his savings on a yacht and sent them to Uruguay without telling us. And I know it was on purpose,

> my dear friend, I know it, though mom might think that the parents
> of Candelaria's friends just forgot about dad and our dollar deposits
> ... I know that's not what happened. I've read Freud and I know they
> did it on purpose, just for the sadistic pleasure of seeing dad beg and
> bringing our family to its knees. Because they see us as nouveau riche
> and they wanted us to feel it. (Vanoli 2010, 22–23)

Like the main character in Hernán Vanoli's novel, published nearly a decade after those stormy hot months in early 2002, many understood that ending up in the corralito or slipping past it was just a question of savvy. The people who had left their money in the bank were those who had not seen the storm coming and trusted in the law Congress had passed to make deposits intangible. They either did not follow or know how to interpret the numbers reported by the Central Bank.

In an investigation by both chambers of Congress, commissions came to a similar conclusion. As did the people on the streets: those who identified as savers and joined some of the organizations that took shape between the end of 2001 and the beginning of 2002 in Buenos Aires and other large cities of Argentina were a motley crew. There was a well-known soccer player and a successful theater producer who had lost important investments to the corralito; there was a female retiree crying over a cash award recognizing fifty years of service with her company and a man who had been fired from his job and had lost his severance. Yet though their levels of prosperity varied, they were all middle class. The ideas they brought to the protests—the defense of property, sacrifice, civic virtue—confirmed this (Luzzi 2008; 2016).

"This bank took my children's future. Give it back to them." The sign was resting on one of the beach chairs a family had set up inside an HSBC branch in the prosperous Buenos Aires neighborhood of Barrio Norte. Besides the beach chairs, Marcelo, Susana, and their teenage son and daughter had brought a beach umbrella, sand buckets, and rakes in a unique protest that caught the attention of the media and many other protesters. "We were planning on going to Villa Gessell[17] like we do every year. But instead we're vacationing at the only place the bank permits: the bank!" exclaimed the father to the press. This was the family's way of demanding that the bank return a family inheritance of US$70,000 they had put into a CD and planned to use to pay for their children's education and a rainy-day fund. Though it was a hefty amount of money for most Argentines, it was nowhere near the amounts the ultra-rich had withdrawn from banks months earlier.

As had occurred at other moments in the past two decades, the so-called savers had formed a group and planned protests together. But unlike the protests that had occurred when the BIR and Banco de Italia had gone belly-up in the 1980s, or when Cajas de Crédito and Banco Mayo went under in the 1990s, these were not all customers from a particular bank. The banking system was in the eye of the storm, and its customers were suffering from a crisis without precedent (Muir 2021). And the dollar was at the core of the conflict.

It was not the only dollar-related controversy. During the 1990s, not only had bank deposits been dollarized: so had loans, especially mortgages. The end of the dollar peg meant that a great number of people earning salaries in pesos (those lucky enough to have not lost their source of income) had debt in dollars. In order to continue making their mortgage payments without losing their homes, they had to make these payments in pesos. While the savers roamed "la City" banging on bank doors, debtors also got organized with a series of creative protests. The first *llaverazos*[18] began at the beginning of January 2002: the protesters demanded that all mortgages be converted to pesos at a one-to-one exchange rate. The first measure introduced by President Eduardo Duhalde had converted bank mortgages denominated in dollars for up to US$100,000 into pesos, provided the property in question was a first family home; the keychain protesters were focused on all other home debtors, including those with peer-to-peer mortgages. Families that had seized on the dollar peg to access a property, when real estate across the country had been bought and sold in dollars since the 1970s, were not the only ones with debt in dollars in 2001. Many small businesses holding loans in the US currency also protested in these months; larger companies, instead of taking to the streets, opted for political lobbying, which tended to be more effective.

Less than a month after Congress ended the "one-to-one" and established a legal framework for debts incurred under the dollar peg, President Duhalde signed a decree translating into pesos all dollar debts in the financial system—independently of their amounts, use, or lender—at a rate of one peso per dollar. Given that the floating dollar was now at around three pesos, those with enormous amounts in the red saw their debt reduced by two-thirds. In order to compensate banks, the state issued a treasury bond. As had occurred in the past, state funding was used to benefit the rich and powerful.

The measure, however, did not apply to debt incurred outside the banking system. This included the peer-to-peer mortgages obtained at notary public offices, real estate agencies, or financial service outlets.[19] The state left this to the courts, and six years would pass until finally, after a number of legislative proposals and court rulings, the Supreme Court set a precedent for these dollar-related conflicts in a series of rulings. During this time, as would occur years later during the subprime crisis—especially in Spain (Ravelli 2020; 2021)—debtor associations in provinces across the country were protesting on the street, across from state legislatures, and in front of courthouses to try to stop auctions that threatened to leave families without a home (and, in many cases, did).

The explosive end to the dollar peg at the end of 2001 also dropped a curtain on this phase in the dollar's popularization in which the greenback's use in

Argentine financial repertoires had been legal, no longer a matter of controversies and illicit dealings. A corollary to this process was the expanded use of banking products among families. What proved entirely new was the movement of "saver" and mortgage debtors: besides joining the landscape of protest of Argentina, they established a novel repertoire of mobilization and a new type of demands. For the first time in history, the dollar was associated with a conflict that played out (at least in part) on the streets and was associated with entreaties for the protection of citizen rights. This articulation is critical to understanding the protests that would unfold a decade later in response to new restrictions on the purchase of foreign currency in Argentina.

*Chapter Six*

# THE FINANCIAL CRISIS FROM THE SOUTHERN CONE (2008–2015)

"Do you know what the dollar's at?"

The reporter and cameraman are standing on a sidewalk in downtown Buenos Aires.

A young man wearing a dress shirt and trousers pulls out his earphone and ventures,

"Four . . . twenty?"

Another young man, this one in a jogging suit, makes the same guess.

On the corner of Florida Street and Corrientes Avenue, the heart of the city's financial district, a third man hesitates before going a bit higher.

"Four thirty."

Two older men give a more precise number, the second even using the decimal separator.

"Four point twenty-eight."

The segment was part of a weekly comedy show (*CQC, Caiga Quien Caiga*) that aired on broadcast television in November 2011. It was two weeks after Cristina Fernández[1] been reelected, winning in a first-round vote just as she had her first term.[2] On camera, the reporter offers his personal conclusion after the interviews as the Pink Floyd song "Money" plays in the background: "It looks like we're all up on the U.S. currency." The conclusion is paradoxical: the newscaster also notes that, according to statistics from the Central Bank, "only 11% of Argentines have purchased dollars so far this year [through September]."

In order to note how Argentina stood out from other countries in this regard, the program offered a comparison between Buenos Aires and Sao Paulo, Brazil's business hub. During a visit to inform on knowledge of the dollar exchange rate in that city, the reporter poses the same question to a series of passersby on Paulista Avenue. Unlike the respondents on the streets of Buenos Aires, none of the Brazilians interviewed ventured to guess the exchange rate.

At the end of the report, a voice-over concludes:

> In recent years, a CD in pesos, real estate, land, shares, bonds, gold, and durable goods have all been better investments than the dollar.
> Yet we keep on buying them. Though not in equal amounts, of course.
> The oddest thing is this: between January and September, three million individuals and companies bought dollars. There's something cultural or psychological behind this.

Toward the end of 2011, the popularization of the dollar had entered a new stage, one with its own distinctive features. The first signs that the dollar was pushing its way back to the center of public debate came in October that year, when the government began restricting the purchase and sale of foreign currencies. Gradually, the restrictions were expanded to the point where it became almost impossible to buy or sell dollars. Argentines are known for their creative jargon: while ten years prior, they had come up with corralito and corralón to refer to measures restricting cash withdrawals from bank accounts, they now began using the term *cepo* to refer to the new foreign exchange measures. In Spanish, cepo is a clamp, the torture instrument known as the thumbscrew, and car boot. It now evoked the closing off of access to the US dollar by the Argentine government. As restrictions on foreign currency tightened, both the media and the public resumed discussion of the dollar.

This chapter, which covers the period from the country's economic recovery in 2003 through 2015, focuses particularly on the final years when the US currency became a prominent topic yet again. This new stage in the dollar's popularization is characterized by two important trends. One of the novelties was that during these years—and for the first time in history—the government would actively work to discourage the use of the greenback in the financial repertoires of Argentines, or to "de-dollarize" the behaviors of local economic actors. On the other hand, the ordinary meanings of the dollar also began shifting; on the street, accessing the exchange market took on a meaning beyond turning a profit or seeking a haven from inflation. Instead, the dollar would become a question of individual rights that the state was expected to protect.

## The Years of Economic Recovery: Booming Exports and Exchange Rate Stability

Compared with the currency fluctuations in the years prior, the official dollar exchange rate between 2003 and 2010 remained surprisingly stable. After topping out at AR$4 in the middle of 2002, the dollar dropped to AR$3.40 by the end of the year and then hovered at around AR$3 until 2007. The years of trade surplus and booming fiscal revenues that lasted until 2008, a source of pride for President Néstor Kirchner (2003–2007), had been accompanied by a stable exchange rate. It was the only recent moment in history, save the currency board—which had maintained a fixed exchange rate by law—that the dollar held steady. The recession faded and the economy began to grow, thanks in part to a stable international economy, during the Kirchner administration. Kirchner was part of a post-neoliberal wave sweeping Latin America, a backlash to the laissez-faire, neoconservative administrations of the 1990s that had offered virtually no assistance for the poor (Levitsky and Roberts, 2011; Etchemendy 2020).

In 2008, Argentine society witnessed a tense economic conflict between the government and farmers, which came out against a system of variable (and rising) export tariffs on agricultural exports (Fairfield 2011; Panero 2018). The media closely followed the tug-of-war, which happened to coincide with a global financial crisis that also had ramifications for the Argentine economy. Still, the situation was nowhere as severe as others in recent memory, like the crisis of 2001 or that of 1989. As the political and economic crisis worsened, the dollar rose to AR$3.40. Yet it did not surpass AR$4 until the end of 2010.

The first years following the 2001 crisis were also characterized by a notable drop in dollar deposits in the banking system. While in the 1990s, more than 50 percent of all bank deposits were in dollars, these represented just 10 percent of the total in 2004. Memories of the mandatory translation into pesos of deposits in 2002 under President Eduardo Duhalde after the end of convertibility remained strong; savers no longer trusted the banks with their dollars. The government had also imposed new restrictions that limited bank loans in foreign currencies, meaning banks had little incentive to encourage deposits in the US currency. Only customers with earnings in dollars could qualify for loans in dollars. The days of the "one-to-one," when banks offered all customers foreign currency loans, were a thing of the past.

Similarly, there was little currency exchange on the informal market during this period. During this time, the "parallel" market was used for illegal transactions, sales or purchases that people did not want on the record, or others that people did not qualify for on the formal market. Yet during those years of a trade surplus and rising fiscal revenues, the difference between the official exchange rate and the parallel market exchange rate was minimal—so minimal, in fact, that it rarely made the news.

Chapter Six

# The Cepo: A Weapon and a Method of Instruction

In October 2011, Cristina Fernández won reelection with 54 percent of the popular vote. Since the death of her husband, Néstor Kirchner, in 2010, "la City" had again been suffering tremors. After a prolonged calm, the price of the dollar on the informal market began ticking upward in the months prior to the election, while the demand for foreign currencies on the official market rose. Little by little, the dollar made its way back into the news and into conversations.

A few days after the election, the Central Bank—in joint efforts with the Federal Revenues Administration and the Financial Information Unit—sent agents into downtown Buenos Aires to investigate illegal exchange offices and arrest arbolitos and coleros[3] in an attempt to halt illegal currency exchange. At the same time, the government introduced a new and even more restrictive forex measure, limiting the purchase of US dollars to individuals authorized by the tax authority. Although the cap on monthly purchases of foreign currency (US$2 million) remained, the Central Bank established that individuals or companies purchasing over US$250,000 per year had to provide evidence of assets and income to back these purchases.[4]

The introduction of the cepo, as these measures soon became known, had immediate effects on the foreign exchange market. Those unfamiliar with the tax administration's paperwork or whose taxes were not in order—the *chiquitaje*,[5] as this group was known in "la City"—rapidly discovered that they could not always get approval for a currency purchase on the Currency Transaction Query web page. This had an instant, detrimental impact on certain markets like tourism and real estate.

In the meantime, demand for dollars remained high among the financial heavyweights, who knew the ins and outs of the tax authority. The high level of dollar purchases and the gradual drop in dollar deposits in the two months leading up to the election were both evidence of this. By late November, there were references in the media of a run on the dollar. The president echoed this in her reelection speech on December 10, where she spoke out against the "five runs on foreign currency by corporations that thought this government would fold." She also recalled that on all five of these occasions,

> The Central [Bank] sold US$15,897,000,000, almost US$16 billion. They wanted to force us to devaluate or mark their territory. If we add what we've paid on the foreign debt [in 2009 and 2010] to the almost US$16 billion, the Central Bank would have US$88,684,000,000 today. That's why I'm asking all sectors to avoid spitting into the wind. It's not a good method and it's never worked for us Argentines. Let's protect what we've achieved in these years, as small businesses have grown to mid-size, mid-size business have expanded to large businesses, and large business

owners have tired of the money they've made. And that's fine: I don't
have anything against making money. I just ask those earning it to make
a sensitive, intelligent contribution—it doesn't even have to be patriotic.
A sensitive, intelligent contribution toward a virtuous economic model
that has yielded incredible profits. (Fernández de Kirchner 2011)

The statistics at year's end, however, were inauspicious: according to Central Bank reports, foreign exchange on the official market had been the highest since 2002, 12 percent more than the previous year and even greater than during the international crisis of 2008. The structure of the demand, however, remained relatively the same. Individuals or companies buying up to US$5,000 per month represented one-third of all purchases.[6] An additional third were buying between US$5,000 and 50,000. Eight percent purchased between US$50,000 and 100,000 dollars, 17 percent between US$100,000 and 1,000,000, and 6 percent more than US$1,000,000 (BCRA 2011b).

The increased demand for dollars can be attributed to diverse factors, one of which was the global crisis of 2008, which had a major impact on international investment. The fact that Argentina had defaulted on its debt at the end of 2001, however, sheltered it from the worst repercussions of the global shakedown. Domestically, inflation spurred demands on the part of certain sectors for the government to raise the exchange rate, which they claimed was artificially low. These critics believed that a higher exchange rate would compensate for the drop in domestic production and make Argentina more competitive on international markets. Finally, upcoming payment deadlines on the foreign debt limited the government's ability to hold the exchange rate steady.

The government had already successfully reduced the purchase of foreign currency through measures introduced at the end of October 2011. In the first months of 2012, the Fernández administration took action to constrict the demand, though this time it targeted larger transactions. Any company wishing to import goods had to present an affidavit, and anyone transferring dollars abroad needed to request authorization from the Central Bank. This applied to import payments and wire transfers by the Argentine affiliates of companies headquartered abroad. Later, the new regulations would also apply to exporters. The government also shortened the lag time for liquidating dollars for sales abroad on the local market.

## One Currency, Multiple Prices

Yet none of these measures was able to quench the thirst for dollars, and, as had occurred in the past, familiar workarounds appeared. The first was the resurfacing of the historic parallel market, where the dollar was now referred to as the "blue."[7]

Yet there was also a second, legal, and more novel way of obtaining dollars, seizing on gaps in the new forex regulations. A relatively sophisticated version involved purchasing dollar bonds on the local market and then liquidating them into an account opened abroad; this blue-chip swap was known as *contado con liquidación*, soon abbreviated to *contado con liqui* or its acronym, CCL. Other workarounds to the new dollar restrictions were more rudimentary—even manual—and did not require knowledge of the economic sciences: drawing cash in foreign currency at ATMs abroad. People in Buenos Aires began taking day trips across the Río de la Plata just to withdraw dollars from teller machines in Uruguay in what became known as *dólar Colonia*, a reference to the Uruguayan city that is less than an hour ride from Buenos Aires on the popular Buquebús ferry. The quantity of withdrawals abroad thus multiplied, leading to a new and profitable (but illegal) financial service: taking someone else's debit card abroad to withdraw cash. These "frequent travelers" would spend days, weeks, and even months going to ATMs in countries both near and far to later bring back "strong currency" for relatives, friends, and even just acquaintances who hired them for this service. These dollars, in turn, would nourish the local "blue" dollar market.

Though these dollar withdrawals abroad did not have a large impact on the country's balance sheet, the administration took note. At the end of April 2012, a new measure limited cash extractions at ATMs abroad to those with bank accounts denominated in dollars. Over the first half of 2012, despite an increasing number of more restrictive forex controls, the country's dollar reserves continued to drain, and the exchange rate on the blue market ticked upward. By the beginning of June 2012, the intensity of purchases and sales of the "blue" dollar led a high-ranking official from the Ministry of Economy to call a meeting with representatives of the most prominent underground foreign exchange offices. He laid out a proposal that would be mutually beneficial: to set an informal limit for the "blue" exchange rate. When the bilateral agreement was reached, a dollar cost AR$4.50 on the official market, compared to a "blue" dollar of AR$5.10. This sort of negotiations between the government and the "parallel" market had occurred in the past; what was novel in this case was that the press reported on them.[8]

## Clamps of All Sorts

The media (newspapers, TV, radio, Internet portals, etc.) regularly covered the "blue" dollar exchange rate along with the official dollar and the contado con liqui. Although the situation was described as surprising ("The country with two exchange rates for the dollar" ran a headline in *La Nación* on May 20, 2012), little was novel about it. The illegal exchange market had become the status quo, and the broad reporting of its rates reflected its expansion. If anything was innovative about this, it was that new technologies allowed people to access the information in real time. There was no longer any need to wait for the evening news or the next morning's paper to check the buy-sell spread; on the websites of newspapers, banks, and financial institutions, rates were constantly updated and shared on social media.

In July, the government decided to prevent any purchase of dollars for savings purposes. Once the measure was introduced, foreign currency could only be purchased at the official exchange rate was for trips abroad or import payments (after obtaining authorization). There were a few other exceptions, such as remittances abroad by migrants living in Argentina or by Argentines with family members living in other countries. This decision to clamp down even harder brought more attention to the "blue" dollar, which jumped 20 percent in the first month following the introduction of the new restrictions. As the gap between the official and unofficial exchange rates continued to grow, people also began withdrawing their bank deposits. These measures had a particularly strong impact on "dollarized" markets like real estate. Since the end of 2011, the number of property sales had been falling; during the first half of 2012, the number of transactions was 16 percent lower than the same period one year earlier.

One month after the "savings dollar," as it had become known, had been eradicated, regulations homed in on controlling the "tourist dollar." The sale of foreign currency became limited to one week prior to a person's declared travel date. In the case of trips to neighboring countries, travelers were not allowed to buy dollars, only the currency of the destination country. For credit card purchases made abroad, 15 percent was tacked on; this amount later rose to 35 percent. Technically, this was not a tax, but an advance payment on income taxes. Finally, only state banks were authorized to buy and sell foreign currency at ports and international airports. Forex offices were thus no longer able to engage in one of their historical lines of business, leading the Argentine Chamber of Foreign Exchange Offices to report an abrupt reduction in transactions at the beginning of September 2012. Since the introduction of the cepo, many of these firms were forced to close or redirect their business to other areas.

As criticism of the administration increased and the public debated the reasons for the constant demand for dollars, the federal government made the final payments on the Boden 2012, ten-year bonds issued in 2002 to return bank deposits frozen in the corralón.[9] At the same time, Argentina continued making regular payments on all its foreign debt, including to the International Monetary Fund (IMF). At the celebration of the 158th anniversary of the stock market, Cristina Kirchner celebrated the payment of nearly US$2.2 billion on those bonds issued nearly a decade earlier. According to the president, paying off that debt marked the end of a cycle. She noted that this was accomplished despite rumors by those who "took the money of Argentines twice: first in 2001, when they claimed everything was going great, and again in recent years, when they said everything was going down the drain and that they [holders of the Boden] should dump the bonds because they weren't worth a thing" (Fernández de Kirchner 2012).

## Black, Parallel, Blue: The Illegal Exchange Market

In each of the periods analyzed in this book, the illegal exchange market expanded whenever forex controls increased. This also held true in 2012. The state regulations aimed at monitoring the exchange market helped shape the new "parallel" market for dollars. Many aboveboard exchange offices were forced to close due to the drop in their clientele or because the Central Bank withdrew their operating licenses. In some cases, former employees of these offices became "blue" entrepreneurs or workers on the illegal exchange market. Those who had worked as coleros before the dollar restrictions evolved into arbolitos and *llamadores*.[10]

As on the official market, technology also influenced the modus operandi of parallel market transactions. The rates of the "blue" dollar on Twitter and Facebook, combined with encrypted WhatsApp chats, were two ingredients of an illegal market, similar to the bolsa negra of the 1930s yet also novel. The state also had other ways of influencing the illegal market. As the initial control measures were gradually relaxed, people with access to the "savings dollar"[11] offered by the Central Bank could turn a profit on the blue market. *Hacer puré* (mashing) was the popular name for this micro-currency speculation that dated back decades: purchasing dollars low at the official exchange rate (in this case, purportedly for "savings") and selling them high on the parallel market. Workers earning relatively high salaries would buy dollars on the official exchange market and then immediately sell (or "mash") them on the blue market, earning up to 70 percent on the transaction when restrictions tightened. The impact of these transactions was especially noteworthy during the first week each month. Often, office workers joined their colleagues in going to the bank to buy dollars on payday and then walked to the nearest *cueva* to exchange them. Journalists and financial market operators speculated about the existence of *cuevas*[12] collaborating with the government to control the "blue" dollar exchange rate, showing just how thin the line was between the official and illegal markets.

The "blue" dollar rate generally mirrored the worth of the US currency in the blue-chip swap known as contado con liqui. This legal transaction allowed powerful players to elude the cepo and purchase dollars. At certain points in time, the contado con liqui was so prevalent that it began draining the country's dollar reserves; at one point, the administration tried to make it a forex crime. In 2015, however, the Supreme Court ruled that it was a perfectly legal transaction.

Founded in 2012, the Prosecutor's Office for Economic Crimes and Asset Laundering (PROCELAC) carried out more than 100 raids at cuevas in its first three years, resulting in fifty cases that went to court. Some of these raids were at the initiative of the Prosecutor's Office; in some cases, it carried out joint investigations with the Central Bank, the Financial Information Unit, and/or the National Securities Commission. In many cases, the media covered these raids in reports that provide valuable insight into the workings of the illegal market during this period. Some of the raids started by following llamadores or arbolitos who worked on the streets into the cuevas. In other cases, these raids relied on anonymous tips of illegal currency trading or information coming from unrelated court cases for drug trafficking or homicide.

The vast majority of these raids took place in the capital's financial district. However, cuevas were also being discovered in other middle-class neighborhoods of Buenos Aires, Greater Buenos Aires, large cities in the interior, and border towns. Traditional jewelry stores, rare coin dealers, tourism agencies, *locutorios* (Internet/phone centers), tanning salons, payment and remittance offices, ticket sale agencies, and credit cooperatives. In fact, every business that handled cash—a lingerie store, a doctor's office, a kiosko[13] with a staircase hidden behind a fridge leading up to a teller window—could potentially operate on the illegal currency exchange market. Frequently, these storefronts were located in shopping galleries, with frosted glass or decals covering the windows. The more sophisticated cuevas also had security cameras.

In order to follow the trail from the legal financial market to the illegal one, financial brokers suspected of illicit currency trading were one focus of investigations. The media reports of the raids reveal that the cuevas are organized for quick transactions: sparsely furnished, they are described as having partition walls, money counting machines, calculators, computers, and, importantly, paper shredders. Besides notebooks, receipts, and accounting records, weapons and drugs were also found in some raids. Police protection—always for a price—is critical to this market. In wiretaps done prior to the raids, *cueveros* can be heard warning the local police station "hired" to keep an eye on things about suspicious characters hanging around near the offices. And often, these suspicious characters were themselves detectives staking out the office.

The Prosecutor's Office also investigated connections between the illegal exchange market and money laundering associated with drug trafficking. High-ranking officials at the office began discussing the need to investigate the sprawling informal market La Salada (Dewey 2020), where dollars were in demand to import merchandise. According to some observers, during moments of high demand, the market located in Ingeniero Budge, Buenos Aires Province, required some US$25 million per day to operate.

Pressure on the official peso-dollar exchange rate continued throughout Cristina Fernández's second term (2011–2015). At the end of January 2014, the country was in the midst of a "currency storm," as the press called it. Soon after the Central Bank began reducing its market interventions, the official exchange rate rose to AR$8 after trading at AR$6 for more than a month. Many described this devaluation of the peso as a necessary, though insufficient, "rectification" of the exchange rate. The government's position on the devaluation was ambivalent. On the one hand, authorities attempted to downplay its repercussions, arguing that a rise in the dollar had only a minimal effect on domestic prices. Yet officials also denounced speculation on the part of certain large companies, which were blamed for the sudden spike in the exchange rate.

Two days after the abrupt rise in the peso, Economic Minister Axel Kicillof stated:

> Certain sectors were speculating on a large-scale devaluation but their attempts have failed, because this was nothing of the sort. In 2002, the devaluation was 214%; the famous "rodrigazo" was 719%. In 1981, it was 226% and in 1989, 2038%. Now those were devaluations. (*Página/12*, January 26, 2014)

Besides the devaluation, the "savings dollar" made a comeback in the early months of 2014. Taxpayers who had met the tax authority's requirements could now purchase dollars on the official exchange market for up to 20 percent of their net monthly income. If they chose not to deposit the dollars purchased, they were subject to a withholding of 20 percent that could later be applied to their income tax. Despite these restrictions, the measure reopened the official market; it was a small step for the legal dollar but a giant leap for the blue market. The difference in the two exchange rates created business opportunities both small and large.

Historically, this type of speculation—buying foreign currency on the legal market before reselling it under the table—had surfaced every time there was both a floating and fixed exchange rate. Something similar occurred with the "tourist dollar," despite the government's best efforts to restrict these purchases to travelers with legitimate needs. Although new technologies made monitoring easier, the authorities continued to face the same problems it had come up against for half a century. In the 1970s, the government had discovered "tourists" declaring trips never taken and even purchasing tickets they never used just to legally obtain greenbacks. In those years, authorities had also attempted to reduce the amount of foreign currency purchased for trips (both real and phony) because a percentage of this money inevitably ended up on the black market.

## Dollarized Markets in Times of the Cepo

The foreign exchange cepo brought tension to the world of soccer yet again, especially because it had become increasingly cross-border. The topic was no longer whether or not players could demand payment in foreign currency, as it had been in the 1980s. Now the question was what exchange rate should be used for US dollar transactions. One of the most memorable cases in those years, one closely followed by the media, was that of midfielder Juan Román Riquelme. When his contract came up for renewal in mid-2014, the player's agent had little trouble agreeing with Boca negotiators on the player's salary in dollars; the problem arose when he demanded that the dollar be translated into pesos at the "blue" exchange rate. The reasoning behind the request was that due to the maximum exchange rate stipulated in his previous contract, Riquelme had been paid far below the under-the-table exchange rate for the last six months. The club managers were reluctant to accept the proposal of the player's representative, fearful of what the "blue" exchange rate might be toward the end of the player's contract in 2015; negotiations turned to an exchange rate halfway between the official and blue dollar rates. The press quickly dubbed this the "Riquelme dollar," yet another category in the local forex domain. Ultimately, no agreement was reached, and Riquelme left Boca Juniors for a brief stint with his first professional team, Argentinos Juniors (*Ámbito Financiero*, June 26, 2014).

The issues associated with calculations in different currencies while maneuvering a range of state regulations—either to adapt to changing rules of play or to find a way around them—became the status quo during the period of forex restrictions between 2011 and 2015. This was even the case within families. The experience of the Torres siblings, who needed to distribute several properties and savings inherited during the peak of the cepo, offers insight into how such agreements could remain elusive.

A few months after their mother passed away, the Torres siblings began discussing the inheritance. Their mother had owned three properties: a small apartment and both units of a duplex home, all located in a suburb north of Buenos Aires. When it came time to see what the properties were worth, the Torres siblings each called a separate real estate agent to appraise the three properties. There were no major differences in the appraisals. The mother had also left her children US$17,000 in savings. From the point of view of how much each sibling would get, it was simply a question of dividing the total amount to be inherited by four. In other words, assuming the three properties sold for US$340,000 plus the US$17,000 in the mother's savings, each sibling should have gotten US$85,000.

Except for the youngest sister, who wanted her inheritance in cash, the siblings each expected to get a property out of the deal. This is where the complications began: although they agreed on calculating the inheritance in dollars, there was no consensus on how payments should be made. Two of the siblings expected to be paid in the same currency in which the properties were appraised, regardless of the dollar-peso exchange rate or how the others would get their hands on the dollars. The other two, however, argued that the houses "are not in Miami, they're in Buenos Aires," an indirect way of refusing to pay for the properties in dollars. Due to the cepo, the only way to come up with that amount in dollars would be to buy them at a much higher rate on the black market. In short, the problem was not about how much the house was worth in dollars (its price): all four siblings and all four appraisers agreed on that. The conflict was about the equivalent (exchange) rate in pesos to reach the dollar amount.[14]

The negotiations and tensions in the Torres family on how to pay heirs in pesos for an inheritance worth a certain amount in dollars are a synecdoche for the real estate market during those years. The cepo had drastically reduced the number of properties being bought and sold. According to statistics from the Buenos Aires municipal government, 7,200 properties had changed hands in 2011; in 2012, it fell to 5,000 and would continue the downward spiral, dropping to 2,883 in 2013, 2,690 in 2014, and 2,846 in 2015. Real estate sales generally involved tense negotiations regarding the price in pesos per dollar (or a consensus on the value of the "real estate dollar"). In some cases, buyers and sellers agreed that part of the payment would be made in dollars and the rest in pesos (buyers approved for a mortgage had a fixed amount of pesos available for the purchase). In other transactions, the sellers demanded that payment be made entirely in dollars, refusing to accept pesos even at the "blue" dollar rate out of fear of taking such a large amount of pesos into a cueva to then buy dollars themselves.[15]

Farmers also clashed with the government regarding the dollar's worth. "Soy is like the dollar," said a farmer in the province of Santa Fe during a visit to his farm on a hot day in September 2014.[16] The area had experienced huge social and economic transformations as a result of the soybean expansion since the 1980s, fostered by the incorporation of technological innovations such as genetically modified seeds and direct seeding. Soybean, which had become a global commodity, contributed billions of dollars to Argentina's economy (Lapegna 2016; Gras and Hernandez 2016). According to Argentina's National Institute of Statistics and Censuses (INDEC), soybean production represented 30 percent of the country's export revenues, or nearly US$20 billion. It is no coincidence that amendments to the tax regime for soy exports had unleashed one of the worst political conflicts of the previous decade (Fairfield 2011; Panero 2018).

Sometime later, these producers would make headlines again due to policies limiting foreign exchange. Government officials blamed these producers, along with the country's biggest traders, of attempting to "destabilize" the Argentine peso. More specifically, they were accused of stockpiling soybeans instead of selling them abroad, lagging to delay the entry of funds into Argentina, and speculating with a devaluation of the peso (a common practice during the 1980s, another period of currency and exchange rate instability).

The basic mathematics of soybean transactions are based on the value of 100 kilograms internationally on the Chicago Board of Trade (in June 2015, US$345.85 per ton). As in construction, farm production costs involve different currencies. Worker salaries, fuel, agricultural machinery rentals (contractors generally charge a percentage of the crop yield, usually 9 percent), and shipping costs are calculated in pesos. The dollar is the currency used for the purchase of seeds and agrochemicals sold by large multinationals like Monsanto. The sale price of the machinery is also expressed in dollars, although the transactions are done in pesos or in soy. In some cases, producers hand over part of their crop yield to pay for machinery.

Trade journals provide information for producers on the cost of each input in dollars so they can estimate their profits. Although some inputs are paid for in pesos (fuel, for example), the total is estimated in dollars in order to have a single benchmark value. This means also converting to dollars whatever has to be paid in taxes. The dollar clearly takes precedence as a unit of account, though it is rarely used as a payment instrument. While pesos are usually the currency of everyday transactions, the most important payment method is the soybean itself. As one farmer said, "The soybean functions like the dollar"; but soybeans are easier to access, and farmers are more accustomed to this currency. Once calculated in dollars, the soybean serves as a payment method and a store of value, allowing its value to be preserved over time. In the context of the cepo, farmers used the official dollar for their calculations, as this is what they received for exports; it soon became known as the "soybean dollar," that is, the official price minus a government withholding of approximately 35 percent.

While the producers of goods for export always have privileged access to foreign currency, the fact that soy is "dollar convertible" gives farmers particular leverage in the context of forex restrictions. Though they do not need to touch a single dollar bill, they can continue carrying out their transactions in dollars (Luzzi and Wilkis 2018).

## Dollars and Screens

From 2012 until December 2015, when the new president, Mauricio Macri (2015–2019), put an end to forex market restrictions, the dollar was a prominent topic in the news. Print outlets and audiovisual news sources frequently reported on its fluctuations on different markets (official, contado con liqui, blue), the exchange rates of the different "types" of dollars (tourist dollar, credit card dollar, savings dollar, etc.), and the level of demand. At the same time, information on the dollar circulated in new formats and devices, like social media accounts dedicated to the dollar or apps developed to provide different values in real time and calculate conversions instantly.

At times, tensions ran high in response to new regulations; at others, police teams were deployed to arrest forex traders in "la City," when the gap between the official and parallel dollars grew. In response, economic news journalists brought back what had become a historical reporting genre: folksy chronicles of the exchange market. In the past, journalistic coverage combining text and images had made San Martín Street synonymous with the forex market, a location familiar even to Argentines who had never stood tiptoe on its sidewalks trying to get a peek at the board. Later on, these chronicles had focused on trading desks, once viewed as an otherworldly setting of money speculations within the financial world. By making them understandable, this type of journalism put trading desks within reach of small and large investors alike.

While the cepo was in place, journalists delved into the universe of the cuevas, providing information on the day-to-day transactions and a firsthand look at the internal dynamics of the market. As María Soledad Sánchez (2016; 2017) has shown, the US currency weaved its way into both traditional and new media in the 2010s, leading to surprising twists. For example, afternoon talk show hosts who never used to offer political or economic analysis began talking about the dollar, inviting panelists or special guests with expert knowledge on the topic to their programs. As for the usual economic experts on radio and television programs, many struck out on their own, exploring other platforms. Since the 1980s, economic journalism, though not always done by experts, had focused on instructing both readers and viewers alike. Besides explaining both actors and transactions in the financial world, these journalists also guided the public in money decisions, providing both tips and recommendations.

Starting in 2012, this economic instruction expanded into a genre relatively new for Argentina, though it had become common abroad—even in neighboring countries like Chile and Brazil—for some time. In publishing, personal finance books and other manuals on economics came to meet the needs of both dedicated readers and those who relied on books exclusively for self-help and expanding their knowledge on certain topics. Besides explaining the workings of the national economy, these books provided practical tips on investment dos and don'ts in a context of high inflation and limited access to dollars.[17] The discussions by these experts, who provided daily reminders of the difficulties facing small investors who wanted to protect their pesos against inflation but could not access the foreign currency market as they had in the past, also influenced public policy.

Thus, the government made attempts, some more successful than others, to create the "investment alternatives" the experts cited. First, in December 2012, just a few months after 51 percent of shares of the oil company YPF returned to state hands, the company began offering a bond with 19 percent returns targeting small savers.[18] Capped at US$50 million, the bonds were available to anyone with a bank account and started at AR$1,000, less than half the monthly minimum salary in September of that year. The bond was a hit, with 10,700 holders purchasing six times more than originally estimated for the first round. Nearly half were in fact small investors, purchasing less than AR$10,000 in bonds. Another instrument, the Certificate of Deposits for Investment (CEDIN), was introduced in mid-2013. Described by Argentina's National Securities Commission as a "tool for both the real economy and the financial sector," these certificates were designed as a response to the cepo's devastating effect on the real estate market, where transactions continued to be done in dollars and largely in cash. A second reason for these CDs was to get undeclared foreign currency aboveboard. The CEDIN offered a legal, albeit temporary way to use undeclared funds. For ninety days, those with dollars they had not declared could exchange them for CEDIN, without forfeiting any part of their capital or answering any questions about the origins of the funds.

The CEDIN could be used as legal tender for real estate transactions, thus standing in for dollars. They could also be signed over to others and used as payment on other markets. These certificates, however, did not have the appeal of the YPF bonds. Although the deadline for "declaring" capital with no questions asked was postponed on four occasions, the CEDIN "swap" fell far below government estimates. Similarly, they did little to dynamize the real estate market, or reduce its reliance on dollars.

## Dollars in the Public Debate

The introduction of the first forex control measures at the end of 2011 led to a series of public debates. The controversy continued throughout the following year as the government added new restrictions. In the media, government officials, economic journalists, and consultants discussed the applicability of state intervention on the foreign exchange market, the efficacy of the new regulations, and the actual worth of the greenback. In each new debate, the national penchant for dollars in the face of an oncoming economic storm came up yet again as Argentines attempted to justify, condemn, or simply comprehend the phenomenon.

In many ways, the discussions brought back a familiar argument between those who defended laissez-faire and those who supported government intervention in the economy. When *La Nación* ran an editorial entitled "In a police state" in June

2012, it reiterated the same arguments that paper had presented at another moment fifty years earlier:

> The national government is feverishly applying new restrictions to the most basic citizen liberties, like the freedom to use the money one earns any way one sees fit. . . . The government's new attack is a confiscation that not only violates the Constitution but also demonstrates what little respect the current government has for the rule of law. (*La Nación*, June 3, 2012)

> Authorizing an honest immigrant with family in Europe to transfer AR$5,000 abroad per quarter—less than US$40—is derisive.[19] And it tramples on the freedom of movement, besides preventing individuals from using their money however they wish, to limit one's purchase to US$750 for any trip beyond our neighboring countries. . . . The recent decree and the regulations it enables are state meddling in the life of individuals, opening many highly unpleasant prospects. (*La Nación*, April 28, 1964)

Another frequent topic in the debate surrounding the dollar was the currency's real (or fictitious) value. As control over the foreign exchange market tightened and the gap between the official and blue dollar widened, the true value of the dollar was an increasing focus of debate. In September 2012, one expert in personal finance explained the different exchange rates of the greenback now that the new regulations were in place. In a column, he declared the "blue" to be "the rate most commonly used to gauge the true purchasing power of every dollar in Argentine pesos." There was nothing novel about this idea; reader comments in one paper's online forum posted in response to similar articles that year noted that the blue "is the only REAL [sic] one, not some artificial [currency] that no longer exists, because it sets the market pace" (*La Nación*, May 16, 2012).

Near the end of the forex cepo, as the presidential elections of 2015 approached, stock market president Adelmo Gabbi had made a similar argument in a televised interview: "Under economic freedom, the market will set the dollar's true price on its own. Let's not fool ourselves: the prices of the economy and at the supermarket are not just nine-something to the dollar. They're higher" (*El Cronista*, September 15, 2015).

Since the 1930s, the debate over fiction versus reality or lies versus truth in exchange rates had resurfaced at every instance of forex controls or dual exchange rates. Whenever a new measure had created a market with different types of exchange rates (legal/illegal, dollar for trade/financial dollar, fixed/floating, etc.), the administration in power had been blamed. When a government insisted on "artificial" currency values, the "true" value remained a mystery, creating a fiction. This meant the exchange rate needed to be rectified.

Analysts, businesspeople, and government officials had used metaphors frequently after President Perón was overthrown and in the years following Frondizi's Stabilization Plan. As noted in the recitals of the Free Foreign Exchange Market Decree,

> Once of the primordial aspects [of the Stabilization Plan] is making exchange rates realistic, putting them at a level compatible with a stable economy. Thus, a single, free-floating exchange regimen is needed and excessive state intervention must end, as it distorts the value of our currency. (*La Nación*, December 31, 1958)
>
> Or, as Economic Minister Federico Pinedo had argued:
>
> Allowing the Argentine currency's real value to be seen is not about devaluing our currency: it is about admitting that one dollar does not equal eighty-three pesos if no one voluntarily hands over one dollar to receive eighty-three pesos on the free exchange market. It is about seeing its actual value once those who purchase dollars are no longer subsidized by the country's reserves. (*Clarín*, April 11, 1962)

This type of criticism of artificially low exchange rates, the result of state control measures, continued into the 1970s.

> Last night, the president opted to set our currency's exchange rate at five pesos per dollar or its equivalent in other currencies . . . This decision aims to ensure the official exchange rate of the Argentine peso accurately reflects its value, adopting measures that combine national interests with the newly devaluated currency. (*La Nación*, August 25, 1971)
>
> Given the clear-cut formulation of the 1976 economic program, it would have been difficult to predict this fictitious exchange rate, a déjà vu of the worst errors of the past. The arbitrarily overvalued peso, incorporated to a set of measures passed in May of this year, has proven ineffective at halting inflation. Yet it also has negative impacts in other areas: discouraging exports, artificially lowering the price of imports, leaving industry unprotected, deterring foreign tourism, and promoting Argentine spending abroad. (*Clarín*, December 14, 1978)

Both the regulations introduced on the forex market and the discussions surrounding them reveal that, in terms of both context and structure, there was nothing unprecedented about the forex cepo of the 2010s. On the contrary, what some were calling the *corralito verde* (green pen) harked back to other experiences of the past. The debates surrounding the cepo, however, did have some novel aspects. While in the 1970s and 1980s, the growing Argentine propensity toward the dollar came up in reporting on forex regulations and their effects, this issue took front and center starting in 2012. Whatever journalists and experts had to say about the measures being introduced, one question always begged for an answer: Why do so many Argentines want to buy dollars?

During the cepo, there were mainly two responses. The first, similar to interpretations of this phenomenon so common in the past, was that in times of high inflation, the dollar was a rational choice. When the national currency could not satisfactorily serve as a store of value, the US currency appeared as a "safe haven." Buying dollars, according to this perspective, was a way to "protect" one's purchasing power as prices rose. According to the other perspectives, however, the preference for the dollar could not be explained in exclusively economic terms. It was a "cultural problem." Without denying the influence of inflation, this interpretation emphasized a dimension of the dollar's allure that was not entirely rational. As the editor of the Economy section in one of the Buenos Aires papers quipped, "This isn't just about economics: it's a cultural standard among economic actors" (*Página/12*, May 19, 2012).

In many of the debates, this contrast between economic rationale and cultural standards led to a more specific discussion, that of normal (e.g., rational) behaviors versus pathological (or irrational) behaviors. Arguing against those who defended the dollar strategy as a way to prevent salaries from eroding, a group of journalists and media outlets considered the insistence on the dollar a malady akin to a psychological disorder. "Obsessive-compulsive dollar disorder," "green psychosis," "a national folkloric obsession," "dollar fever," and "dollar-drug dependence" were some of the terms used to pathologize the Argentine preference for the dollar. Those in favor of this argument acknowledged how inflation reduced the peso's standing as a store of value but emphasized that in the current-day national and international economy, the dollar was far from the best investment alternative.

According to this perspective, an economic actor made a rational choice when choosing the most profitable option. Yet there were other investment options on the local market—typically, stocks, bonds, and certificates of deposit—that yielded higher returns. Another strike against the US dollar was that its value had dropped since the 2008 economic crisis. Now that saving in dollars was not such a solid savings option, the affinity for the dollar could be seen as pathological, as some analysts engaged in the public debate argued.

In his work on inflation in Argentina and Brazil (Neiburg 2006; 2010; 2011), anthropologist Federico Neiburg has noted the use of medical metaphors in explanations surrounding money. References to the instability ("illness") of currency, Neiburg shows, has a long tradition in the Western world. In the public discussions about the dollar's central role in Argentina, this trend of pathologizing the greenback was evident. Within the framework of the forex cepo, however, there was a novel aspect to the trend: the health and medical metaphors were applied not to the country's monetary policies but to certain money behaviors and practices by Argentines conceived of as "sick" or as "symptoms" of illness.

> Dollar-related OCD [obsessive-compulsive disorder] is a symptom that dates back years, with varying degrees of severity, but a new aggressive recurrence can now be attributed to the tax authority's abrupt decision to ban the purchase of foreign currencies, regardless of the amount requested or the financial standing of the applicant. . . . As occurs with alcoholics, treatment must be progressive to avoid the desperation caused by withdrawal syndrome. A strategy consisting of the abrupt cessation of nearly all greenback purchase transactions has worsened an already severe case of economy uncertainty among the dollar-drug dependents. (*Página/12*, June 3, 2012)

This type of argument, which brings noneconomic factors to bear in the public debate surrounding the Argentine fixation on the dollar, was particularly frequent among elected officials. Two days after Cristina Fernández spoke of the runs on foreign currency during her second inaugural speech, for example, Central Bank president Mercedes Marcó del Pont gave an interview to the press. In this interview, she mentioned speculation in the year leading up to the election on the part of sectors "with a vested interest in generating a more extreme devaluation [of the peso] while doing political damage." Del Pont also spoke of the differences between the recent run on foreign currency and those that preceded it:

> In this case [2011], there was no talk of capital flight, because the majority of the dollars being purchased stayed in Argentina. Many argued for a passive approach, saying, "The culture of saving in dollars has to pass," but that requires too much time. Sometimes, change requires a push. For example, the introduction of restrictions on dollar purchases. . . . This represents a step towards the *pesificación* of the economy. (*Página/12*, December 31, 2011)

Axel Kicillof, the minister of economy of the final two years Cristina Kirchner was president, made a similar argument in January 2014. In response to the peso's recent devaluation and the return of the "savings dollar," Kicillof said,

> In Argentina, the dollar represents a cultural problem. It's not only about major speculators or the richest sectors wagering on foreign currency: it's that the desire to have dollars is culturally rooted in the minds of Argentines. There is no economic explanation for this, nor can it be attributed to recent events. Countries like Brazil, Chile, and Uruguay have all devaluated their currencies, but none of these economies rely on dollars like Argentina's. There was a time when investments in dollars were not as profitable as certificates of deposit, stocks, or bonds, but among the lower middle and middle-income earners, the demand for dollars continued. If people are constantly demanding dollars, there is a cultural pressure on the exchange rate, not to mention the way this influences factors in the real economy. This measure [new criteria for authorizing purchases of the "saving dollar"] is designed to address precisely that. (*Página/12*, January 26, 2014)

With statements like these by the minister of economy and many other officials, the dollar as a "cultural issue" became an argument to justify decisions at the highest levels of government. "De-dollarization" thus became a way to battle Argentine society's economic reliance on the US dollar and its cultural components: behaviors and decisions that were, to some degree, irrational.

## The Streets Speak

While the forex market restrictions tightened and this type of discussion became more frequent in the media, a brief and unsigned message began circulating on social media accounts in the capital and Greater Buenos Aires toward the end of May 2012.

> To make Argentina the country we want it to be, we say ENOUGH. Enough of medication shortages.
> Enough of import and export restrictions. Enough limits on the dollar.
> Enough cases like Ciccone.[20]
> Enough verbal violence. Enough expropriations. Enough strongmen.
> Enough impunity. Enough authoritarianism. Enough of the lack of dialogue.
> Enough INSECURITY. Enough corruption.

CACEROLAZO and/or BOCINAZO[21] on Thursday, May 31st. 8:30 pm.

Spread the word . . . If you want to do something to change our Argentina!

This was the first anti-government protest since the massive demonstrations that had taken place in 2008 during the so-called countryside conflict. As had occurred that year, the sounds of pots banging and horns honking could be heard in the upscale neighborhoods on the north side of the capital city. On a handful of iconic corners, small groups gathered with pots and wooden spoons, but no signs or slogans in common. As one journalist recounted in a chronicle published the following day in an international paper, the demonstrators "did not appear to be protesting anything particular": what brought them together was contempt for the administration, particularly President Cristina Fernández.

The protest did coincide with the introduction of new and stricter requirements on "tourist dollar" purchases. That same week, statistics were released on the drop in real estate sales and the rise in bank deposit withdrawals. Though it was just one reason that residents of the city of Buenos Aires had taken to the streets, the dollar cepo appears to have been a strong motivator. Later in 2012, two similar protests took place. The most important, held on November 8 and referred to as #8N, extended beyond the capital to cities across the country. Unlike the first and more improvised of these protests, this one was preceded by a call to action that circulated for several weeks before the day of the protest, mainly on social media and, in some cases, by groups created solely to encourage turnout. However, there was still no clear leader of these protests, no announcements, and no speakers. There were no common slogans, nor did political organizations participate. Attendees seemed to agree only on the Argentine flag and the national anthem. As had occurred with the demands that had circulated in the invitations for the first *cacerolazo*, a range of grievances coexisted, though most could be categorized within two categories. Demands for the government to end the forex cepo had disappeared while claims of government corruption and restrictions on the freedom of expression had taken its place.

In 2013, on April 18 (#18A) and November 13 (#13N), two additional *cacerolazos* were organized against the Cristina Fernández administration. Again, the summons to both were sent on social media and focused on government corruption and authoritarian measures. However, unlike in 2012 when political figures had been largely absent from the two protests, members of the opposition attended the ones held in 2013. Again, an end to the cepo was not one of the most common demands among protesters interviewed on television cameras, or in social media messages, or the signs the demonstrators carried. In other words, discontent over the dollar restrictions—visible in media debates, captured in reader comments of the major papers, and in daily humor—did not translate into a robust entreaty for the government to take action.

During the 2001 crisis, the mobilizations of bank account holders had resulted in a street slogan ("We deposited dollars, we want dollars back") and court petitions. Between 2012 and 2014, despite the general upset over restrictions on foreign currency access, people did not characterize this as a violation of their rights, come out against it in public, or demand a response on the part of institutions. Far from a protest slogan, the upset regarding dollar restrictions served only as a catalyst to take to the streets. In other words, it contributed politically to a general sense of anger as opposed to a public demand on the part of citizens for specific action.

## The "Election Dollar" and Foreign Exchange Campaigning in 2015

While running for president in 2015, Buenos Aires mayor Mauricio Macri turned the forex cepo into one of the key political weapons of his campaign. The candidate for Cambiemos, a newly formed coalition of opposition parties, made this promise in March: "Starting in December, the cepo will be over and done and then we will gradually work to end inflation." (*Infobae*, March 17, 2015). The governor of Buenos Aires Province, Daniel Scioli, was quick to respond. Scioli—the candidate for the ruling party coalition, Frente para la Victoria—referred to the proposal as "irresponsible," and warned that it would lead "to an abrupt devaluation." Central Bank president Alejandro Vanoli was quick to agree with this assessment. In Scioli's view, by reintroducing the "savings dollar" in recent months, the Cristina Fernández administration was playing it safe: progressively eliminating the restrictions without jeopardizing the peso's value. At the same time, the economists on the Cambiemos team began backpedaling on amendments to the foreign exchange market regulations: "Don't take 'the *cepo* will be over and done December 11$^{th}$' too literally" (*El Cronista*, March 18, 2015).

Macri's pledge to abolish the cepo, however, became one of his core campaign messages. Even analysts who favored the opposition's candidate and proposals warned that this particular vow was "brazen." Macri was at risk of being unable to meet the promise, as occurred back in 2002 when President Duhalde vowed, "whoever deposited dollars will get dollars back."[22] More important than the feasibility of the proposal was the fact that the presidential candidate had incorporated a topic sensitive for both voters and markets to his agenda.

As the months passed, Macri continued to insist on an end to the cepo as a central part of his campaign. The Cambiemos economic advisors soon joined him, working to dissipate doubts surrounding a sudden and definitive end to exchange rate controls. The coalition's future minister of the interior, Rogelio Frigerio, had this to say about the official dollar exchange rate: "There is no dollar in Argentina worth nine pesos: that's a virtual dollar. We need a single exchange rate. We need to end the forex *cepo*." Like Macri, Frigerio argued in favor of ending the forex restrictions on the president's first day in office, "because the forex *cepo* does more to prevent dollars from flowing into the country than to keep them from flowing out." The closer the election came, the more prominent the question of exchange rate restrictions became. All the main candidates began talking about the cepo, which also led accusations to fly.

In their statements to the press, economists sought to leverage their technical knowledge to influence public opinion for or against a candidate. Miguel Bein, an economic advisor to Scioli, explained that the cepo

> is capital control. There are restrictions and limitations . . . I would call it a light *cepo*. When he takes office, the president will keep capital controls in place. Eliminating them would lead to a brusque devaluation of the peso, annihilating the purchasing power of the people. (*La Nación*, c. October 15, 2015)

Alfonso Prat-Gay, former president of the Banco Central who would be appointed minister of economy once Macri took office, focused instead on the benefits of a floating rate on the currency exchange market:

> The dollar cepo is the easiest problem of them all. We plan to open up the cepo to let in dollars that should have been coming. These are trade dollars. Since the cepo, exports have plummeted and our regional economies are hurting. It's necessary to create incentives for the sector that generates foreign currency so this sector can do precisely that. It's that simple. (*El País*, October 16, 2015)

Other economists who supported Macri lamented the "artificially low exchange rate" of Cristina Fernández's second term but promised a "floating" exchange rate once Cambiemos was in power to ensure it would reflect the peso's true value. In the Cambiemos proposal, doing away with the cepo was a decisive step in a set of institutional reforms that President Macri saw as essential; he associated the Cristina Fernández administration and its manipulation of statistical data—which he characterized as lying to Argentines about the true state of the economy—as a populist ploy to retain support. Under such an administration, argued Macri, people rightly turned to the forex market as a source of truth and certainty. "Of course everyone wants to buy dollars: how could it be otherwise?" he asked in July 2015. "It makes perfect sense. After all, this administration lies about absolutely everything" (*El Cronista*, July 16, 2015).

However, the Banco Central had solid numbers to back its argument that the country lacked the reserves necessary to end the forex cepo in one fell swoop. As the elections grew closer, the sales of the "savings dollar" rose, thus further reducing foreign currency reserves. At the same time, the "blue" dollar continued its upward climb. At the end of July 2015, with elections scheduled for November, the Central Bank upped the benchmark interest rate for investments. Working to discourage the purchase of foreign currencies in a context where demand was putting pressure on the forex market, the monetary authority took an active role on the dollar futures market. By offering new contracts for future dollars with pesos as the base currency, the Central Bank sought to attract investments to the futures market, limiting the contado con liqui transactions and preventing the "stock market dollar"—and the blue dollar—from rising.

For the critics of the administration, the financial body was "raffling off" the country's reserves with these contracts; the fixed price of the quoted currency (the dollar) in the contracts was lower than what its actual price would likely be, given the high chance of a devaluation of the peso. In the view of these detractors, instead of giving individuals the change to invest and take a chance on profits or losses on the futures market, the Central Bank was instead providing them with an exchange rate "insurance," that is, allowing them to purchase dollars at a fixed anticipated rate. The sole condition for investors was to wait until a certain date to receive the "physical currency," but in exchange, the price in pesos for these dollars was guaranteed. Thus, in March 2016, the Central Bank was offering a future dollar at AR$10, when five months earlier, the "blue" dollar was already trading at AR$15.

In October 2015, when the dollar at AR$16, Prat Gay—then a legislator with the opposition party—petitioned the courts to investigate the dollar futures transactions. According to the former president of the Central Bank, this exchange rate "insurance" threatened to empty the country's foreign currency reserves. Those accused in the lawsuit were high-ranking government officials, including the president herself, and the Central Bank authorities. This politically driven litigation of the exchange market represents a chapter unto itself in the election campaign.

The first round of the presidential elections took place at the end of October 2015. Over the course of that month, 1.2 million Argentines purchased "savings dollars" for a total of US$700 million. It was a record number for a single month since the government had loosened the forex cepo by introducing this new option for dollar purchases in January 2014. The rising demand for dollars could be attributed to the upcoming elections and the fear of further depreciation of the peso. Observers noted that many of the individuals buying the "savings dollar" in October that year had never dabbled in purchases on the official foreign currency market in the past.

Without the restrictions on the "savings dollar" by the Central Bank, the quantity of dollars purchased for savings would have been even higher.

Before the first round of the election, another tremor shook the financial system: a withdrawal of nearly US$170 million in bank deposits. In October, the country's reserves had plummeted by nearly US$6 billion, a 20 percent decrease. On the day of the election, October 25, none of the candidates won enough of the votes to be declared a winner in the first round. Yet the ruling party received fewer votes than expected, and it seemed very likely that the Cambiemos candidate would triumph in the second round. On Monday, October 26, *La Nación* noted that the "blue" dollar had opened lower than the previous week, a piece of good news it attributed to the blow dealt to Frente para la Victoria a day earlier.

The two candidates who would go head to head in the second round, Daniel Scioli and Mauricio Macri, made both promises and prophecies in relation to the future of the exchange market. While the Frente para la Victoria candidate predicted a dollar worth no more than AR$10 in January, the man for Cambiemos anticipated that the dollar would be worth AR$16 at the start of the following year, taking as a reference the current value of the "blue" dollar. His position, both popular and controversial, was based on the notion that the true value of the US currency was its purchase price in cuevas (the blue dollar), not that of Banco Nación (the official dollar). Therefore, according to Macri's line of reasoning, once he freed the country from the cepo and the dollar rose to AR$16, it would mean "coming clean," not a "devaluation." Some of his advisors argued that "sixteen pesos is too high" and that a single floating exchange rate would be lower. Macri was elected on November 22; twenty-eight days later, he took office. Seven days after being sworn in, he fulfilled his campaign promise and ended the forex cepo. The end of the restrictions caused a 40 percent depreciation of the peso.

"The *cepo* is a trauma I carry," said the head of the Central Bank when the foreign exchange controls were implemented in 2011. Mercedes Marcó del Pont, who held the post for nearly three years, had been invited to speak at the presentation of a book about monetary policy attended mainly by young students in the social sciences. It was 2016, and several months had passed since President Macri had put an end to all currency restrictions as promised during his campaign. Back when the cepo had been introduced, however, this public official had actively defended the restrictions as a weapon in a "cultural battle" oriented toward "de-dollarizing the minds" of Argentines. The "trauma" that plagued her in 2016 could likely be attributed to having lost that battle, given that the Argentine penchant for dollars held strong despite nearly five years of foreign exchange restrictions.

Regulations to limit multiple exchange rates like those implemented between 2011 and 2015 in Argentina must address practices and beliefs that take root over time. Phrased in psychoanalytical terms, the "trauma" of the Argentine Central

Bank's former president denoted how these measures limiting access to US dollars clashed with established uses and robust meanings of that currency among Argentines.

By exploring the most recent stage of the dollar's popularization, this chapter has shown how practices and connotations of the US dollar constructed over time are brought to bear in response to certain situations. It also analyzed innovations during the period that followed the 2001–2002 crisis, particularly de-dollarization as state policy and the idea—born in 2001 but reinterpreted during this period—that access to the dollar is a fundamental right. Both point to the production of new meanings and uses for the greenback, as well as the central role conceptualizations of money play in political conflicts, pivotal moments in the dollar's gradual popularization in Argentine society.

*Conclusion*

# THE DOLLAR BEYOND ITS BORDERS

Thousands of peoples come through the Callao subway station in Buenos Aires, Argentina's capital, every day. The walls behind the subway platform feature a series of blown-up comic strips by Landrú, a famous Argentine graphic artist whose work dates back to the 1960s.

Drawing on a particularly Argentine humor, Landrú's comic strips usually depict two typical characters the public can easily identify: office worker and boss, parent and child, husband and wife, doctor and patient. In one of them, an apprehensive mother consults with her son's pediatrician. "I'm so worried, doctor! The little one swallowed a dollar." The doctor is reassuring in his response: "Don't worry, ma'am. It will go down."

Dating back to the 1930s, the popularization of the dollar in Argentina has been a lengthy process. At the beginning, interest in the dollar was limited to financial market or foreign trade experts; over the years, it expanded to an increasing number of social groups and became a political flashpoint.

As knowledge about the dollar expanded, so did its use as a regular, frequently used currency. A series of specific mediations proved essential to the dollar's integration to the savings, investment, loan, and consumer practices of Argentines with scarce experience on the finance and forex market. The most important of these was undoubtedly the US currency's transformation into an artifact of popular culture. The dollar became familiar, easy to understand, and capable of providing cognitive, emotional, and practical guidance to anyone exploring new economic universes.

The first stage of the dollar's popularization extends from the end of the 1950s to the beginning of the 1970s, years of political and economic upheaval as well as periodic devaluations of the national currency. The dollar, once a benchmark for economic or policy experts, became a familiar reference for an ever-expanding public. The press covered the rapid movements of the forex market, advertisers made the dollar into an icon, and the US currency gradually became a litmus test of Argentina's economic and political reality. In the 1970s, the dollar's meanings and uses expanded. Spiraling inflation—and, later, the liberalization of the forex market—made it a pressing topic in the public debate, while increasingly diverse social groups incorporated it to their financial repertoires.

At the same time, certain domestic markets began using the dollar as a unit of reference and medium of exchange. In 1977, rising inflation and property investments drove real estate agents to start publishing home prices in dollars, thus avoiding the renegotiations that came with a fluctuating exchange rate. The institutional setting shifted with the return to democracy in 1983, contributing to an economic, political, and cultural proliferation of the dollar. The hyperinflation of 1989 left two indelible marks: an almost ubiquitous use of the dollar in local transactions and a correlation between election outcomes and forex market dynamics. Over time, this connection would evolve into a distinctive feature of Argentine politics.

Hyperinflation instigated a terminal currency crisis that exacerbated the use of a second currency (the dollar) as one of its most notable offshoots. Therefore, the creators of the currency board (1991–2001) presented the dollar peg as a way to legalize de facto practices. A certain level of economic discipline and a profound transformation of the financial system accompanied this decade of currency stability. The country opened up to foreign capital while bank customers increasingly opted for savings and loans denominated in US dollars. The crisis of 2001 laid bare the dramatic consequences of this process.

In its aftermath—and as a new political cycle led to the election of President Néstor Kirchner in 2003—the dollar's integration to local financial repertoires continued, albeit with some novel features. The 2001–2002 crisis represented the first time in which social actors like the holders of savings accounts and mortgage loans voiced specific demands around the buck. Their protests revealed yet another facet of the dollar's popularization that resurfaced in 2011–2015 as Argentines insisted that access to the forex market was a right they were being denied. Two novel features of the dollar's popularization during this period (2011–2015) are, first, the way in which it was articulated with the logic of right, and second, the government's efforts to challenge the dollar's popularity while building a political discourse around the need to decrease it.

This took shape as a "cultural battle" over the "de-dollarization" of the national economy, as the Kirchner administration introduced new forex restrictions and the public debate intensified. In the 2015 elections, a new political coalition, Cambiemos, rose to power after twelve years of Kirchner presidencies (Néstor Kirchner first, followed by his wife Cristina Fernández, who served two terms); the coalition's win was strongly influenced by its depiction of access to foreign exchange as a "right."[1]

# The Popular Dimensions of a Global Currency

Vivana Zelizer's compelling work describes the limits of currency unification in her analysis of the US dollar at the turn of the twentieth century (1994). This book has taken up where Zelizer left off, tracing the history of the dollar as it evolved into a "global currency." Yet the focus here differs from that of studies of the dollar as a dominant currency in the international monetary system. This book is an attempt to shed light on the unexplored aspects of "global currencies," that is, what happens when they become "popular currencies" outside their national borders.

The sociology of money has demonstrated that monies have no momentum of their own: the practices surrounding monies involve complex learning processes—processes too often treated as natural—for people to appropriate, trust them, and use them. In Zelizer's seminal work, this process—in which macroeconomic dynamics and policies are connected to the widespread use of a given currency—is reconstructed "from the bottom up." The question of how people incorporate a new unified currency in their day-to-day lives is thus considered, along with the way in which it becomes compatible with their social relations, their family and gender dynamics, etc. This model of analysis, the cornerstone of the contemporary sociology of money, is based on the idea that a currency's expansion is about more than just a government decision or certain macroeconomic conditions. Instead, the popularization of a currency is the result of a process we might refer to as "currency familiarization" that sociologists must reconstruct.

According to this perspective, there is no direct causal relationship between macroeconomic dynamics and the widespread use of a currency. Instead, the focus is on the cultural mediations that link contexts and practices surrounding a currency, serving as money lessons. These mediations help people incorporate the cognitive tools (interpretations, languages, and calculations) they need to make these new monies their own. In order for these lessons to have an impact on a broader public—especially one with no economic expertise—and disseminate a currency across a society, myriad formats must be used. It could even be said that the less these formats rely on expert knowledge, and the closer they are to mass culture, the more likely they are to be effective. This way, new currencies are more likely to become popular, part of mass culture, and accessible in their multiple uses and meanings for broad swaths of society.

This is precisely what has been happening with the US dollar in Argentina since the end of the 1950s. Gradually, the dollar carved out a prominent place in mass culture through a wide variety of cultural mediations. These included everything from press chronicles that described the forex market in an accessible language to advertisements, comic strips, television, theater, film, and—more recently—social media and memes.

It is important to identify the multiple uses and connotations attributed to the US currency locally. By referring to the dollar as a "global currency," the emphasis is on the buck's role in the international monetary system. The concept of "popular currency," in contrast, captures a different dimension of this function of the dollar, other uses and meanings, and its changes over time. One of the core hypotheses of the sociology of money—the same hypothesis that lays the groundwork for this book—is that money is never exactly the same. At each stage of the dollar's popularization, uses and meanings inherited from the past were adapted and innovated.

Over time, the dynamics changed. The number of social groups that incorporated the dollar to their financial repertoires varied, as did its use as a medium of exchange and the public attention it garnered. The public and transactional lives of the dollar were often in step with one another, but not always. Thus, the pace at which the US currency expanded and reached broader social segments (vis-à-vis its integration to financial repertoires and multiple markets) did not always match that of its intensification (as a lens into politics and economics), revealing its relative autonomy within these different spheres.

## Global Currency vs. National state

The learning of a financial repertoire based on the articulation of different currencies means pushing numbers, paying, and saving, but also imagining and planning in several units at the same time. In our case, these units are the Argentine peso and the US dollar. At the most critical junctures of history, this savvy often surprises foreign observers. As one Buenos Aires visitor asked a journalist in June 1989: "How can you live like this?" (*Clarín*, June 18, 1989). It was a frequent question among non-Argentines. The unique economic socialization of the local population has given them practical tools and knowledge to guide them through unstable times. It is the ability to keep one's head above water—and even prosper—during times of currency instability, and often even profit from them (Guyer 2004).

This training, accumulated over years, constitutes a great cognitive and symbolic tool, a cluster of knowledge and practices. At different moments in relatively recent history—the hyperinflation of 1989, the end of the currency board in 2001, the forex restrictions in 2011–2015—this training in a context of monetary plurality had provided autonomy. Though the lessons, people gain more maneuvering room in the face of a state widely viewed as calamitous and the financial system it regulates. Essentially, it keeps them from going down with the ship.

Moreover, as we have shown throughout this book, the building of a financial repertoire that combines different currencies and monetary functions is an ongoing, flexible process. Despite certain continuities from one period to the next—rising inflation and forex restrictions among them—scenarios are never quite the same, and people develop novel strategies that build on lessons from the past (Luzzi and Wilkis 2018). At the same time, this room for innovation enables profit-making. Yet while some scholars have treated the use of the dollar as a unit of account or store of value as an "automatic" response to inflation, our fieldwork shows that people's decisions adapt to each specific juncture. Transactions are often innovative and always anchored in historic processes of economic socialization; they are reactivations of individual and collective lessons learned in unique contexts.

As this book has shown, Argentines embraced the dollar as part of their social lives in multiple ways. First and foremost, the dollar proves a valuable, meaningful piece of information. Tracking the ups and downs of this currency allows Argentines to assess the domestic state of affairs at any given moment. Importantly, these assessments can also provide guidance on what to do with the dollar. After all, as a currency, the dollar is not only an asset but also a medium that enables actions. Or to put it another way, during times of financial turbulence, the dollar serves not only as a bellwether but also as a possible solution to a problem. Now that the US currency has been part and parcel of the Argentine economy for decades, it represents a familiar, simple, and relatively immediate strategy to weather financial instability (or elude it altogether) among many Argentines. For residents of Buenos Aires, it was once as easy as heading downtown to San Martín Street. For Argentines across the country, it is now as easy as logging on to home banking. Although the efficacy (or potential for profit) of this solution can never be known beforehand, in the midst of a crisis, it allows people to "do something" or at least imagine that something can be done.

In several Latin American countries, the state has failed to keep drug traffickers or guerrilla groups from controlling their territory. In Argentina, the main issue the state has faced is entirely different: it failed to establish a currency that provides its people with protection and certainty. Incorporating the dollar to family financial repertoires means operating independently from the state, freeing oneself from its controls. It allows Argentines to develop knowledge and learn lessons on working around currency regulations and cyclical state breakdowns. In this book, we have shown how the configuration of monetary pluralism connects with views on the state, its capacities for regulation, and the resistance it encounters. Unlike the peso, the US dollar is critically positioned outside the scope of the state, immune to its ails.

## Money Cultures as Political Cultures

Culture is a difficult word when analyzing the place of the dollar in Argentine society. When we began analyzing the popularization of the dollar—and the peculiar money culture at its origin—we found ourselves in a debate that far exceeded academia.

## Conclusion

The publication of the Spanish-language version of this book caused a stir in the press and in political and intellectual circles. In 2020, in yet another context of forex instability, Central Bank president Miguel Pesce appeared on prime-time television. The question of the dollar in Argentine society was a "question of culture," he said, and thus outside the control of the monetary authority; he proceeded to recommend our book as a guide to understanding this.

Over the last decade, the word "culture" has been ubiquitous in the press and in statements by public officials discussing the persistent and ostensibly irreversible penchant for the dollar among Argentines. Others, in contrast, argue that any talk of a "cultural trend" overlooks the rational behaviors of economic agents that could explain this preference. The research behind this book shows that neither of these arguments fully explains the phenomenon. On the one hand, the social history of the popularization of the dollar in Argentina reveals that while the US currency relied on myriad economic and political dynamics to gradually gain prominence, it also required meaningful social and cultural mediations. Like all historical and social processes, this popularization is not set in stone: it is subject to change and could even be reversed. On the other hand, the idea of economic agents guided exclusively by an urge for maximum individual benefits provides little insight into the diverse—and not always evident—meanings and uses of the dollar within this money culture.

The study of money cultures matters because people's relationship with money is about more than automatic responses to material conditions. Money does not always operate the same way; context and place both play a part. In order to understand the role the dollar has played in Argentina since the second half of the twentieth century, this perspective led us to speak of a *global* currency, the term used in economic history and political economics to refer to the dollar's expansion outside the United States. However, this is articulated herein with the sociological notion of a *popular* currency in order to consider how these strong monies not only expand but also are integrated—and thus transformed—in other territories, and even refashioned as local monies. These hypotheses allowed us to take another step forward and discover not only how the dollar has been integrated to the financial repertoires of Argentines but also the political meanings and uses of the US currency within the money culture that popularization has engendered.

At different points in time over the lengthy period analyzed herein, government officials, journalists, and economic experts sought to shift the debate away from the dollar. In doing so, they argued that the dollar was an issue that concerned but a small minority of Argentines—those capable of investing on the forex market. As this book has highlighted, however, the dollar is in fact a currency of the masses. Furthermore, this predilection for the dollar is about more than its relative strength in comparison to the Argentine peso; the buck consistently provides trustworthy interpretations of the national state of affairs.

While these attempts to sway attention away from the dollar rely on a traditional understanding of currency's functions, the history reconstructed here shows uses and implications of monies that exceed this definition. The dollar's role as a tool for interpretation and political decision-making proves as important as its ability to serve as a unit of account, a medium of exchange, a form of payment, and a store of value.

After a spike in the dollar's worth in August 2018, a journalist headed to one of the most densely populated districts of Greater Buenos Aires to interview locals. This had been one of the epicenters of the looting that accompanied the economic crisis of 2001. Now, when consulted by the journalist about what could be expected, a shopkeeper quipped, "There will probably be looting again." A change in the value of the US dollar allowed this merchant to make predictions on what was to come with a relative degree of certainty. His attention to the exchange rate was independent of how strongly the dollar—or the dual currency system—figured into his own personal finances. Instead, he had appropriated this numerical value as political insight into predictable consequences, some of which could have a direct impact on him (the possibility that the devaluation could lead to a more profound economic crisis following by store looting, as had occurred in the past).

At the end of 2018, almost a year before the presidential elections of 2019, joint efforts by the Cambiemos coalition administration and Central Bank temporarily stabilized the exchange rate, raising the approval ratings of President Mauricio Macri. According to national surveys, it was the first improvement in the president's image after runs on the dollar in mid-2018 had led to a severe drop in his popularity. A few months into 2019, after a new run on the dollar, the same polls showed that the president's chance of winning reelection was waning, and, in fact, he went on to lose to candidate Alberto Fernández later that year. As in 2011 and 2015, yet with even greater intensity, the forex market became a political flashpoint during the campaign of 2019. This revealed that this connection between elections and foreign exchange turbulence had become a characteristic feature of local political life.

Argentine political scientist Guillermo O'Donnell (1996) has suggested that "other [informal] institutions" must be considered in order to understand the workings of democracy. The popularization of the dollar, which plays a central role in both the economy and politics, has affirmed the forex market as an informal democratic institution in Argentina since democracy was reinstated in 1983. As seen throughout this book, the forex market shaped not only expectations for democratic political actors during four decades but also their chances of continuing in office. This did not happen once or only occasionally; instead, it was a gradual process that started in 1983 and eventually became the status quo. Therefore, the forex market can be treated as an institution that helped determine democratic behaviors thanks to a money culture organized around the dollar and inextricably entwined with political culture.

Over the past four decades, the more the dollar rises and the less the government is able to keep it in check, the less likely it is to win reelection. Political actors from the opposition have also gauged their chances through the dollar's ups and downs. At the same time, it has become impossible for Argentines to ignore the dollar. After all, the dollar is a bellwether for a continuously shifting and often profoundly unstable reality, offering insight into where the economy is heading and what will happen in the next elections. Were Argentines to abandon or renounce the dollar today, they would be left feeling less able to interpret the political context and take action accordingly. Opting not to check the exchange rate, which appears in the news as frequently as the weather, would be akin to withdrawing from public life. The forex market has conditioned the democratic participation of politicians and citizens alike for the past four decades.

In Argentina, the consolidation of democracy has been inextricably tied to the popularization of the dollar and to the forex market's increasing role as an informal democratic institution. This shows that the political sociology of money is critical to any analysis of the workings of democracy in countries like Argentina. It is our hope that this book contributes to a research agenda that is still only beginning in Latin America.

For decades, economists and journalists specializing in the economy cited the macroeconomics of the trade deficit and/or inflation as the only way to explain the "Argentine penchant" for dollars. In a uniquely configured public debate, economists hold a monopoly on knowledge and are treated as the only whose opinion on this key topic matters. Sociologists, in contrast, have largely overlooked this "penchant" in their research. Our reconstruction of the long, slow process of the dollar's popularization allowed us to go further than economists ever had in their debate on why Argentines developed this affinity for the dollar.

What set our work apart was, first and foremost, the fact that we did not limit ourselves to explaining *why* the dollar occupies the place it has earned in Argentine society. Instead, we homed in on *how* this process occurred: the conditions, the map of actors, and the innovations that could be seen at each stage of the popularization. Second, we treated the dollar not only as a particular currency but also as a tool for interpretation and political action. Knowledge of forex market fluctuations guides financial decisions but also political expectations and experiences. Keeping up on this market is a way of participating in political life; it allows citizens to assess a government's performance—or the opposition's chances to win an upcoming election. Incorporating the dollar in family financial repertoires means putting into practice a relationship with the Argentine state that is, to some degree, autonomous.

In response to the recurring question on the Argentine preference for the US dollar, we showcased previously unnoticed uses and meanings of money, revealing how the dollar provides protection and resistance in the face of a perpetually weak state. So when people ask why Argentines buy dollars whenever they get the chance, we respond, who doesn't look out for their best interest—and how did they learn what that best interest was?

As we trust this book has shown, only a sociological perspective is capable of truly assessing how a global currency becomes popular outside its national borders, in this case, the history of the place of the US dollar in Argentine society, culture, and politics. This perspective must consider the conditions and shifting forms this popularization takes over time in order to ask the necessary questions and work backward to find the answers.

# NOTES

## Introduction

1. On several opportunities, Zelizer clarified that her theory was not intended to be applied exclusively to the domestic sphere; Zelizer originally wanted to incorporate other money situations outside the household in *The Social Meaning of Money*. In the afterword to the book's most recent edition, the author even suggests that, were she to rewrite the book now, she would consider other non-domestic currency realms (Zelizer 2017).

## Chapter One

1. In September 1930, General José Felix Uriburu overthrew President Hipólito Yrigoyen, who had begun his second presidency in 1928. Yrigoyen was a member of Unión Cívica Radical (Radical party), a political party associated with the new urban middle classes. Uriburu was part of a fascist-supporting, corporate, anti-liberal group within the Argentine army, and his would be the first of many military coups over the course of the twentieth century (Rock 1975).

2. Federico Pinedo serviced as minister of economy on three occasions (1933–1935, 1940–1941, and for a brief stint in 1962). During his first period as minister, he launched the National Economic Action Plan to increase government intervention in the economy. New institutions were created like the Regulation Boards for Meats and Grains, which regulated prices for export goods. Besides maintaining measures to control the foreign exchange market, Pinedo oversaw the founding of the Central Bank during his time as minister.

3. The first Five-Year Plan (1947–1952) was guided by President Perón's conviction that the

government should have a hand in the economy. The plan emphasized industrialization and economic development as a way to consolidate national autonomy (Gerchunoff and Antúnez 2002).

4. Literally "black sack," another euphemism for the forex black market.

## Chapter Two

1. General Pedro Eugenio Aramburu, a member of the liberal, anti-Peronist wing of the Argentine army, served as president of the de facto regime after overthrowing President Perón in November 1955. In May 1958, Aramburu handed over power to a new democratically elected president. Under the general, Peronism had been banned, so no Peronist candidate was allowed to run in this election; the prohibition of the party would continue until 1973.

2. Arturo Frondizi was the democratically elected president from May 1958 until March 1962, when yet another coup d'état led by the military ousted him from power. The election of Frondizi had been overshadowed by the ban on Peronism, yet certain aspects of Frondizi's developmentalism were similar to the Peronist platform. Frondizi was a candidate presented by a faction of Unión Cívica Radical (Radical party) that was critical of the military government and more willing to engage in dialogue with sectors of Peronism (Altamirano 1998a).

3. Arturo Frondizi's overtures toward former Peronists left the armed forces wary that the democratically elected administration could lift the ban on the party and allow it to return to power. The military thus forced him to resign in March 1962 and replaced him with another civilian, José María Guido, who held the presidency until October 1963 (O'Donnell 1997; Cavarozzi 2006).

4. Arturo Illia won the presidential elections the following year and with just 25 percent of the votes; a high percentage of the electorate cast blank or spoiled ballots to protest the ongoing ban on Peronism (James 2003). Illia held office from October 1963 to June 1966.

5. In June 1966, the military intervened yet again, forcing Illia to resign and placing General Juan Carlos Onganía in the presidency in June 1966. The administration of Onganía, who held power until June 1970, was characterized by widespread repression and authoritarianism, in a period of popular uprisings and leftist militancy (O'Donnell 1982).

6. Launched in March 1967 under Onganía, the "Krieger Vasena plan"—named for the minister of the economy—introduced drastic measures in an attempt to reduce inflation. Besides ordering a 40 percent devaluation, collective bargaining and worker raises were banned, a prize freeze was ordered, and a new hydrocarbon law was passed to foster private sector participation in energy (Gerchunoff and Llach 2018).

7. The exclusive Uruguayan beach town.

# Chapter Three

1. In the elections of March 1973, Héctor Cámpora was elected president. Juan Domingo Perón, who had been living in exile since 1955 and was unable to run in the elections due to an express ban by the military regime, gave Cámpora his seal of approval. Political youth groups, some with ties to armed Peronist organizations like Montoneros that had arisen in recent years, fervently supported Peronism's return to power. Leftist Peronist groups had expanded since the end of the 1960s as part of a broader trend of rising political activism among young influenced by the Cuban Revolution, the ban on Peronism, and the authoritarian regimes (and ensuing repression) in Argentina and in other countries of the region (Gillespie 1982; James 2003; Manzano 2014).

2. General Lanusse headed the military regime from March 1971 and May 1973, when the Peronist candidate Héctor Cámpora was sworn in after a triumph at the polls two months earlier. In a feverish social and political climate characterized by waning public support for the military regime, Lanusse was under great pressure to set a date for elections.

3. Upon Perón's death, his widow María Estela Martínez de Perón (popularly known as "Isabelita") took office. Despite the insistence of his closest advisors to choose a running mate with political experience, Perón had put his wife on the September 1973 ticket as vice president. After a bout of high inflation in 1975, widespread union protests, attacks by armed groups that opposed the administration, and a growing sense among many military officers that another coup was in order, her time as president ended abruptly when the armed forces seized power on March 24, 1976 (Franco 2012).

4. José Ber Gelbard, a spokesman for Argentine entrepreneurs since the 1940s and businessman himself, served as minister of economy from May 1973 to October 1974. The "Gelbard Plan" was based on an agreement between workers and business owners geared to increasing industrial exports, public investments, and worker salaries to guarantee growth (de Riz 1981) and keep inflation in check. Through this social pact, Gelbard—the figurehead of Peronist economic policy in those years—forged a consensus among these key actors.

5. Following Ber Gerbard's resignation as minister of economy, the former president of the Central Bank, Alfredo Gómez Morales, took the helm. Gómez Morales had also served as minister of finance and economic affairs during Perón's first two terms. In June 1975, he tendered his resignation, and Celestino Rodrigo held the post of economic minister for forty-nine days. The measures Rodrigo introduced, known as the "rodrigazo," included severe cutbacks, a cap on salary increases, and a major price hike.

6. After the death of President Perón, political violence had surged across the country. Attacks by armed leftist guerrilla organizations—some but not all with ties to Peronism—were as prevalent as the kidnapping, torture, and murder of political activists by parapolice and paramilitary (Franco 2012; Carassai 2014).

7. The population of the Buenos Aires area was approximately seven million people.

8. The military junta that took over the country in 1976 had three members: Jorge Rafael Videla (Army), Emilio Massera (Navy), and Orlando Agosti (Air Force). Videla was appointed president of the de facto regime, a post he held until March 1981.

## Chapter Four

1. Interview conducted by the authors in Buenos Aires in May 2015 as part of a series of interviews with economic journalists of different ages for print media, radio, and television outlets.

2. The recent book by Juan Carlos Torre (2021), an Argentine sociologist and former official of the Ministry of Economy, provides valuable insight into the tensions the economic team faced during these years as the country attempted to hammer out a deal with the IMF.

3. As the printing of the new austral bills took time, the government decided to reuse old Argentine peso bills for the first few months after the creation of the new currency. These old bills had a seal stating their adjusted value (1,000 Argentine pesos were equal to one austral).

4. During times of crisis or immediately before announcing new regulations, the Argentine government had been declaring bank and/or forex "holidays"—that is, days on which a temporary halt was ordered on all financial activity or only foreign exchange transactions—for at least the past three decades.

## Chapter Five

1. The idea the song conveys is the narrator who buys dollars at AR$7,000 because he hears the exchange rate will be going up to AR$15,000. Inflation continues to rise, but the dollar never gets as high as he was told.

2. Carlos Saúl Menem (1930–2021) was an Argentine politician and a member of the Peronist party. He served as president from 1989 until 1995 and then, following a constitutional amendment that he himself introduced in 1994, he was reelected for a second term (this one four years) in 1995.

3. A reference to the fact that one peso was worth one US dollar. Initially, the Convertibility Act established a fixed exchange rate of ARA 10,000 per dollar. Months later, starting in January 1992, Argentina changed its official currency back to the peso and the new exchange rate became one peso (the equivalent of ARA 10,000) per dollar.

4. Besides these fundamental measures, the Convertibility Act did away with indexation and automatic price adjustments based on inflation. Now that the dollar was a legal currency, contracts could be stated in dollars, and people could open savings accounts and take out loans in dollars (Sgard 2014; Luzzi 2016).

5. In Spanish, the pun that makes the joke funny is that *bolsa* can refer to the stock market or to a pouch.

6. A town in Greater Buenos Aires.

7. Over the course of our fieldwork, we interviewed some twenty people from the world of finance, including financial advisors, officials, and workers from exchange offices, financial companies, banks, and the Central Bank. The interviews were conducted between 2014 and 2016. Certain public figures like the one quoted here, preferred to remain anonymous.

8. An Argentine writer, sociologist, and former advertising executive, Fogwill (1941–2010) won Argentina's National Prize for Literature in 2004.

9. In addition to the economic plan analyzed here, Menem's administration undertook sweeping state reforms largely aligned with the Washington Consensus, policy prescriptions that strongly influenced Latin America throughout the decade (Vellinga 1998). In the case of Argentina, in just five years, the country privatized all public utility companies and the retirement/pension system, besides a partial privatization of the national oil company (it would be fully privatized a few years later) (Gerchunoff and Torre 1998, 1999; Oszlak 2006). The revenues from the sales of these state-owned companies were key to maintaining the currency board for its first few years.

10. The unemployment crisis that began in the mid-1990s peaked during the crisis of 2001–2002 (Damill, Frenkel, and Maurizio 2002), leading to the formation of a robust movement of unemployed people (the *piquetero* movement) that became synonymous with the contentious politics of these years (Svampa and Pereyra 2003; Garay, 2007; Rossi 2017).

11. Although it surrounds the capital city of Buenos Aires, the province is a separate administrative entity from the capital.

12. This process continued for two years. Finally, as part of new negotiations with the International Monetary Fund, the Currency Unification Program was launched in 2003, and the federal government repurchased all bonds still in circulation. Cf. Luzzi 2012; 2015.

13. At that time, a one-bedroom apartment in the city of Buenos Aires rented for around US$/AR$400. Minimum monthly wage, which remained the same for years, was US$/AR$200, the same amount people received on unemployment.

14. Arbolitos (literally, little trees) is the slang term in Buenos Aires for those on the lowest rung of the illegal forex market: street vendors looking for potential buyers and sellers of foreign currency.

15. People out of work who would wait in line for someone else outside banks or state offices, often for hours. When they neared the front of the line, the person they were waiting for would come to take their place, paying them a handful of pesos for their time.

16. Incorporated to the Argentine Constitution in 1994, the writ of amparo is a legal instrument that provides rapid injunctive relief for individuals in the face of a violation of fundamental rights. During the crisis, it was a tool that allowed many of those affected by the corralito to contest the mandatory rescheduling/translation into pesos of their certificates of deposit in dollars, as ordered at the beginning of 2002. Given that the Argentine legal system

has nothing like a class action suit, the thousands of writs of amparo presented in 2002 served, in practice, as a collective legal action.

17. Villa Gessell is a popular and solidly middle-class beach destination in Argentina. Argentine anthropologist Diego Zenobi (2006) has noted the characteristic of this particular protest by Argentine savers and its repercussions.

18. During this "keychain protest," people made noise by shaking their house keys.

19. For decades, peer-to-peer mortgages were a common financial instrument in major Argentine cities. For investors looking to make money despite high inflation, this was a safe way to obtain a higher level of returns on investment than what the bank offered on CDs. In the 1990s, peer-to-peer mortgages were the only option for those who did not qualify for a bank loan (informal workers, shop owners, small business owners unable or unwilling to declare all their earnings, etc.) but did own a property (generally, a family home) they could present as collateral (Luzzi 2012; 2017).

# Chapter Six

1. The widow of Nestor Kirchner, she is alternately referred to in the Argentine media as Cristina Fernández, Cristina Fernández de Kirchner, and Cristina Kirchner. For the sake of consistency, Cristina Fernández is used here.

2. Fernández served for two consecutive terms: 2007–2011 and 2011–2015. A Peronist leader, she served as senator for the province of Santa Cruz from 1995–1997 and later, as senator for the province of Buenos Aires between 2001 and 2005. Her husband, Néstor Kirchner, preceded her in the presidency. In 2015, she was succeeded by Mauricio Macri, a leader of the center-right PRO, a coalition that included the country's traditional Unión Cívica Radical, party of former presidents Raúl Alfonsín (1983–1989) and Fernando de la Rúa (1999–2001).

3. As noted in chapter 5, the coleros make a living waiting in line for others. In 2011, their services included waiting in line to buy foreign currency and even then carrying out the transaction using their social security number; this was added value once the government placed a limit on the monthly amount of foreign currency any individual could purchase.

4. Regulations and controls grew progressively tougher until July 2012, when the purchase of dollars or other currencies for savings was banned altogether. These restrictions were partially lifted in January 2014, when it became possible to purchase dollars for savings once again, though with certain limits. Cf. Central Banks Statements A 236 (10/27/2011); A 5318 (7/5/2012) and A 5330 (7/27/2012); Statement A 5526 (1/27/2014).

5. The term used in the financial world and economy to refer to small investors with little savvy and limited access to insider knowledge. In a historical comparison, they could be considered the modern-day version of the *especulador hormiga* of the 1960s.

6. At the end of 2011, the monthly minimum wage in Argentina was approximately US$660.

7. As María Soledad Sánchez has noted, use of the term "blue" to refer to the dollar in

Argentina's financial community arose in the mid-2000s. It was a nod "to blue chip stocks, those well-established corporate assets that assure profits whether the economy is booming or ailing" (Sánchez 2016, 96).

8. *El Cronista*, June 1, 2012; *Clarín*, June 2, 2012.

9. In May 2002, an executive decree ordered the issue of the ten-year bonds in dollars for bank deposits originally made in dollars and later translated into pesos and rescheduled between December and January 2011. This was a measure aimed at making a better offer to savers, given that the bonds represented a reversal of the *pesificación*, or conversion to pesos, of the original deposits but could not be cashed for ten years. Cf. Decree 905/2002.

10. Llamadores, or callers, are those who offer currency exchange on the street but do not do the transaction themselves; instead, they lead the customer to the storefront or office where they can swap dollars for pesos, or vice versa.

11. The measure established that companies or individuals purchasing foreign currency must declare the purpose of the transaction (import payments, travel, savings). On several occasions, getting approval for a foreign currency purchase depended on the stated purpose. Between 2012 and 2014, the purchase of the "savings dollar" was prohibited. At the time of writing (2022), the savings dollar is limited to US$200 per person per month, with additional restrictions on who can purchase.

12. Cueva, or cave, is the slang term for sites offering under-the-table currency exchange. In some cases, these are regular storefronts of a variety of businesses that exchange currency in addition to offering other business services; in others, they exclusively deal in illegal currency. The manager of the storefront or person handling the transaction is known as the *cuevero*.

13. A kiosko is a small store, sometimes only a window on the street, selling candy, cigarettes, nonalcoholic beverages and other small items.

14. This case study is presented in a previous work (Luzzi and Wilkis 2018).

15. Nicholas D'Avella (2019) has researched the place of real estate ("bricks") and dollars in Argentine ecologies of investment, especially in the period following the 2001 crisis.

16. The research for this book also included a series of interviews with key informants from different economic sectors, especially those that operate on dollarized markets, including real estate agents, farmers, and agricultural service providers.

17. Books by business administration specialist Mariano Otálora (2012; 2013) and by financial journalist Mariano Gorodisch (2013) are a good example of this trend.

18. The returns were officially above annual inflation, which stood at around 10 percent. However, due to state interventions in the National Institute of Statistics and Censuses between 2007 and 2016, the consumer price index had ceased to be a reliable gauge of inflation (Daniel and Lanata Briones 2019). Alternative sources placed inflation in 2011 at close to 25 percent (CIFRA 2012).

19. In 1960, 13 percent of Argentina's population was foreign born. More than 75 percent of these foreigners had been born in Europe and had arrived in Argentina during a wave of immigration that began at the end of the nineteenth century and extended into the first decades of the twentieth century (Hudson 2012).

20. Also known as "Boudougate," this was a lawsuit in which Vice President Amado Boudou was accused of using his influence while serving as economic minister to ensure a state contract was assigned to a printing company with which he had ties.

21. A prominent form of protest during the crisis of 2001–2002, a cacerolazo involves banging on a pot or pan (*cacerola*), often with a wooden spoon or other kitchen utensil; a more recent development, from the comfort of one's own car, is the *bocinazo*, repeatedly honking the car horn (*bocina*). For a history of pot-and-pan banging as part of a repertoire of protest in Argentina and a specific analysis of the cacerolazos of 2012 and 2013, see Tomás Gold and Rocío Annunziata (2018) and Tomás Gold and Alejandro Peña (2019).

22. Duhalde made this pledge in January 2002 in response the increasingly violent protests on the part of savers whose deposits had been frozen and converted to pesos at a fixed exchange rate below the market rate. Later, he proved unable to meet this promise.

# Conclusion

1. During the election campaign of 2015, opposition candidate Mauricio Macri promised voters that he would eliminate all forex restrictions upon taking office. A week after being sworn in, he did just that, but the measure had negative repercussions that would overshadow his entire administration. In order to keep the forex market unregulated, the government relied heavily on foreign loans, plunging Argentina into debt once again. However, when international aid organizations suddenly cut off funding in 2018, the Argentine peso suffered a severe devaluation.

# BIBLIOGRAPHY

## Primary Sources

### Archives and Libraries

Archivo General de la Nación, Departamento Archivo Intermedio, Fondo documental Series Históricas III: documentos de la Dirección Nacional de Vigilancia de Precios y Abastecimiento. Años 1949–1955.
Archivo Espigas, Fundación Espigas—Universidad Nacional de San Martín, Fondo Marta Minujín.
Archivo del Museo del Club River Plate.
Biblioteca Nacional, Hemeroteca.
Biblioteca del Honorable Congreso de la Nación, Hemeroteca.
Biblioteca del Honorable Congreso de la Nación, Sala de Colecciones Especiales, Biblioteca Peronista.
Biblioteca Dr. Raúl Prebisch, Banco Central de la República Argentina.
Centro de Documentación e Información, Ministerio de Economía de la Nación.

### Periodicals

Unless otherwise noted, place of publication is Buenos Aires, and the periodicals listed were consulted for the entire period covered.

#### NEWSPAPERS

*Ámbito Financiero* (1977 onward)
*Clarín* (1945 onward)
*La Nación*

*La Opinión* (1971–1977)
*La Prensa* (1931–1935)

### MAGAZINES
*Análisis* (1961–1971)
*Caras y Caretas* (1931–1941)
*Economic Survey* (1941–1979)
*El Economista* (1952–1979)
*Humor* (1978–1999)
*Mercado* (1977–1999)
*Mundo Peronista* (1951–1955)
*Primera Plana* (1962–1969)
*Plaza de Arte* (1979)
*Pulso* (1967–1972)
*Somos* (1985)
*The Review of the River Plate* (1931–1949)

### Print
Academia Nacional de Ciencias Económicas. Anales.
Banco Central de la República Argentina. 2010. *Informe de Medidas Cautelares*. Buenos Aires: BCRA—Superintendencia de Entidades Financieras y Cambiarias.
Banco Central de la República Argentina. 2011a. "Comunicaciones A 236." BCRA.
Banco Central de la República Argentina. 2011b. "Evolución del Mercado Único y Libre de Cambios y Balance Cambiario. Cuarto Trimestre de 2011." BCRA.
Banco Central de la República Argentina. 2012a. "Comunicaciones A 5318 y A5330." BCRA.
Banco Central de la República Argentina. 2012b. "Evolución del Mercado Único y Libre de Cambios y Balance Cambiario. Cuarto Trimestre de 2012." BCRA.
Banco Central de la República Argentina. 2013. "Evolución del Mercado Único y Libre de Cambios y Balance Cambiario. Cuarto Trimestre de 2013." BCRA.
Banco Central de la República Argentina. 2014a. "Comunicación A 5526." BCRA.
Banco Central de la República Argentina. 2014b. "Evolución del Mercado Único y Libre de Cambios y Balance Cambiario. Cuarto Trimestre de 2014." BCRA.
Banco Central de la República Argentina. 2015. "Evolución del Mercado Único y Libre de Cambios y Balance Cambiario. Cuarto Trimestre de 2015." BCRA.
Banco Central de la República Argentina. Boletín Estadístico.
Banco Central de la República Argentina. Memorias Anuales.
Bioy Casares, A. 1996. *En viaje (1967)*. Buenos Aires: Norma.
Centro de Investigación y Formación de la República Argentina (CIFRA-CTA). 2012. *Propuesta*

*de un indicador alternativo de inflación.* CIFRA_CTA. http://www.centrocifra.org.ar/docs/CIFRA%20-%20IPC-9%20(Marzo %202012).pdf.

Comisión Especial Investigadora de la Cámara de Diputados sobre Fuga de Divisas de la Argentina durante el año 2001. 2005. *Fuga de Divisas en la Argentina.* Buenos Aires: FLACSO-Siglo XXI Editores.

de Pablo, J. C. 1980. *La economía que yo hice.* Buenos Aires: El Cronista Comercial.

Department of the Treasury et al. 2006. *The Use and Counterfeiting of United States Currency Abroad. Part 3: The Final Report to the Congress.* Washington, DC: United States Treasury Department.

Fernández de Kirchner, C. 2011. "Discurso de la Presidenta de la Nación en el Acto de Asunción de mando en el Congreso de la Nación." Presidencia de la Nación.

Fernández de Kirchner, C. 2012. "Discurso de la Presidenta de la Nación en la Celebración del 158° Aniversario de la Bolsa de Comercio de Buenos Aires." Presidencia de la Nación.

Fogwill, R. 1998. *Vivir afuera.* Buenos Aires: Sudamericana.

Gorodisch, M. 2013. *60 opciones para invertir en pesos y ahorrar en dólares: Estrategias para ganarle a la inflación.* Buenos Aires: Penguin Random House.

Hudson, C. F. 2012. "El Censo Nacional de 1960 en Argentina." Preprint. *Diacroni: Studi di Storia Contemporanea* 12 (4). https://doi.org/10.4000/diacronie.2569.

Hurtado, L. 1953. *Pigmalión.* In *Diez cuentos policiales argentinos*, edited by R. Walsh. Buenos Aires: Hachette, 25–40.

Instituto Nacional de Estadística y Censos (INDEC). 2022. *Informe de la Encuesta Nacional de Gastos de los Hogares 1996–1997. Total del país.* INDEC.

Organización Techint, Boletín Informativo.

Otálora, M. 2012. *Del colchón a la inversión.* Buenos Aires: Booket.

Otálora, M. 2013. *¿Qué hacemos con los pesos?* Buenos Aires: Planeta.

Perón, J. D. 1955. *Discursos del Presidente Gral. Juan D. Perón (1946–1955)*, Presidencia de la Nación, Subscretaría de Informaciones, Dirección General de Prensa.

Poder Ejecutivo Nacional. 2002. Decreto PEN 905/2002.

Prebisch, R. 1993. "El control de cambio en la República Argentina." In *Obras Completas 1919–1949*, Tomo III. Buenos Aires: Fundación Raúl Prebisch.

Presidencia de la Nación. Secretaría de Informaciones, Dirección General de Prensa.

Rejtman, M. 1996. *Velcro y yo.* Buenos Aires: Planeta.

Silberstein, E. 1967. *Charlas económicas.* Buenos Aires: Peña Lillo Editor.

Silberstein, E. 1970. *Vida y milagros de nuestro peso.* Buenos Aires: Centro Editor de América.

Secretaría de Comercio Interior de la Nación (1989) "Resolución n° 51/1989."

Vanoli, H. 2010. *Pinamar.* Buenos Aires: Interzona.

## Multimedia

"Raúl Alfonsín y Juan V. Sourrouille presentan el Plan Austral" June 14, 1985. Buenos Aires: Archivo Histórico de la Radiotelevisión argentina. https://www.youtube.com/watch?v=oZ4HAJJu_5g.

# Secondary Sources

Abeles, M., P. Lavarello, and H. Montagu. 2013. "Heterogeneidad estructural y restricción externa en la economía argentina: Hacia un desarrollo inclusivo." In *Hacia un desarrollo inclusivo: El caso de la Argentina*, edited by Ricardo Infante and Pascual Gersentel, 23–96. Santiago de Chile: CEPAL-OIT.

Aglietta, M., and V. Coudert. 2014. *Le dollar et le système monétaire international*. Paris: La Découverte.

Aglietta, M., and A. Orleán, eds. 1998. *La monnaie souveraine*. Paris: Odile Jacob.

Alary, P. et al., eds. 2020. *Institutionalist Theories of Money: An Anthology of the French School*. Cham: Palgrave Macmillan.

Altamirano, C. 1998a. *Arturo Frondizi o, el hombre de ideas como político*. Buenos Aires: Fondo de Cultura Económica.

Altamirano, C. 1998b. "Desarrollo y desarrollistas." Prismas. *Revista de historia intelectual* (2): 75–94.

Amato, M., and L. Fantacci. 2012. *The End of Finance*. Cambridge: Polity Press.

Andrada, J. C. 2018. "¿Cuánto vale conocer el precio del arte? Valuaciones monetarias y jerarquías estéticas en publicaciones periódicas argentinas de los años sesenta." In *El poder de (e)valuar: La producción monetaria de jerarquías sociales, morales y estéticas en la sociedad contemporánea*, edited by Ariel Wilkis, 155–72. Bogota: UNSAM edita-Editorial Universidad del Rosario.

Arrarte, J. 1944. *El control de cambios*. Buenos Aires: Sudamericana.

Auyero, J. 2001. *Poor People's Politics: Peronist Survival Networks and the Legacy of Evita*. Durham, NC: Duke University Press.

Auyero, J., 2007. *Routine Politics and Violence in Argentina: The Gray Zone of State Power* Cambridge Studies in Contentious Politics. Cambridge: Cambridge University Press.

Auyero, J., and T. P. Moran. 2007. "The Dynamics of Collective Violence: Dissecting Food Riots in Contemporary Argentina." *Social Forces* 85 (3): 1341–67.

Basualdo, E. 2013. *Estudios de historia económica argentina desde mediados del siglo XX a la actualidad*. Buenos Aires: Siglo XXI Editores.

Basualdo, E. 2017. *Endeudar y fugar: Un análisis de la historia económica argentina, de Martínez de Hoz a Macri*. Buenos Aires: Siglo XXI.

Basualdo, E. M., C. Nahon, and H. J. Nochteff. 2007. "La deuda externa privada en La Argentina (1991–2005): Trayectoria, naturaleza y protagonistas." *Desarrollo Económico* 47 (186): 193–224.

Beunza, D. 2019. *Taking the Floor: Models, Morals, and Management in a Wall Street Trading Roomo*. Princeton, NJ: Princeton University Press.

Blanc, J. 2000. "Unité et diversité du fait monétaire." Paris: L'Harmattan.

Blanc, J. 2009. "Usages de l'argent et pratiques monétaires." In *Traité de sociologie économique*, edited by P. Steiner and F. Vatin, 649–88. Paris: Presses Universitaires de France.

## Bibliography

Blanc, J. 2018. *Les monnaies alternatives*. Paris: La Découverte.

Bohannan, P. 1959. "The Impact of Money on an African Subsistence Economy." *Journal of Economic History* 19 (4): 491–503.

Bulmer-Thomas, V. 2014. *The Economic History of Latin America since Independence*. Cambridge: Cambridge University Press.

Callon, M., Y. Millo, and F. Muniesa. 2008. *Market Devices*. Malden, MA: Blackwell.

Canelo, P. 2008. *El proceso en su laberinto: La interna militar de Videla a Bignone*. Buenos Aires: Prometeo.

Canitrot, A. 1980. "La disciplina como objetivo de la política económica: Un ensayo sobre el programa económico del gobierno argentino desde 1976." *Desarrollo Económico* 76: 453–75.

Carassai, S. 2014. *The Argentine Silent Majority: Middle Classes, Politics, Violence, and Memory in the Seventies*. Durham, NC: Duke University Press.

Carruthers, B. 2017. "The Social Meaning of Credit, Value and Finance." In *Money Talks: Explaining How Money Really Works*, edited by Nina Bandelj, Frederick F. Wherry, and Viviana A. Zelizer, 73–88. Princeton, NJ: Princeton University Press.

Carruthers, B., and S. Babb. 1996. *The Color of Money and the Nature of Value: Greenbacks and Gold in Postbellum America*. Chicago: University of Chicago Press.

Castellani, A., and M. Szkolnik. 2011. "'Devaluacionistas' y 'dolarizadores': La construcción social de las alternativas propuestas por los sectores dominantes ante la crisis de la Convertibilidad. Argentina 1999–2001." *IDAES—Documentos de investigación social* 18. http://www.unsam.edu.ar/escuelas/idaes/docs/DocIS_18_Castellani_Szkolnik.pdf.

Cavarozzi, M. 2006. *Autoritarismo y democracia, 1955–2006*. Buenos Aires: Ariel.

Cortés Conde, R. 2005. *La economía política de la Argentina en el siglo XX*. Buenos Aires: Edhasa.

Corso, E. 2014. "Mar del Plata, nuestro 'shadow banking' junto al mar." *Alquimias económicas* (blog). September 30, 2014. https://alquimiaseconomicas.com/2014/09/30/mar-del-plata-nuestro-shadow-banking-junto-al-mar/.

D'Avella, N. 2019. *Concrete Dreams: Practice, Value, and Built Environments in Post-crisis Buenos Aires*. Durham, NC: Duke University Press.

Dalla Corte-Caballero, G. 2014. "Hacia los 25 años de los saqueos de la ciudad de Rosario, Argentina." *Historia Actual Online* (33): 7–19.

Dalton, G. 1961. "Economic Theory and Primitive Society." *American Anthropologist New Series* 63 (1): 1–25.

Damill, M., and R. Frenkel. 1990. *Hinperinflación y estabilización: La experiencia argentina reciente*. Buenos Aires: Centro de Estudios de Estado y Sociedad (CEDES).

Damill, M., R. Frenkel, and R. Maurizio. 2002. "Argentina: A Decade of Currency Board: An Analysis of Growth, Employment and Income Distribution." ILO—Employment Paper 42. https://www.ilo.org/wcmsp5/groups/public/---ed_emp/documents/publication/wcms_142375.pdf.

Damill, M., R. Frenkel, and M. Rapetti. 2005. "La deuda argentina: Historia, default y reestructuración." *Desarrollo Económico* 45 (178): 187–233.

Daniel, C. 2013. *Números públicos: Las estadísticas en Argentina (1990–2010)*. Buenos Aires: Fondo de Cultura Económica.

Daniel, C. J., and C. T. Lanata Briones. 2019. "Battles over Numbers: The Case of the Argentine Consumer Price Index (2007–2015)." *Economy and Society* 48 (1): 127–51.

de Riz, L. 1981. *Retorno y derrumbe: El último gobierno peronista*. México City: Folios Ediciones.

Decker, S., and McKinlay, A. 2020. "Archival Ethnography." In *The Routledge Companion to Anthropology and Business*, 17–33. New York: Routledge.

Dellatorre, R., and N. Restivo. 2016. *El rodrigazo: El lado oscuro del ajuste que cambió la Argentina*. Buenos Aires: Capital Intelectual.

Devlin, R., and R. French-Davis. 1995. "The Great Latin American Debt Crisis: A Decade of Asymmetric Adjustment." In *Poverty, Prosperity, and the World Economy: Essays in Memory of Sidney Dell*, edited by S. S. Dell and G. K. Helleiner, 43–80. Basingstoke, UK: MacMillan Press.

Dewey, M. 2020. *Making It at Any Cost: Aspirations and Politics in a Counterfeit Clothing Marketplace*. Austin: University of Texas Press.

Dezalay, Y., and B. G. Garth. 2010. *The Internationalization of Palace Wars: Lawyers, Economists, and the Contest to Transform Latin American States*. Chicago: University of Chicago Press.

Diamand, M. 1972. "La estructura productiva desequilibrada Argentina y el tipo de cambio." *Desarrollo Económico* 12 (45): 25–47.

Díaz Alejandro, C. 1966. *Exchange Rate Devaluation in a Semi-industrialized Country: The Experience of Argentina, 1955–1961*. Cambridge, MA: MIT Press.

Dinerstein, A. C. 2003. "¡Que se vayan todos! Popular Insurrection and the Asambleas Barriales in Argentina." *Bulletin of Latin American Research* 22 (2): 187–200.

Dominguez, V. 1990. "Representing Value and the Value of Representation: A Different Look at Money." *Cultural Anthropology* 5 (1): 16–44.

Drake, P. 1989. *The Money Doctor in the Andes*. Durham, NC: Duke University Press.

Eichengreen, B. 2010. "The Breakup of the Euro Area." NBER working paper series, no. w13393. Cambridge, Mass: National Bureau of Economic Research. https://www.nber.org/papers/w13393.

Eichengreen, B. 2011. *Exorbitant Privilege: The Rise and Fall of the Dollar and the Future of the International Monetary System*. Oxford: Oxford University Press.

Eichengreen, B. 2015. *Hall of Mirrors: The Great Depression, The Great Recession, and the Uses—and Misuses—of History*. Oxford: Oxford University Press.

Eichengreen, B., and M. Flandreau. 2008. "The Rise and Fall of the Dollar, or When Did the Dollar Replace Sterling as the Leading International Currency?" National Bureau of Economic Research, Inc., NBER Working Papers.

Eichengreen, B., A. Mehl, and L. Chitu. 2019. *How Global Currencies Work: Past, Present, and Future*. Princeton, NJ: Princeton University Press.

Elena, E. 2011. *Dignifying Argentina: Peronism, Citizenship, and Mass Consumption.* Pittsburgh: University of Pittsburgh Press.

Epstein, E., and D. Pion-Berlin. 2006. *Broken Promises?: The Argentine Crisis and Argentine Democracy.* Lanham, MD: Lexington Books.

Etchemendy, S. 2020. "The Politics of Popular Coalitions: Unions and Territorial Social Movements in Post-Neoliberal Latin America (2000–15)." *Journal of Latin American Studies* 52 (1): 157–88.

Fairfield, T. 2011. "Business Power and Protest: Argentina's Agricultural Producers Protest in Comparative Context." *Studies in Comparative International Development* 46 (4): 424–53.

Fodor, J. G., A. A. O'Connell, and M. R. Santos. 1973. "La Argentina y la economía atlántica en la primera mitad del siglo XX." *Desarrollo Económico* 13 (49): 3–65.

Ford, A., and J. Rivera. 1985. "Los medios masivos de comunicación en la Argentina." In *Medios de comunicación y cultura popular*, edited by A. Ford, E. Romano, and J. Rivera, 24–41. Buenos Aires: Llegada.

Fourcade, M. 2010. *Economists and Societies: Discipline and Profession in the United States, Britain, and France, 1890s to 1990s.* Princeton, NJ: Princeton University Press.

Fourcade, M., and S. Babb. 2002. "The Rebirth of the Liberal Creed: Paths to Neoliberalism in Four Countries." *American Journal of Sociology* 108: 533–79. 10.1086/367922.

Franco, M. 2012. *Un enemigo para la nación: Orden interno y violencia subversiva (1973–1976).* Buenos Aires: Fondo de Cultura Económica.

French, J. D. 1989. "Industrial Workers and the Birth of the Populist Republic in Brazil, 1945–1946." *Latin American Perspectives* 16 (4): 5–27.

Frenkel, R. 1979. "Decisiones de precio en alta inflación." *Desarrollo Económico* 1 (75): 291–330.

Frenkel, R. 1990. "El régimen de alta inflación y el nivel de actividad." In *Inflación rebelde en América Latina*, edited by José Pablo Arellano, 163–88. Santiago de Chile: CIEPLAN-Hachette.

Fridman, D. 2010. "A New Mentality for a New Economy: Performing the Homo Economicus in Argentina (1976–83)." *Economy and Society* 39 (2): 271–302.

Gaggero, A., and P. Nemiña. 2022. "Origen y consolidación de la dolarización del mercado inmobiliario en Argentina." *Ensayos de Economía* 32 (60): 136–59. https://revistas.unal.edu.co/index.php/ede/article/view/92443.

Gamarnik, C. 2016. "La fotografía de prensa en Argentina durante la década del 60: Modernización e internacionalización del periodismo gráfico." *Revista Photo & Documento* (2): 1–20.

Gamarnik, C. 2020. *El fotoperiodismo en Argentina: De 7 días ilustrados (1965) a la Agencia Sigla (1975).* Buenos Aires: Pretéritos Imperfectos.

Garay, C. 2007. "Social Policy and Collective Action: Unemployed Workers, Community Associations, and Protest in Argentina." *Politics & Society* 35 (2): 301–28.

Gerchunoff, P. 2010. "Circulando en el laberinto: La economía argentina entre la depresión y la guerra (1929–1939)." Working paper. IELAT-Instituto de Estudios Latinoamericanos, Universidad de Alcalá, N. 10.

Gerchunoff, P., and D. Antúnez. 2002. "De la Bonanza a la Crisis de Desarrollo." In *Los años peronistas (1943–1955)*, edited by J. C. Torre, 125–97. Buenos Aires: Sudamericana.

Gerchunoff, P., and L. Llach. 2018. *El ciclo de la ilusión y el desencanto*. 2nd ed. Buenos Aires: Planeta.

Gerchunoff, P., and J. C. Torre. 1998. "Argentina: The Politics of Economic Liberalization." In *The Changing Role of the State in Latin America*, edited by M. Vellinga, 115–48. New York: Routledge.

Germani, G. 1954. *Estructura social de la Argentina*. Buenos Aires: Raigal.

Germani, G. 1972. *Política y sociedad en una época de transición*. Buenos Aires: Paidós.

Gillespie, R. 1982. *Soldiers of Perón, Argentina's Montoneros*. Oxford: Oxford University Press.

Gold, T., and R. Annunziata. 2018. "Manifestaciones ciudadanas en la era digital: El ciclo de cacerolazos (2012–2013) y la movilización #NiUnaMenos (2015) en Argentina." *Desarrollo Económico* 57 (223): 363–87.

Gold, T., and A. M. Peña. 2019. "Protests, Signaling, and Elections: Conceptualizing Opposition-Movement Interactions during Argentina's Anti-Government Protests (2012–2013)." *Social Movement Studies* 18 (3): 324–45.

Gómez, G. M. 2015. *Argentina's Parallel Currency: The Economy of the Poor*. New York: Routledge.

González Bombal, M. I., and M. Luzzi. 2006. "Middle-Class Use of Barter Clubs: A Real Alternative or Just Survival?" In *Broken Promises? The Argentine Crisis and Argentine Democracy*, edited by E. Epstein and D. Pion-Berlin, 143–60. Lanham, MD: Lexington Books.

Gowan, P. 1999. *The Global Gamble: Washington's Faustian Bid for World Dominance*. New York: Verso.

Gras, C., and V. Hernández. 2016. *Radiografía del nuevo campo argentino: Del terrateniente al empresario transnacional*. Buenos Aires: Siglo XXI Editores.

Gregory, C. 1997. *Savage Money: The Anthropology and Politics of Commodity Exchange*. Milton Park, UK: Taylor & Francis.

Guyer, J. 1995. "Introduction: The Currency Interface and Its Dynamics." In *Money Matters! Instability, Values and Social Payments in the Modern History of West African Communities*, edited by J. Guyer, 1–33. Portsmouth, NH: Heinemann.

Guyer, J. 2004. *Marginal Gains: Monetary Transactions in Atlantic Africa*. Chicago: University of Chicago Press.

Guyer, J. 2011. "Describing Urban 'No Man's Land' in Africa." *Africa* 81 (3): 474–92. doi:10.1017/S0001972011000258.

Guyer, J. 2016. *Legacies, Logics, Logistics: Essays in the Anthropology of the Platform Economy*. Chicago: University of Chicago Press.

Guyer, J., and F. Neiburg, eds. 2020. *The Real Economy*. Chicago: HAU Books.

Guyer, J., and K. Salami. 2013. "Life Courses of Indebtedness in Rural Nigeria." In *Transitions and Transformations: Cultural Perspectives on Aging and the Life Course*, edited by C. Lynch and J. Danely, 207–17. New York: Berghahn Books.

Guyer, J. I. 2012. "Soft Currencies, Cash Economies, New Monies: Past and Present." *Proceedings of the National Academy of Sciences of the United States of America* 109 (7): 2214–21.

Hart, K. 1986. "Heads or Tails? Two Sides of the Coin." *New Series* 21 (4): 637–56.

Helleiner, E. 2003a. "Dollarization Diplomacy: US Policy towards Latin America Coming Full Circle?" *Review of International Political Economy* 10 (3): 406–429.

Helleiner, E. 2003b. *The Making of National Money: Territorial Currencies in Historical Perspective*. Ithaca, NY: Cornell University Press.

Helleiner, E. 2009. *The Future of the Dollar*. Ithaca, NY: Cornell University Press.

Helleiner, E. 2017. "The Macro-Social Meaning of Money: From Territorial Currencies to Global Money." In *Money Talks: Explaining How Money Really Works*, edited by Nina Bandelj, Frederick F. Wherry, and Viviana A. Zelizer, 145–58. Princeton, NJ: Princeton University Press. doi:23943/princeton/9780691168685.001.0001.

Helleiner, E., and J. Kirshner. 2009. *The Future of the Dollar*. Ithaca, NY: Cornell University Press.

Heredia, M. 2014. *Cuando los economistas alcanzaron el poder*. Buenos Aires: Siglo XXI Editores.

Heredia, M., and C. Daniel. 2019. "The Taming of Prices: Framing and Fighting Inflation in the Second Half of the Twentieth Century in Argentina." *Economic Sociology: The European Electronic Newsletter* 20 (2): 6–13.

Ho, K. 2012. *Liquidated: An Ethnography of Wall Street*. Durham, NC: Duke University Press.

James, D. 2003. *Nueva Historia Argentina, Tomo 9: Violencia, proscripción y autoritarismo, 1955–1976*. Buenos Aires: Sudamericana.

Knight, A. 1998. "Populism and Neo-populism in Latin America, Especially Mexico." *Journal of Latin American Studies* 30 (2): 223–48.

Knorr Cetina, K., and A. Preda. 2012. *The Oxford Handbook of the Sociology of Finance*. Oxford: Oxford University Press.

Krippner, G. 2012. *Capitalizing on Crisis: The Political Origins of the Rise of Finance*. Cambridge, MA: Harvard University Press.

Landi, L. 1978. *La tercera presidencia de Perón: Gobierno de emergencia y crisis política*. Buenos Aires: CEDES.

Lapavitsas, C. 2013. "The Financialization of Capitalism: 'Profiting without Producing.'" *City* 17 (6): 792–805.

Lapegna, P. 2016. *Soybeans and Power: Genetically Modified Crops, Environmental Politics, and Social Movements in Argentina*. New York: Oxford University Press.

Leiras, M. 2004. "Organización partidaria y democrática: Tres tesis de los estudios comparativos y su aplicación a los partidos en la Argentina." *Revista SAAP: Sociedad Argentina de Análisis Político* 3 (1): 515–60.

Lemon, A. 1998. "'Your Eyes Are Green Like Dollars': Counterfeit Cash, National Substance, and Currency Apartheid in 1990s Russia." *Cultural Anthropology* 13 (1): 11–55.

Levitsky, S., and M. V. Murillo, eds. 2005. *Argentine Democracy: The Politics of Institutional Weakness*. University Park: Penn State Press.

Levitsky, S., and K. Roberts, eds. 2011. *The Resurgence of the Latin American Left*. Baltimore: Johns Hopkins University Press.

Losada, L. 2008. *La alta sociedad en la Buenos Aires de la Belle Époque*. Buenos Aires: Siglo XXI.

Losada, L. 2009. *Historia de las elites en la Argentina: Desde la conquista hasta el surgimiento del peronismo*. Buenos Aires: Editorial Sudamericana.

Luzzi, M. 2005. *Réinventer le marché?: Les clubs de troc face a la crise en Argentine*. Paris: L'Harmattan.

Luzzi, M. 2008. "La institución bancaria cuestionada. Actitudes y representaciones de los ahorristas frente a los bancos en el contexto de la crisis de 2001 en Argentina." *Crítica en Desarrollo: Revista Latinoamericana de Ciencias Sociales* (2): 173–90.

Luzzi, M. 2012. "La monnaie en question: Pratiques et conflits à propos de l'argent lors de la crise de 2001 en Argentine." PhD diss., École des Hautes Études en Sciences Sociales.

Luzzi, M. 2013. "La moneda en cuestión: Del estallido de la convertibilidad a las discusiones sobre el 'cepo cambiario.'" In *La grieta: Política, economía y cultura después de 2001*, edited by S. Pereyra, G. Pérez, and G. Vommaro, 195–209. Buenos Aires: Biblos.

Luzzi, M. 2015. "Socialisation économique et hiérarchies monétaires dans un contexte de crise: Argentine, 2001–2003." *Critique internationale* 69 (4): 21–37.

Luzzi, M. 2016. "Quelle est la monnaie de l'épargne?" Preprint. *La Vie des idées*. https://laviedesidees.fr/Quelle-est-la-monnaie-de-l-epargne.html.

Luzzi, M. 2017. "La financiarización de los hogares bajo el prisma de otras crisis." *Civitas— Revista de Ciências Sociais* 17 (1): 43.

Luzzi, M., and A. Wilkis. 2018. "Soybean, Bricks, Dollars, and the Reality of Money: Multiple Monies during Currency Exchange Restrictions in Argentina (2011–15)." *HAU: Journal of Ethnographic Theory* 8 (1–2): 252–64.

MacKenzie, D. 2008. *An Engine, Not a Camera: How Financial Models Shape Markets*. Cambridge, MA: MIT Press.

Mancusi, D., and S. Grandi. 2018. *Operación Sinatra*. Buenos Aires: Aguilar.

Manzano, V. 2014. *The Age of Youth in Argentina: Culture, Politics, and Sexuality from Perón to Videla*. Chapel Hill: University of North Carolina Press.

Marques-Pereira, J., and B. Théret. 2014. "Dualidad monetaria y soberanía en Cuba (1989–2001)." In *La moneda develada por sus crisis*, edited by B. Théret, 290–328. Bogota: Universidad Nacional de Colombia. doi:10.15446/achsc.v44n1.61240.

Maurer, B. 2006. "The Anthropology of Money." *The Annual Review of Anthropology* 35: 15–36.

Mauss, M. 1967. *The Gift: Forms and Functions of Exchange in Archaic Societies*. New York: Norton.

Milanesio, N. 2013. *Workers Go Shopping in Argentina: The Rise of Popular Consumer Culture*. Albuquerque: University of New Mexico Press.

Muir, S. 2021. *Routine Crisis: An Ethnography of Disillusion*. Chicago: University of Chicago Press.

Murmis, M., and J. C. Portantiero. 2011. *Estudios sobre los orígenes del peronismo*. Buenos Aires: Siglo XXI Editores.

Neiburg, F. 2006. "Inflation: Economists and Economic Cultures in Brazil and Argentina." *Comparative Studies in Society and History* 48 (3): 604–33.

Neiburg, F. 2010. "Sick Currencies and Public Numbers." *Anthropological Theory* 10 (1–2): 1–2.

Neiburg, F. 2011. "La guerre des indices: L'inflation au Brésil (1964–1994)." *Genèses: Sciences sociales et histoire* 84 (3): 25–46.

Neiburg, F. G. 2007. "As moedas doentes, os números públicos e a antropologia do dinheiro." *Mana* 13 (1): 119–51.

Nelms, T. 2015. "Making Popular and Solidarity Economies in Dollarized Ecuador: Money, Law, and the Social after Neoliberalism." PhD diss., University of California, Irvine. ProQuest ID: Nelms_uci_0030D_13365. Merritt ID: ark:/13030/m5qz4j31. Retrieved from https://escholarship.org/uc/item/3xx5n43g.

Nemiña, P., and J. Larralde. 2018. "Etapas históricas de la relación entre el Fondo Monetario Internacional y América Latina (1944–2015)." *América Latina en la historia económica* 25 (1): 275–313.

Novaro, M., and V. Palermo. 2003. *La dictadura militar, 1976–1983: Del golpe de Estado a la restauración democrática*. Buenos Aires: Paidós.

O'Donnell, G. 1982. "Notas para el estudio de procesos de democratización política a partir del estado burocrático-autoritario." *Desarrollo Económico* 22 (86): 231–48.

O'Donnell, G., P. Schmitter, and L. Whitehead, eds. 1986. *Transitions from Authoritarian Rule*. Baltimore: John Hopkins University Press.

O'Connell, A. 1984. "La Argentina en la depresión. Los problemas de una economía abierta." *Desarrollo Económico* 23 (92).

O'Donnell, G. 1996. "Another Institutionalization: Latin America and Elsewhere." Working Paper n.222, Kellog Institute. https://kellogg.nd.edu/sites/default/files/old_files/documents/222_0.pdf.

O'Donnell, G. 1997. "Estado y alianzas en la Argentina, 1956–1976." In *Contrapuntos: Ensayos escogidos sobre autoritarismo y democratización*, 31–68. Buenos Aires: Paidós.

O'Donnell, G. A. 1988. *Bureaucratic Authoritarianism: Argentina, 1966–1973, in Comparative Perspective*. Berkeley: University of California Press.

Orléan, A. 2009. "De l'euphorie à la panique: Penser la crise financière." Paris: Cepremap, Éditions Rue d'Ulm.

Orléan, A. 2013. "Money: Instrument of Exchange or Social Institution of Value?" In *Financial Crises and the Nature of Capitalist Money: Mutual Developments from the Work of Geoffrey Ingham*, edited by J. Pixley and G. C. Harcourt, 46–69. London: Palgrave MacMillan.

Ortiz, H. 2021. *Everyday Practice of Valuation and Investment: Political Imaginaries of Shareholder Value.* New York: Columbia University Press.

Oszlak, O. 2006. "From Smaller to Better Government: The Challenge of the Second and Third Generations of State Reform." *International Journal of Organization Theory & Behavior* 9 (3): 408–35.

Panero, M., ed. 2018. *Actores, políticas públicas y conflicto agropecuario.* Villa María: EDUVIM.

Panitch, L., and S. Gindin. 2013. *The Making of Global Capitalism: The Political Economy of American Empire.* New York: Verso.

Parbonni, R. 1981. *The Dollar and Its Rivals.* New York: New Left Books.

Pastoriza, E., and J. C. Torre. 2019. *Mar del Plata, un sueño de los argentinos.* Buenos Aires: Edhasa.

Pedersen, T. 2002. "The Storm We Call Dollars: Determining Value and Belief in El Salvador and the United States." *Cultural Anthropology* 17 (3): 431–59.

Petras, J., and M. Zeitlin. 1968. *Latin America: Reform or Revolution?* Greenwich, CT: Fawcett Publications.

Polillo, S. 2017. *Money Talks: Explaining How Money Really Works.* Princeton, NJ: Princeton University Press.

Portantiero, J. C. 1977. "Economía y política en la crisis argentina: 1958–1973." *Revista Mexicana de Sociología* 39 (2): 531–65.

Potash, R. A. 1996. *The Army and Politics in Argentina, 1962–1973: From Frondizi's Fall to the Peronist Restoration.* Stanford, CA: Stanford University Press.

Preda, A. 2009. *Framing Finance: The Boundaries of Markets and Modern Capitalism.* Chicago: University of Chicago Press.

Pucciarelli, A. 1999. *La primacía de la política: Lannusse, Perón y la Nueva Izquierda en los tiempso del GAN.* Buenos Aires: EUDEBA.

Pucciarelli, A. 2004. *Empresarios, Tecnócratas y Militares: La trama corporativa de la última dictadura militar.* Buenos Aires: Siglo XXI Editores.

Rapoport, M. 2008. "Argentina y el MERCOSUR: ¿dilema o solución?" *Ciclos hist. econ. soc.* 17: 33–34.

Ravelli, Q. 2020. "In the limbo of debt economic crisis and social movements: From Wall Street bankers to Spanish activists." *Revue francaise de sociologie* 61 (4): 641–71.

Ravelli, Q. 2021. "Debt Struggles: How Financial Markets Gave Birth to a Working-Class Movement." *Socio-Economic Review* 19 (2): 441–68.

Rock, D. 1975. *Politics in Argentina, 1890–1930: The Rise and Fall of Radicalism.* Cambridge: Cambridge University Press.

Roig, A. 2016. *La moneda imposible: La convertibilidad argentina de 1991.* Buenos Aires: Fondo de Cultura Económica.

Rosenberg, E. 2004. *Financial Missionaries to the World. The Politics and Culture of Dollar Diplomacy, 1900–1930.* Durham, NC: Duke University Press.

Rossi, F. M. 2017. *The Poor's Struggle for Political Incorporation: The Piquetero Movement in Argentina.* Cambridge: Cambridge University Press.

Rougier, M. 2018. "El Banco Central durante el primer peronismo 1946–1955: Un instrumento clave de la política económica y la promoción de los sectores productivos." In *Historia necesaria del Banco Central de la República Argentina*, edited by M. Rougier and F. Sember, 77–101. Buenos Aires: Lenguaje Claro-CICUSS.

Rougier, M., and M. Fiszbein. 2006. *La frustración de un proyecto económico: El gobierno peronista de 1973–1976*. Buenos Aires: Manantial.

Rouquié, A. 1981. "Dictadores, militares y legitimidad en América Latina." Crítica & Utopía. *Latinoamericana de Ciencias Sociales* 5: 11–28.

Rozenwurcel, G., L. Bleger, and D. Kampel. 1997. "El sistema bancario argentino en los noventa: De la profundización financiera a la crisis sistémica." *Desarrollo Económico* 37 (146): 163–93.

Ruiz, F. 2005. *El señor de los mercados: Ámbito Financiero, la City y el poder del periodismo económico de Martinez de Hoz a Cavallo*. Buenos Aires: Editorial El Ateneo.

Salera, V. 1941. *Exchange Control and the Argentine Market*. New York: Columbia University Press.

Sánchez, M. S. 2016. "Economía y moral en blue: Un estudio sociológico sobre el mercado ilegal del dólar en la Argentina de la posconvertibilidad." PhD diss., Facultad de Ciencias Sociales, Universidad de Buenos Aires.

Sánchez, M. S. 2017. "El dólar blue como 'número público' en la Argentina posconvertibilidad (2011–2015)." *Revista Mexicana de Sociología*: 28.

Schvarzer, J. 1986. *La política económica de Martinez de Hoz*. Buenos Aires: Hyspamérica.

Schvarzer, J. 2006. "The Costs of the Convertibility Plan: The Economic and Social Effects of Financial Hegemony." In *Broken Promises? The Argentine Crisis and Argentine Democracy*, edited by E. Epstein and D. Pion-Berlin, 73–91. Lanham, MD: Lexington Books.

Serulnikov, S. 2017. "Como si estuvieran comprando: Los saqueos de 1989 y la irrupción de la nueva cuestión social." In *La larga historia de los saqueos en la Argentina: De la Independencia a nuestros días*, edited by G. Di Meglio and S. Serulnikov, 137–76. Buenos Aires: Siglo XXI Editores.

Servet, J.-M., B. Théret, and Z. Yildirim. 2020. "Universality of the Monetary Phenomenon and Plurality of Moneys: From Colonial Confrontation to Confluence of the Social Sciences." In *Institutionalist Theories of Money: An Anthology of the French School*, edited by P. Alary, 157–98. Cham: Palgrave Macmillan. doi:10.1007/978-3-030-59483-1_6.

Sgard, J. 2014. "Money Reconstructured: Argentina and Brazil after Hyperinflation." In *The Manufacturing of Markets*, edited by E. Brousseau, 315–32. Cambridge: Cambridge University Press.

Smulovitz, C. 2006. "Judicialization of Protest in Argentina: The Case of Corralito." In *Enforcing the Rule of Law: Social Accountability in the New Latin American Democracies*, edited by E. Peruzzotti and C. Smulovitz, 55–74. Pittsburgh: University of Pittsburgh Press.

Sidicaro, R. 2002. *Los tres peronismos*. Buenos Aires: Siglo XXI.

Sigal, S., and G. Kessler. 1997. "Comportements et representations dans une conjoncture de dislocations des regulations sociales." *Culture & Conflicts* (24–25): 35–72.

Sivak, M. 2013. *Clarin: Una historia*. Buenos Aires: Planeta.

Svampa, M. 2014. "Revisiting Argentina 2001: From '¡Que se vayan todos!' to the Peronist Decade." In *Argentina since the 2001 Crisis: Recovering the Past, Reclaiming the Future*, edited by C. Levey, D. Ozarow, and C. Wylde, 155–73. New York: Palgrave Macmillan.

Svampa, M., and S. Pereyra. 2003. *Entre la ruta y el barrio: La experiencia de las organizaciones piqueteras*. Buenos Aires: Editorial Biblos.

Taroncher Padilla, M. Á. 1998. "Un caso de renovación periodística en la Argentina de los años sesenta: la revista Primera Plana." *Estudos Ibero Americanos* 24 (2): 43–167.

Telechea, R. 2006. "Historia de los cacerolazos: 1982–2001." *Razón y Revolución* 16: 141–84.

Théret, B. 2007. *La monn aie dévoilée par ses crises*. 2 vols. Paris: Éditions del'EHESS.

Théret, B. 2008. "Les trois etats de la monnaie Approche interdisciplinaire du fait monetaire." *Revue économique* 59 (4): 813–42.

Théret, B., ed. 2007. *La monnaie dévoilée par ses crises*. Paris: Editions de l'Ecole des hautes Etudes en sciences sociales.

Tilly, C. 1999. "Survey Article: Power—Top Down and Bottom Up." *Journal of Political Philosophy* 7: 330–52. https://doi.org/10.1111/1467-9760.00080.

Torre, J. C. 2005. "Citizens vs. Political Class: The Crisis of Partisan Representation." In *Argentine Democracy: The Politics of Institutional Weakness*, edited by S. Levitsky and M. V. Murillo, 165–79. University Park: Penn State Press.

Torre, J. C. 2021. *Diario de una temporada en el quinto piso*. Buenos Aires: Edhasa.

Torre, J. C., and P. Gerchunoff. 1999. *La economía política de las reformas institucionales en Argentina: Los casos de la política de privatización de Entel, la reforma de la seguridad social y la reforma laboral*, Research Department Publications. 3047. Inter-American Development Bank, Research Department. https://ideas.repec.org/p/idb/wpaper/3047.html.

Torre, J. C. 1983. *Los sindicatos en el gobierno 1973–1976*. Buenos Aires: CEAL.

Torre, J. C. 1990. *La vieja guardia sindical y Perón. Sobre los orígenes del peronismo*. Buenos Aires: Sudamericana—Inst Di Tella.

Truitt, A. 2013. *Dreaming of Money in Ho Chi Minh City*. Seattle: University of Washington Press.

Ulanovsky, C. 2005. *Paren las rotativas: diarios, revistas y periodistas*. Buenos Aires, Argentina: Emecé.

Vellinga, M. 1998. *The Changing Role of the State in Latin America*. New York: Routledge.

Visconti, M. 2017. *Cine y dinero: Imaginarios ficcionales y sociales en la Argentina (1978–2000)*. Buenos Aires: CICCUS.

Wainer, A. 2021. *¿Por qué siempre faltan dólares?: Las causas estructurales de la restricción externa en la economía argentina del siglo XXI*. Buenos Aires: Siglo XXI Editores.

Weber, M. 1978 [1921–22]. *Economy and Society: An Outline of Interpretive Sociology*. Berkeley: University of California Press.

Wilkis, A .2017a. *The Moral Power of Money: Morality and Economy in the Life of the Poor.* Stanford, CA: Stanford University Press.

Wilkis, A. 2017b. "La sociología moral del dinero: Algunos aportes a la sociología política." In *La vida social del mundo político. Investigaciones recientes en sociología política*, edited by G. Vommaro and M. Gene, 211–31. Buenos Aires: UNGS.

Wilkis, A. 2018. "Quand l'argent vient de l'État: Hiérarchies monétaires et antagonismes moraux dans la politique d'assistance aux classes populaires argentines." *Raisons Pratiques* 26: 9–34.

Zaloom, C. 2006. *Out of the Pits: Traders and Technology from Chicago to London.* Chicago: University of Chicago Press.

Zelizer, V. 1994. *The Social Meaning of Money: Pin Money, Paychecks, Poor Relief, and Other Currencies.* Princeton, NJ: Princeton University Press.

Zelizer, V. 2005. *The Purchase of Intimacy.* Princeton, NJ: Princeton University Press.

Zelizer V. 2012. "How I Became a Relational Economic Sociologist and What Does That Mean?" *Politics and Society* 40 (2): 145–74.

Zelizer, V. 2016. " My Money Obsessions." La vie des ideés. https://booksandideas.net/Twenty-Years-After-The-Social-Meaning-of-Money.html.

Zelizer, V. 2017. "Afterword to the 2017 edition." In *The Social Meaning of Money: Pin Money, Paychecks, Poor Relief, and Other Currencies*, 217–26. Princeton, NJ: Princeton University Press.

Zenobi, D. 2006. "'Ahorristas estafados' de vacaciones: De Villa Gessell al HSBC." *Estudios de Antropología Social* (1): 217–34.

# INDEX

advertising, 44, 61, 65, 66, 103, 108, 113, 130, 131, 140, 203
Alfonsín, Raúl, 107-9, 111, 112, 117-21, 124, 125, 135, 143, 147, 204
Alsogaray, Álvaro, 78, 97
Amato, Massimo, 69, 89, 104
Angeloz, Eduardo, 120–24
anti-Peronist, 35, 200. *See also* Perón, Juan Domingo
Aramburu, Pedro Eugenio, 200
*Arbolitos*, 157, 166, 170, 171, 203
Argentina's Industrial Union (UIA), 70, 122, 123
Argentine Constitution, 178, 203
Argentine Exchange Controls Commission. *See* foreign exchange market
Argentine Foreign Ministry, 139
Argentine Industrial Council (CAI), 126
Argentine Revolution, 68, 73, 78
Asís, Jorge, 93. *See also* journalism
*austral* (ARA), 118, 123 –128, 138–40, 142, 202
Austral Plan, 117–19

Banco Central (Banco Central de la República Argentina [BCRA]), 29, 30, 33, 27, 46, 49, 58, 62, 63, 74, 76, 79, 81, 87, 90, 94, 104, 109, 110, 114–16, 118, 120–24, 136, 137, 139, 141–43, 147, 150, 156–58, 160, 164, 167, 170, 171, 181, 184-87, 194, 195, 199, 201, 203
Basurto, Jorge, 116. *See also* comic strips
Bioy Casares, Adolfo, 36, 62
black market, 31, 36, 37, 39, 40, 46, 55, 57, 71–77, 79, 81, 87, 89, 104, 108, 110, 116, 172, 174, 200; "blue" dollar, 16, 40, 41, 54–57, 68, 73–77, 79–81, 83, 86, 87, 89, 93, 94, 104, 108, 110–12, 117, 156, 165, 167–70, 172–75, 178, 186, 187, 204; *bolsa negra*, 36–39, 55, 56, 170; *cueva/ cueveros*, 170, 171, 174, 205
*blindaje*, 152, 153
bonds, 4, 25, 30, 69, 71, 72, 74, 79, 86, 87, 108, 113, 116, 117, 120, 141, 145, 153, 164, 168–70, 177, 180, 182, 203, 205; Boden 2012, 169, 170; Bonex, 108, 113, 116; Lecop, 154; Patacones, 25, 116, 141, 153, 154; Repatriation for Development bond, 71

# Index

Borges, Jorge Luis, 36
Boudou, Amado, 206
Bozán, Sofía, 22
Bretton Woods, 2, 5, 19, 22, 28, 44, 72
Bróccoli, Alberto, 117. *See also* comic strips
Brodersohn, Mario, 125

*cacerolazo*, 183, 206. *See also* social movements
Cafiero, Antonio, 119
*Caja Nacional de Ahorro*, 145
Caloi (Carlos Loiseau), 96
cambiemos, 184, 185, 187, 190, 195
Cámpora, Héctor J., 68, 78, 201
*carestía de la vida*, 52. *See also* inflation
cartoons, 126. *See also* comic strips
Casas, David, 91, 148. *See also* journalism
Castro, Fidel, 46
Cavallo, Domingo, 110, 136, 137, 139, 143, 144, 147, 153, 154, 156. *See also* currency board
*cepo*, 164, 166, 169, 170, 173–76, 178, 180, 181, 183–87. *See also* foreign exchange market
Central Bank. *See* Banco Central de la República Argentina
cold war, 47
comic strips, 35, 60, 73, 117, 120, 126, 189, 191; Basurto, Jorge, 116; Bróccoli, Alberto, 117; Caloi, 96; *Caras y Caretas* (magazine), 24; *Diógenes y el linyera*, 120; Dobal, Felipe Miguel Ángel, 60; Fontanarrosa, Roberto, 151; Fortín, Raúl, 115; Gómez Laborde, Tabaré, 120; *Humor* (magazine), 115, 148; Ian, 113; Landrú, 106, 189; Maicas, Eduardo, 115; *Mister Whisky and Soda*, 35;
Viuti (Roberto López), 96
Commission for Latin America and the Caribbean (ELAC), 37

Confederación General del Trabajo (CGT), 12
*contado con liquidación (CCL)*, 168
*corralito*, 156, 158–60, 164, 203; *corralito verde*, 180; *Corralón*, 156, 159, 164, 169
Convertibility Act, 136, 138, 202. *See also* currency board
Criminal Exchange Act (Law 19,359), 77
Cuban Revolution, 201
*cueva*, 170, 174, 205. *See also* black market
cultural artifact, 3, 16
currency board, 6, 15, 20, 137, 165, 190, 192, 203

de-dollarization, 182, 188, 190. *See also* dollarization
De la Rúa, Fernando, 152–56, 20
democracy, 13, 14, 19, 21, 68, 106, 107, 147, 154, 190, 195, 196
devaluation, 17, 19, 23, 24, 29, 34, 44, 45, 47, 49, 50, 52, 59–65, 70–74, 81–84, 89–92, 94, 95, 97, 99–101, 104, 106, 108, 117, 118, 123, 124, 128, 139, 141, 146, 148, 155, 157, 158, 172, 175, 181, 184–86, 187, 195, 200, 206; micro–devaluation(s), 70, 71; mini–devaluation(s), 71
developmentalism, 200
Dobal, Felipe Miguel Ángel, 58. *See also* comic strips
*dólar*, kinds of: "blue" dollar, 167–70, 173–75, 178, 186, 187; *dólar billete*, 49; *dólar calesita*, 53; *dólar Colonia*, 168; *dólar giro / dólar transferencia*, 49; *dólar planchado*, 119
*dolarazo*, 132
dollar fever, 132, 180
dollar peg, 136, 138, 139, 141, 143–45, 147–57, 161, 190. *See also* currency board

## Index

dollar uses, as a reference for household economy, 9, 13–15, 46, 58, 60, 65, 128, 149, 155; as savings tool/method, 62, 130, 138, 180–82, 192; for tourism and travel, 14, 24, 16, 61, 62, 64, 65, 74, 80, 82, 83, 86, 88, 89, 97, 166, 169, 171, 179, 205; in art market, 101; in car market, 101, 131, 145, 164; in financial markets, 81; in international trade, 35; in real estate, 2, 14, 16, 61, 71, 92, 98–100, 111, 113, 118, 127–29, 145, 150, 151, 161, 164, 166, 169, 173, 174, 177, 183, 190, 205; in soccer player market, 59, 67, 95, 96, 129, 132, 148, 160, 173; in the political arena, 11–15, 19–21, 27, 34, 36, 41, 42, 44, 55, 69, 73, 78, 135, 136; invoicing in dollars, 127
Duhalde, Eduardo, 121, 156, 161, 165, 184, 206

economic pedagogy, 51, 66; money lessons, 191
economic socialization, 7, 66, 192, 193
economic sociology, 12
elites, 11, 14, 19, 23, 27, 42
*especulación hormiga*. See *pequeña especulación*
*especuladores hormigas*. See *pequeña especulación*
Exchange Control Commission, 24. See also foreign exchange market
exchange rate controls, 32, 34, 89. See also foreign exchange market
Executive Decree 28,337/49, 39
experts, 3, 5, 11, 14, 52, 53, 55, 58, 59, 65, 94, 104, 121, 132, 136, 141, 143, 144, 146, 154, 176, 177, 180, 189, 190, 194

Fantacci, Luca, 69, 89, 104
Fernández de Kirchner, Cristina, 167, 169, 170, 181, 190, 204

Fernández, Roque, 139
financial liberalization, 17, 69
financial repertoires, 3, 4, 7, 13–15, 18–20, 41, 44, 63, 64, 66, 68, 83, 103, 131, 134, 136, 162, 164, 190, 192–94, 196; ordinary financial practices, 10
financial capitalism. See financialization
financialization, 2, 5, 12
First World War, 4
Fogwill, Rodolfo, 150, 203. See also literature
Fontanarrosa, Roberto, 151. See also comic strips
foreign currency accounts, 58, 87, 115. See also foreign currency deposits
foreign currency deposits, 62, 64, 94, 110, 116, 118, 1465, 153
foreign exchange market, 1, 12, 13, 15–17, 18, 21, 23, 24, 25, 26–28, 31, 32, 35, 37, 41, 46, 47, 48–51, 54, 55, 57, 59, 61, 62, 63, 65, 66, 70, 71, 74, 75, 76–81, 86, 87, 89, 91, 94, 95, 110, 119, 120, 121–23, 125, 131, 132, 134, 135, 137, 139–41, 143, 166, 175, 176, 177, 178, 179, 180, 182, 184, 185, 186, 189, 190, 191, 194–96, 199, 203, 206; Argentine Exchange Controls Commission, 37; cepo, 164, 166, 169, 170, 173–78, 180, 181, 183–87; Exchange Control Commission, 24; exchange market regulations, 14, 18, 49, 184; exchange rate controls, 32, 34, 89; Free Foreign Exchange Market Decree, 179; foreign exchange market liberalization, 47
forex market. See foreign exchange market
Franco, Marina, 81, 201
Free Foreign Exchange Market Decree, 179. See also foreign exchange market
Frente para la Victoria (coalition), 184, 18

# Index

Fridman, Daniel, 85
Frigerio, Rogelio, 18
Frondizi, Arturo, 33, 34, 45–47, 50, 52, 56, 78, 143, 179, 200

Gaggero, Alejandro, 98
Gelbard, José Ber, 79, 20
Gerchunoff, Pablo, 23, 24, 32, 52, 69, 107, 200, 203
global currency, 2–5, 10, 11, 18, 19, 21, 22, 28, 191, 192, 194, 197
Gómez Laborde, Tabaré, 120. See also comic strips
Gómez Morales, Alfredo, 33, 34, 79, 201
González, Erman, 139
Granados, Osvaldo, 114. See also journalism
Great Depression, 5, 18, 23, 24
Gregory, Chris, 5
Grinspun, Bernardo, 111, 112
Guido, José María, 200
Guyer, Jane, 2, 5, 6, 8, 10

hacer puré, 170. See also pequeña especulación
hegemony of the dollar, 11, 12
Heredia, Mariana, 52, 88, 107, 144
Home, David. See Casas, David
Hurtado, Leopoldo, 36, 38. See also literature
Hussein, Saddam, 139

Ian, 113. See also comic strips
Illia, Arturo, 50, 62, 68, 200
imperialism, 11, 67, 68
inflation, 6, 7, 12, 15, 17, 19, 20, 32, 45, 52, 58, 61, 62, 68–70, 74, 77, 78, 81, 84, 85, 87–89, 93, 94, 99, 101, 103–105, 107, 108, 110, 112, 116–19, 121, 123, 125–28, 132, 133, 135, 136, 138, 143–45, 151, 152, 164, 167, 176, 179, 180, 184, 190, 193, 196, 200–02, 204, 205; anti-inflation policies, 88; *carestía de la vida*, 52; high inflation regime, 104; hyperinflation, 7, 14, 15, 17, 19, 125, 128–30, 133, 134, 135, 137, 146, 147, 151, 155, 190, 192, 201
International Monetary Fund (IMF), 28, 46, 70, 107, 108, 117, 147, 169, 202, 203

journalism, 52, 55, 132, 140, 141, 176; Asís, Jorge, 93. Casas, David, 91, 148; chronicle, 38, 46, 48, 50, 51, 56, 70, 82, 83, 114, 137, 143, 148, 157, 158, 183; Granados, Osvaldo, 114; Nudler, Julio, 73; photographs (in economic reporting), 47–52, 140, 141, 149, 153; Roth, Roberto, 71, 72; Silberstein, Enrique, 54, 56, 57
Justicialist Liberation Front, 78

Kaplan, Marcos, 22. See also theater
Kicillof, Axel, 172, 181
Kirchner, Néstor, 165, 166, 190, 204
Krieger Vasena, Adalbert, 50, 57, 63, 64, 200

la City, 46, 49–51, 64, 69, 77, 85, 86, 91–94, 102, 103, 106, 111, 112, 115, 116, 121, 122, 131, 132, 138, 140, 143, 156, 157, 158, 161, 166, 176. See also San Martín Street
Landi, Oscar, 69, 78, 155
Landrú, 106, 189. See also comic strips
Lanusse, Alejandro Agustín, 70, 72, 201
La Salada, 171
Law 12,830, 38
Law 12,893, 38
Law 14,773, 45, 46
Lecop. See bonds
Levingston, Roberto Marcelo, 70, 72
Liberators' Revolution, 47
Liendo, Horacio, 136

Llach, Juan Carlos, 52, 69, 107, 136, 200
Luder, Ítalo Argentino, 107, 108

Machinea, José Luis, 120, 121
Macri, Mauricio, 175, 184, 185, 187, 195, 204, 206
Malvinas War, 103
Maradona, Diego Armando, 95, 96
Marcó del Pont, Mercedes, 181, 187
Mar del Plata, 60, 61, 89
Martínez de Hoz, José Alfredo, 85, 88, 90, 92, 99, 102, 103, 119, 125; *tablita*, 88–92, 95, 99, 101, 119, 122, 125
Martínez de Perón, María Estela, 81, 201
Marx, Karl, 8, 9
mass culture, 3, 22, 19, 44, 66, 111, 189, 191
Massera, Emilio, 202
Mauss, Marcel, 133
Menem, Carlos Saúl, 119, 121, 124, 125, 135, 144, 146, 149, 151, 202, 203
middle class(es), 28, 61, 67, 68, 83, 88, 98, 99, 102, 145, 154, 160, 171, 199, 204
mini-devaluations, 52. *See also* devaluation
minister of finance, 48, 72, 201
ministry of economy, 37, 53, 58, 62, 71, 72, 112, 122, 143, 168, 20
Ministry of Technical Affairs Decree 32,214, 40
Minujín, Marta, 97, 98
*modelo de convertibilidad*, 20. *See also* currency board
monetary functions, 6, 192; medium of exchange, 15, 190, 192, 195; medium of payment, 9, 10; monetary functions desegregation, 6; store of value, 2, 6, 10, 16, 175, 180, 193, 195; unit of account, 10, 11, 64, 65, 84, 126, 127, 175, 193, 195

monetary plurality, 6, 192
money culture. *See also* popularization of the dollar
money lessons. *See also* economic pedagogy
Montoneros, 201

National Bureau of Price and Supply Controls, 38, 39
National Bureau of Price and Supply Monitoring, 40
National Economic Action Plan, 199
National Institute of Statistics and Censuses (INDEC), 155, 174, 205
Nemiña, Pablo, 98, 107
neoliberalism, 2, 5, 19, 133
New Deal, 24
new journalism. *See* journalism
Nixon, Richard, 2, 5, 72
Nudler, Julio, 73. *See also* journalism

Olmedo, Alberto, 102
Onganía, Juan Carlos, 50, 62, 70, 200
ordinary financial practices, 10. *See also* financial repertoires
Ortega, Ramón "Palito," 96, 97
over-invoicing, 104

parallel market dollar. *See* black market, "blue" dollar; *dólar*, kinds of, "blue" dollar
Paris Club, 46
patacones. *See* bonds
*pequeña especulación*, 49, 59, 204; *hacer puré*, 170; micro–currency speculation, 170; pocket economist, 49, 51
Perón, Juan Domingo, 12, 23, 28, 29, 31, 34, 35, 41, 45–47, 51, 78, 81, 179, 200, 201; Peronism, 28, 32, 35, 36, 41, 45, 52, 68, 76, 78, 200, 201; anti-Peronist, 35, 200

## Index

Peronism. *See* Perón, Juan Domingo
Pesce, Miguel, *194*
*pesificación*, *181*, 205
*peso ley 18,188 (peso ley)*, 70
Pinedo, Federico, 25, 37, 179, 199
Pink Floyd, 163
political autonomy, 200; autonomous way of relating to the Argentine state, 13; engaging with the state in a relationship that is autonomous, 193, 196; autonomy provided by monetary plurality, 192
popular culture. *See* mass culture
popular currency. *See* popularization of the dollar
popularization of the dollar, 14, 19, 20, 41, 60, 66, 84, 88, 95, 105, 107, 133, 149, 164, 189, 193–96; currency familiarization, 191; money culture, 21, 193–95; prehistory of the dollar's, 23; proto-popularization of the US currency, 22; popularization
Porcel, Jorge, 102
Prat–Gay, Alfonso, 18
Prebisch, Raúl, 37
price control committee, 123
prosecutor's office for economic crimes and asset laundering (PROCELAC), 171
proto-popularization of the US currency. *See* popularization of the dollar
public culture, 66
public numbers, 3, 107
Puerta, Ramón, 156
Pugliese, Juan Carlos, 124, 125
Punta del Este, 56, 89, 111

que se vayan todos, 155
Quilici, Juan, 72

radical party, 33, 57, 78, 107, 121, 122, 124, 125, 152, 199, 200. *See* Unión Cívica Radical
real estate market, 2, 14, 61, 98, 99, 100, 111, 128, 129, 145, 174, 177
regulation boards for meats and grains, 26, 199
Rejtman, Martín, 145. *See also* literature
repatriation for development bond. *See* bonds
*revista criolla*, 22. *See also* theater
*revista porteña*, 22. *See also* theater
Rocamora, Oberdan. *See* Asís, Jorge
*rodrigazo*, 17, 83, 84, 125, 128, 172, 201
Rodrigo, Celestino, 17, 81–83, 201. *See also rodrigazo*
Rodríguez Saá, Adolfo, 156
Roig, Alexandre, 136
Roosevelt, Franklin D., 24
Roth, Roberto, 71, 72. *See* journalism
Rougier, Marcelo, 33, 69, 78
Ruckauf, Carlos, 153
Rural Society, 70

San Martín Street, 38, 39, 43, 46–51, 54, 55, 57, 60, 63, 64, 68, 82, 94, 116, 138, 140, 142, 157, 176, 193. *See also* la City
Sánchez, María Soledad, 176, 204, 205
Scioli, Daniel, 184, 185
Second World War, 2, 4, 41, 44
Sigaut, Lorenzo, 91, 95
Silberstein, Enrique, 54, 56, 57
Simmel, Georg, 8, 9
Sinatra, Frank, 96
Socialist Bloc, 19, 77, 133
social movements, *cacerolazo*, 183, 206; *piquetero* movement, 203; savers (protest), 63, 68, 62, 85, 94, 95, 108, 114, 115, 120, 147–49, 151–53, 158–61, 165, 177, 204, 205, 206

sociology of money, 3, 7–11, 13, 14, 191, 192, 196
Sofovich, Gerardo, 83. *See also* theater; television
Sourrouille, Juan Vital, 112, 117–19, 123, 124
Spring Plan, 119, 121, 122, 124, 125
stabilization plan, 46–48, 52, 56, 59, 73, 143, 179
sterling pound, 4, 5, 14, 22, 23, 24, 29, 34; sterling pound devaluation, 23
stock market crash of 1929, 41
"stop-go" cycle, 32

Tato Bores (Mauricio Borensztein), 43, 50, 58, 72, 135. *See also* television
television: Channel 13 news, 90, 114; CQC (*Caiga quien caiga*), 163; *Polémica en el bar*, 67, 68, 83; *Realidad* 80, 90; Tato Bores, 43, 50, 58, 72, 135
Tequila effect, 146, 149, 152, 159
theater: Bozán, Sofía, 22; *El dólar está cabrero*, 22; Kaplan, Marcos, 22; *La risa es la mejor divisa*, 22, 32; *Los verdes están en el Maipo*, 83; *revista criolla*, 22; *revista porteña*, 22; Sofovich, Gerardo, 83
total social fact, 133
treasury bonds. *See* bonds
two-bit speculation. See *pequeña especulación*

Ubaldini, Saúl, 121
under-invoicing, 104
Unión Cívica Radical, 78, 107, 199, 200, 204. *See also* radical party
Unión de Centro Democrático (UCD), 97, 127
United Kingdom, 19, 103, 104, 133, 139
United States, 2, 4–6, 10, 11, 19, 20, 22, 25, 28, 29, 31, 35, 38, 46, 47, 60, 64, 69, 101, 112, 133, 139, 194
*uno a uno*, 136. *See also* currency board
Uriburu, José Félix, 17, 24, 27, 199

Vanoli, Alejandro, 184
Vanoli, Hernán, 160. *See also* literature
*Videla, Jorge Rafael*, 202
*Viola, Roberto*, 91
Visconti, Marcela, 10

Wall Street, 11, 50
Walsh, Rodolfo, 36. *See also* literature
Washington Consensus, 203
Weber, Max, 36
Wehbe, Jorge, 104, 106
World Bank, 18, 107, 123

Yrigoyen, Hipólito, 199

Zelizer, Viviana, 3, 8–10, 18, 42, 44, 66, 191

www.ingramcontent.com/pod-product-compliance
Lightning Source LLC
Chambersburg PA
CBHW020651230426
43665CB00008B/391